RETHINKING LEADERSHIP IN A
COMPLEX, MULTICULTURAL,
AND GLOBAL ENVIRONMENT

RETHINKING LEADERSHIP IN A COMPLEX, MULTICULTURAL, AND GLOBAL ENVIRONMENT

New Concepts and Models for Higher Education

Edited by

Adrianna Kezar

STERLING, VIRGINIA

Published by Stylus Publishing, LLC
22883 Quicksilver Drive
Sterling, Virginia 20166-2102

Library of Congress Cataloging-in-Publication-Data

Rethinking leadership in a complex, multicultural, and
global environment : new concepts and models for higher
education / edited by Adrianna Kezar.
    p. cm.
  Includes bibliographical references and index.
  ISBN 978-1-57922-281-9 (cloth : alk. paper)—
  ISBN 978-1-57922-282-6 (pbk. : alk. paper)
  1. Education, Higher—United
States—Administration. 2. Educational
leadership—United States. 3. College administrators—In-
service training—United States. I. Kezar, Adrianna J.
LB2341.R47 2009
378.1′010973—dc22   2008025909

13-digit ISBN: 978-1-57922-281-9 (cloth)
13-digit ISBN: 978-1-57922-282-6 (paper)

Printed in the United States of America

All first editions printed on acid free paper
that meets the American National Standards Institute
Z39-48 Standard.

Bulk Purchases

Quantity discounts are available for use in workshops
and for staff development.
Call 1-800-232-0223

First Edition, 2008

10 9 8 7 6 5 4 3

CONTENTS

ACKNOWLEDGMENTS   *vii*

PREFACE   *ix*
Adrianna Kezar

1. REVOLUTIONIZING LEADERSHIP DEVELOPMENT   *1*
   Lessons From Research and Theory
   Adrianna Kezar and Rozana Carducci

2. THE HERS INSTITUTES   *39*
   Revolutionary Leadership Development for Women
   Lynn M. Gangone

3. DEVELOPING LEADERS OF COLOR IN HIGHER
   EDUCATION   *65*
   **Can Contemporary Programs Address Historical Employment
   Trends?**
   *Bridget R. McCurtis, Jerlando F. L. Jackson, and Elizabeth M.
   O'Callaghan*

4. FACING ORGANIZATIONAL COMPLEXITY AND CHANGE   *93*
   A Case-In-Point Approach to Leadership Development
   Tricia Bertram Gallant and Cheryl Getz

5. CREATING A NEW BREED OF ACADEMIC LEADERS
   FROM STEM WOMEN FACULTY   *117*
   The National Science Foundation's ADVANCE Program
   Sue V. Rosser

6. SPIRITUALITY, RELIGIOUS PLURALISM, AND HIGHER
   EDUCATION LEADERSHIP DEVELOPMENT   *131*
   Robert J. Nash and Lara Scott

7. LEADERSHIP PROGRAMS FOR A FAMILY-FRIENDLY
   CAMPUS   *151*
   Jaime Lester

8. CREATING FACULTY ACTIVISM AND GRASSROOTS
   LEADERSHIP   *169*
   An Open Letter To Aspiring Activists
   Jeni Hart

9. CHANGING OF THE GUARD IN COMMUNITY
   COLLEGES   *185*
   The Role Of Leadership Development
   Pamela Eddy

10. HIGHER EDUCATION LEADERSHIP DEVELOPMENT
    PROGRAMS IN THE MARKETPLACE   *213*
    Sharon A. McDade

11. REFLECTIONS ON THE LEADERSHIP MARKETPLACE   *233*
    Adrianna Kezar and Laurel Beesemyer

   ABOUT THE CONTRIBUTORS   *239*

   INDEX   *243*

ACKNOWLEDGMENTS

I would like to thank several people who have been instrumental in the development of this book. Rozana Carducci, Melissa Contreras-McGavin, Tricia Bertram Gallant, and Jaime Lester have spent the last three years with me on the journey to explore leadership in new ways. Thank you to all the chapter authors who tirelessly made revisions in chapters that reflect novel ways of conceptualizing leadership. I also want to thank Laurel Beesemyer for her thoughtful comments, sense of humor, and editorial support. A special note to Helen (Lena) Astin for her intellectual leadership in this area and for inspiring me to work on rethinking leadership. Most of all, I want to extend my appreciation to Lynn Gangone who initiated my work in leadership development by asking me to help develop the Institute on Emerging Women Leaders and working with me as codirector for several years. She has worked with me in the trenches for over a decade to help transform the way people in higher education think about leadership development. Working collectively, in the spirit of empowerment, as full spiritual, emotional, and cognitive beings we can create experiences that truly transform people and change the nature of the world.

The quickest way of changing an institution is to change its leadership.
                                    —James Perkins, former president
                                                of Cornell University

One of the most important conditions for the health and future of higher education is the development of its leaders. Leaders create change and innovation or maintain important long-standing values. I am convinced that the future of higher education rests on creating a new set of leaders across campuses who embrace new concepts and abilities of leadership. One of the ways to ensure that higher education has the needed leadership pool is to create training programs. Since the 1960s programs have emerged at the national, regional, and institutional level to meet this need. In the late 1980s Sharon McDade published a well-received ASHE-ERIC monograph in which she created an inventory of leadership development programs in higher education, providing an overview of the various programs offered and the advantages of these programs. She explored the skills and knowledge required for leaders in higher education and the benefits of professional development programs. This monograph became a resource to help people identify leadership development programs as well as to understand how to create leadership development opportunities. Surprisingly, little has been written about faculty and administrative leadership development programs since the publication of this monograph (outside student leadership development programs). A void exists in the literature in higher education on the topic of faculty and staff leadership development.

While the field of higher education has languished in producing publications on leadership development programs, a plethora of new research has emerged about ways to develop leaders in other fields, such as business, public policy, community development, and politics, for example. In fact, in the past 20 years, there has been a revolution in the way that leadership is conceptualized and the way leaders are trained across most fields and disciplines. This revolution has moved beyond the doors of the academy, as evidenced by the fact that practitioner and professional journals, popular management texts, and leadership development programs now reflect "revolutionary" views of leadership that result in different skills and competencies needed among leaders.

What is the revolution that has transpired? Historically, leadership has usually been conceptualized as hierarchical in nature and emphasizing social control.[1] However in the past 20 years, nonhierarchical, increasingly democratic forms of leadership that focus on process and values have been conceptualized. Moving away from hierarchical, authority-based, context-free, highly structured, and value-neutral leadership frameworks, contemporary scholars have embraced context-specific, globalized, and process-oriented perspectives of leadership that emphasize empowerment, cross-cultural understanding, collaboration, cognitive complexity, and social responsibility for others. The heroic, controlling, and distant leader of the past has given way to a focus on teams and collectives and social change. These many exciting changes in theory were summarized in *Rethinking the "L" Word in Higher Education: The Revolution of Research on Leadership* (Kezar, Carducci , & Contreras-McGavin, 2006) that described cultural, cognitive, chaos, and team theories of leadership driven by social constructivist and critical studies of the phenomenon.

The changes in leadership development reflect the changing context for leaders. In the 1960s and 1970s, traditional notions of authority were questioned and hierarchical and individualistic notions of leadership undermined. In the 1980s and 1990s, the world economy shifted creating a more interdependent system that has been called a globalized economy. The emphasis on interdependence reinforces the importance of collaboration and working in teams for enacting leadership. As people throughout the world connect and work together with greater frequency, cultural and social differences have become recognized and have been studied in relation to leadership. Various forms of technology have sped up decision time and connected people across the globe, making more local forms of leadership possible and the emphasis on context and culture more important (Lipman-Blumen, 1996). This has led to the democratization of leadership as well as making the process more complex and diffuse. While we do not summarize all the forces and conditions here, we recognize that the world in which leadership

---

1. Other images have emerged over time but were not the predominant view. Versions of servant leadership have come and gone based on religious leaders like Jesus Christ or Buddha. Human relations theories in the 1900s advocated for more democratic and participatory forms of leadership.

is practiced has changed dramatically, and that leadership development and practice need to evolve as well (see Lipman-Blumen, 1996; Vaill, 1996; Wheatley, 1999 for more detailed descriptions of the forces and conditions).

While much has been written about needed changes to traditional frameworks of leadership in higher education (Heifetz, 1994; Lipman-Blumen, 1996), equal attention has not yet been paid to the way that leadership development programs should change in order to reflect the leadership revolution. Most of the leadership development programs in higher education reflect outdated perspectives and approaches to leadership development. The programs bring together hierarchical, positional leaders; focus on skill and trait development; and reinforce the importance of social control and persuasion, and teaching competencies that transcend context. These outdated approaches to leadership are discussed more in chapter 1.

In this volume we examine the implications of new theories and concepts about leadership and the ways these concepts can be integrated to develop new leadership development programs for higher education. We also present examples or models of leadership development programs that integrate these new concepts to provide guidance for redeveloping programs in higher education. We showcase the few higher education leadership development programs that have begun to integrate the new leadership concepts into their curriculum and approach. Higher education will be ill prepared for future challenges if leaders continue to be trained in outdated modes that no longer fit the complexities and challenges of our times.

The ideas presented here are important for a variety of audiences, including (a) individuals who develop institution-based leadership development programs, (b) individuals who create regional or national leadership development programs, (c) participants or clients of leadership development programs, (d) leaders on college campuses who are concerned with the development and pipeline of emerging leaders, and (e) scholars of leadership.

Most large college campuses have some form of leadership development for faculty and staff/administrators. Leadership development among faculty is often offered by centers for faculty development. One of the main audiences for this book is the administrators in faculty development offices who are planning and creating workshops and who often have no background in leadership training. Another major audience is staff in human resource departments that offer training for staff and administrators. In addition to institution-based programs, some programs are offered regionally (University of California system, Vermont network, New Hampshire collaborative) and nationally (through the American Association of Community Colleges, National Association of Land Grant and State Universities, American Council of Education, and through disciplinary societies, for example). Regional programs are emerging and being created to train faculty and staff, and organizers are seeking ideas on how to create programs, as those in charge are often not from a leadership development background. Local, regional, and national programs will greatly benefit from the ideas presented here.

In addition to those who create programs locally, regionally, and nationally, another major audience is consumers of programs—participants and institutions that pay for such programs. Campus administrators and faculty need to understand the qualities and characteristics of programs that will help them be effective higher education leaders. This book provides them with the background for allocating resources within divisions. In speaking with leaders across the country, administrators and faculty often look for a resource on how to choose between different leadership development programs and where they should send their staff for training. We hope this book helps provide campus administrators with ideas for mentoring faculty and staff and for leadership opportunities. In particular, the chapters related to leaders of color and to community college leaders will be informative for clients seeking these programs, as the authors review a host of programs across the country and provide ideas on which programs might be best for people seeking certain experiences.

Finally, one of the most extensive areas of research in higher education is leadership, and this book will be of great interest to scholars in this field of study. The review of new concepts of leadership drawn from interdisciplinary resources is a helpful tool for leadership scholars in research, graduate students in their studies, and for teaching courses. In addition, the text may also be used within higher education programs as part of the leadership curriculum. What better way to prepare future leaders within these programs than to introduce them to key ideas and practices that can advance their leadership abilities?

This book fills a gap in our understanding and practice of leadership in the following ways: (a) there are few texts on faculty and staff leadership development, (b) the resources published on faculty or staff development in higher education tend to take a very traditional approach and are therefore not as rich as they could be, (c) this book adds entirely new concepts to the dialogue on leadership development in higher education and can improve the practice of leadership development, and (d) a growing audience for the text exists as many campuses are recognizing the importance of developing leaders among faculty (fostered by outside agencies such as the National Science Foundation), department chairs, deans, and midlevel staff.

Now that you have an understanding of the main purpose of the text and the audience, we invite you to read the chapters in any order. They are not arranged in any particular sequence. While they all relate to the ways concepts from the leadership revolution can be applied to development, they all have distinctive and independent messages for different groups—individuals in community colleges, leaders of color, faculty leaders, department chairs, women leaders, leaders with no authority—and each chapter has a different area of focus: spirituality, chaos, globalization, organizational learning. We do encourage you to read the introductory chapter first, as it frames the entire book, but after that, each is a stand-alone chapter to be referenced as needed. Each chapter helps shed light on one or more of the concepts within the leadership revolution. I briefly review the main focus of each chapter and its contribution and identify the main message for leadership development planners or clients of leadership development programs.

Chapter 1, by Rozana Carducci and me, "Revolutionizing Leadership Development: Lessons From Research and Theory," provides a foundation for understanding the following chapters. We review traditional leadership assumptions embedded within most of the current higher education leadership development programs and then describe how these traditional assumptions are problematic and will not well serve higher education leaders of the future. We then review the revolutionary concepts of leadership that should be included in future leadership development programs, which are highlighted in programs described in the book. The main concepts are organizational learning, sensitivity to context and culture, ethics/spirituality, emotions, complexity and chaos, globalization, empowerment and social change, and teams/collaboration. Carducci and I identify key resources for teaching in each of these concepts. Finally, we describe how these concepts fundamentally change the way we think about leadership development—expanding program timeframes, balancing action and reflection, promoting interdependence, situating leadership in context, and focusing on values.

Chapter 2, "The HERS Institute: Revolutionary Leadership Development," by Lynn Gangone, reviews one of the most well-known national leadership institutes for administrators and faculty in higher education that reflects three revolutionary concepts of leadership: social change, empowerment, and a global/international focus. The HERS (Higher Education Resource Services) Institute emerged from the 1960s when many of the revolutionary concepts about leadership originally emerged. HERS was the first leadership development opportunity that incorporated these new concepts. In 2008 it remains the only leadership development opportunity that intentionally and consistently attempts to create change agents who challenge the status quo; institute planners want to change the nature of higher education through the development of a new cadre of leaders. The program planners believe that women can lead from any position (nonhierarchical) but still believe in the importance of women obtaining positions of power in order to alter postsecondary institutions. The revolutionary concepts of leadership presented in this chapter have been part of the institute for almost 40 years now.

In chapter 3, "Developing Leaders of Color in Higher Education: Can Contemporary Programs Address Historical Employment Trends?" Bridget R. McCurtis, Jerlando F. L. Jackson, and Elizabeth M. O'Callaghan review a contemporary concern related to the leadership revolution in higher education—the preparation of leaders of color. The authors remind us that little has been written about leaders of color, and their development has been ignored for the most part. In recent years, a few programs have emerged nationally that are specifically aimed at leaders of color, and the authors review these programs but demonstrate how they are incomplete for truly harnessing this growing talent on campuses. The authors propose a new leadership development model that reflects various elements of the leadership revolution, including sensitivity to the cultural background of leaders, leaders' being aware of their institution's culture and context, the importance of organizational learning, and an awareness of power dynamics such as racism, which can hamper us from enabling all leaders to contribute on campuses. This chapter is revolutionary in its own right for focusing on the needs and development of women leaders and leaders of color who have long been excluded from full participation in higher education. My hope, as editor, is that a change agent will create a leadership development institute such as the one proposed by the authors.

Another exciting example of the way these new concepts about leadership have already been included in leadership development programs in higher education is described in chapter 4 by Tricia Bertram Gallant and Cheryl Getz, "Facing Organizational Complexity and Change: A Case-in-Point Approach to Leadership Development." The authors remind us that faculty and staff working in higher education increasingly face complex organizational issues that are not easily resolved in an era of constant and fast-paced change. Many administrators and staff trained in traditional leadership programs may not have the capacity to work and lead under various dynamic and multifaceted conditions because they lack exposure to real-world, nontraditional leadership theories and experiences. The authors describe case-in-point pedagogy, which helps leaders address complexity in their institutions and which has been used at several campuses. This chapter not only reinforces the importance of chaos and complexity for today's leaders but also the key roles of emotional intelligence, working in teams, and ongoing organizational learning (core elements of the leadership revolution). It also demonstrates how leadership can be found in change agents throughout the organization and not just in those in authority.

In chapter 5, Sue Rosser examines a newer effort to integrate the revolutionary leadership concepts: the National Science Foundation's (NSF's) ADVANCE program. Rosser reviews a novel leadership development experience for department chairs that can serve as a model for other emerging programs by including important new approaches to leadership development, such as responsiveness to a multicultural environment, the importance of collaboration and teams and encouraging interdisciplinary work, and nonpositional leadership (all revolutionary principles). Department chairs are receiving greater attention in leadership development efforts as institutions, as well as national organizations such as NSF, recognize that bottom-up leadership is often more successful for truly changing the culture of campuses. Rosser reflects on the ways programs can be created that build leadership among faculty, which can potentially encourage more women to enter underrepresented fields such as math or science. The examples provided by Rosser of campuses with ADVANCE programs makes the revolutionary concepts of leadership real for readers.

Robert J. Nash and Lara Scott investigate and propose a way to integrate spirituality into leadership development in chapter 6, "Spirituality, Religious Pluralism, and Higher Education Leadership Development." One of the most prominent changes in the leadership revolution is the rising importance of spirituality in leadership development. The authors refer to some representative, in-place curricular, pedagogical, and programmatic elements that have emerged in higher education leadership programs, providing specific examples from practice. Nash and Scott also reflect on working with difficult concepts such as spirituality and religious pluralism that can only be understood through many years of working with these concepts in the classroom. They describe challenges they have faced, new methods they have learned, and strategies for best approaching what can be a delicate and tricky set of ideas. The authors also provide a powerful explanation and rationale for why spirituality is so important to leadership development—it creates leaders with integrity.

Another difficult concept to integrate into leadership development is awareness of new policies that challenge the existing organizational culture and higher education norms. In chapter 7, Jaime Lester describes the experiences of campuses that incorporate family-friendly policies in leadership development courses. She reminds us that, in the last decade, a demographic shift (an increase in women leaders) among faculty and staff has created a need for colleges and universities to consider the creation of new family-friendly policies and flexible work arrangements. She demonstrates how the inclusion of family-friendly policies in leadership development introduces many of the topics that are part of the leadership revolution. Implementation of family-friendly policies requires involvement from faculty and staff change agents (who may not be in positions of authority) leading from the bottom up. Leadership development has to examine sexism, racism, and other abuses of power that might make campus leaders hesitant to use family-friendly policies. Organizers also find that these programs are more effective if they help leaders understand how organizational culture operates in general, as well as the specific levers for change on their own campus. Therefore, leadership in this new era requires revolutionary skills of nonpositional leaders who understand how to examine issues of power and can analyze institutional culture while retaining and defending the fundamental values of higher education and democracy.

All of these chapters point out the need to create leadership among faculty and staff who are not necessarily in positions of power—a core assumption of the leadership revolution. Jeni Hart takes on this challenge directly in chapter 8, "Creating Faculty Activism and Grassroots Leadership: An

Open Letter to Aspiring Activists." In a globalized environment where decisions are being made increasingly at the lower levels of organizations, faculty need to take greater leadership roles than in the past. In this chapter, the author explores faculty activism as a form of leadership and the ways that faculty need to increasingly play a leadership role on campus that differs from previous models based solely on involvement in a faculty senate. Addressing fellow faculty activists/leaders, Hart attempts to persuade them that the work they are currently involved in can be labeled leadership (and asks faculty to increasingly pick up the mantle to do this work). She also provides advice to faculty about how to be effective grassroots leaders based on her own research and resources such as Meyerson's (2003) book *Tempered Radicals*. I hope her chapter will inspire faculty to consider playing a larger role in leadership. My colleagues and I (Kezar, Lester, Carducci, Bertram Gallant, & Contreras-McGavin, 2007) wrote about our concern that fewer and fewer faculty are taking up the leadership mantle because of the growth of part-time and contract faculty, academic capitalism, and increasing publications standards for tenure and promotion. These many forces make it increasingly difficult for faculty to take an active role. In our article, we suggest ways administrators can make the environment more supportive for faculty leaders, and we offer advice for faculty grassroots leaders. Hart's chapter, paired with Kezar et al., provides helpful guidance for ensuring that institutions capitalize on the leadership of faculty that has long characterized college campuses.

Adding to the crisis among faculty leadership is the growing concern about creating enough qualified leaders for community college campuses that are experiencing unprecedented turnover in employees, including positional leaders such as presidents. Pamela Eddy examines this challenge in chapter 9, "Changing of the Guard in Community Colleges: The Role of Leadership Development." This leadership transition is one of the most significant that higher education will face in coming years. The great majority of students in postsecondary education, particularly from the neediest and most underserved populations, attend community colleges. One could argue that the leadership of community colleges affects the overall economy and social stability of the country given the summation of the impact on local communities. This chapter explores the opportunity for markedly changing the nature of leadership in community colleges based on the turnover and retirements in faculty, administration, and staff in coming years. Eddy reviews existing leadership programs aimed at community college staff, faculty, and administrators and suggests new programs to meet the needs of the future that reflect attention to context, succession planning, organizational learning, and the diversity of new leaders—all key concepts within the leadership revolution.

Sharon McDade's important synthesis in chapter 10 examines the revolutionary principles within what she calls the *marketplace* of leadership development. She reminds leadership developers and consumers that existing programs can be seen as a reflection of marketplace demands. She explores the potential of the revolutionary principles within a market-based view of leadership development, highlighting particular opportunities she sees within specific programs for incorporating the ideas presented as well as some areas where we may see less progress. She also reminds readers how little we know about current leadership development programs nationally (pointing to a paucity of empirical research) and suggests that we have little knowledge about the extent to which some of these ideas may be entering the curriculum of programs. Nonetheless, she appreciates the call to arms raised in this book, suggesting that all leadership developers should examine their programs. In the last chapter, Laurel Beesemyer and I examine this notion of the marketplace, so aptly brought up by McDade. We argue that it is the marketplace (which typically supports corporate interests and those in power) that created top-down command and control views of leadership. We question whether the market is a good source for shaping leadership development in a more global, multicultural, and interdependent leadership context. We also offer some ethical considerations with using market forces as a way to develop and shape the future of leadership.

A final thought as you move forward reading this book: the concepts described will be challenging to implement. Our society and institutions reinforce traditional notions of leadership—they are hard to escape. Even if you embrace the ideas, they may be challenging to put into practice. You may find yourself slipping back into traditional notions while teaching, professionals in your program may resist the concepts at some level, and institutions may need to be convinced of the value of these ideas. While business, government, and nonprofits have mostly been convinced of the value of these ideas, higher education has not had the same education and consciousness raising as these other sectors.[2] Some leadership developers will and have struggled to incorporate these new ideas because they are outside traditional assumptions. We recommend that you make the traditional notions explicit and deconstruct them for participants, which is helpful when introducing these new concepts. Unless they can see the limitations in the old values, they may be unable to embrace these new ones.

While traditional notions of skills and traits remain important areas to emphasize in the development of leaders, we argue that leadership development can be greatly enhanced if programs incorporate these new ideas around cognitive complexity, spirituality, empowerment, and globalization. We also encourage program developers to reconceptualize the orientation of programs that typically focus on the identification and cultivation of positional leaders and instead direct their energies toward recognizing and fostering a broader audience for leadership development. There is so much untapped leadership potential that our campuses could be harnessing.

> Adrianna Kezar
> University of Southern California
> 2008

References

Heifetz, R. A. (1994). *Leadership without easy answers.* Cambridge, MA: Belknap Press.

Kezar, A., Carducci, R., & Contreras-McGavin, M. (2006). Rethinking the "L" word in leadership: The revolution of research on leadership. *ASHE Higher Education Report, 31*(6). San Francisco: Jossey-Bass.

Kezar, A., Lester, J., Carducci, R., Bertram Gallant, T., & Contreras-McGavin, M. (2007). Where are the faculty leaders? *Liberal Education, 93*(4), 14–21.

Lipman-Blumen, J. (1996). *The connective edge: Leading in an interdependent world.* San Francisco: Jossey-Bass.

McDade, S. (1988). *Higher education leadership: Enhancing skills through professional development programs. ERIC/ASHE Higher Education Research Report, 24, 1.* Washington, DC: ERIC Clearinghouse on Higher Education.

---

2. There are of course businesses that still operate in a traditional leadership fashion, and colleges and universities that operate within the revolutionary principles of leadership. I am speaking in general.

Meyerson, D. (2003). *Tempered radicals: How everyday leaders inspire change at work.* Boston: Harvard Business School Press.

Vaill, P. B. (1996). *Learning as a way of being.* San Francisco: Jossey-Bass.

Wheatley, M. J. (1999). *Leadership and the new science: Discovering order in a chaotic world* (2nd ed.) San Francisco: Berrett-Koehler Press.

REVOLUTIONIZING LEADERSHIP DEVELOPMENT

Lessons From Research and Theory

Adrianna Kezar and Rozana Carducci

Today's leadership development coordinator: I think it was much easier when I could isolate the few characteristics that people could use in all situations to be successful leaders.

Tomorrow's leadership development coordinator: I like demonstrating how leadership is affected by context, culture, and situational elements. It really feels authentic to me to help people carefully observe and interpret their environment and the people within it to be successful leaders.

Today's leadership development coordinator: It helps when you can clearly identify who leaders are in organizations. When lines of authority are clear, organizational communication and coordination are much easier. This also assists with helping leaders predict the outcomes of their work.

Tomorrow's leadership development coordinators: Breaking the illusion of hierarchical power relationships and demonstrating how people have always had agency to follow their own visions and helping to understand how we can move to more collective forms of leadership by empowering people rather than trying to mandate change is exciting.

In future years, these may well be the comments of administrators responsible for leadership development on college campuses as leadership development programs move away from traditional scientific management approaches to developing leaders and instead embrace a more revolutionary perspective of academic leadership. As noted in the preface, conceptions of leadership have changed markedly in the last 20 years. Leadership has moved from being leader centered, individualistic, hierarchical, focused on universal characteristics, and emphasizing power over others to a vision in which leadership is process centered, collective, context bound, nonhierarchical, and focused on mutual power and influence processes. These revolutionary assumptions are reflected in the emphasis contemporary leadership scholars place on empowerment, the global dimensions of leadership, cross-cultural understanding, cognitive complexity, and social responsibility for others. These changes are shown in Figure 1.1.

Although leadership development curricular changes are well under way in the business sector, academic leadership programs are just beginning to embrace complexity, globalization, and team-based leadership—three constructs closely associated with revolutionary views of leadership. This book is an attempt to translate and expedite the transfer of revolutionary concepts of leadership into the higher education dialogue and more specifically into the design and implementation of leadership development programs (see Kezar, Carducci, & Contreras-McGavin, 2006, for more details on revolutionary leadership theories and concepts).

In this chapter, we provide an overview of traditional and revolutionary assumptions of leadership and discuss the impact of these assumptions on the format and content of leadership development programs. After synthesizing these two divergent sets of leadership assumptions, we move on to the

FIGURE 1.1
The Revolution in Leadership Research

Then		Now
Search for universal leadership characteristics	⟶	Context bound
Examine power and hierarchy	⟶	Focus on mutual power and influence
Study individuals	⟶	Emphasis on the collective and collaborative
Predict behavior and outcomes	⟶	Promote learning, empowerment, change
Leader centered	⟶	Process oriented

main focus of the chapter, which is to provide an overview of revolutionary leadership concepts—organizational learning, sensitivity to context and culture, ethics/spirituality, emotions, complexity and chaos, globalization, empowerment and social change, and teams/collaboration. Many of these concepts will be described in greater detail in later chapters. In contrast to the depth provided by these subsequent chapters, our goal is to provide a foundation for understanding and interpreting revolutionary leadership concepts as well as to highlight the characteristics and advantages associated with applying these new perspectives in higher education leadership development programs. The chapters that follow present actual cases of new leadership development programs or hypothesize ways to integrate these new concepts into the curriculum. Another objective of this chapter is to demonstrate the interconnected nature of revolutionary leadership constructs. One of the common dilemmas is that leadership development coordinators become interested in one concept that they add to their program's curriculum but ignore the many other important innovations that need to be covered in order to create leaders who can be effective in coming years. In this chapter we seek to demonstrate some of the similarities and the synergy that exist between concepts and how they naturally fit together in leadership development curricula.

In the end, these revolutionary concepts will require a journey, especially for individuals embedded in traditional scientific management theories. Texts such as Bolman and Deal's (1995) *Leading With Soul* and Parker Palmer's (1990) *Leading From Within: Reflections on Spirituality and Leadership* underscore how the new assumptions of leadership—social change, empowerment, learning, collective action, mutual power—require leaders to let go of authority, control, power, individualism, and a scientific view of leadership and to embrace what might be a spiritual journey. So to start the journey, readers need to first acknowledge and examine traditional leadership assumptions and how they shape leadership development programs.

Traditional Leadership Development Assumptions and Program Formats

Four main assumptions undergird most contemporary leadership development programs:

1. Leadership is conceptualized as an individual, hierarchical leader.
2. Universal and predictable skills and traits that transcend context best epitomize the work of leaders.
3. Leadership is related to social control, authority, and power.
4. Representations of leadership are value free.

Most leadership development programs tend to focus on individuals who are already (or aspiring to be) in positions of authority. These programs bring in individual leaders rather than teams. Few leadership programs are designed to cultivate all employees as part of the leadership process, a practice at odds with revolutionary leadership principles. Additionally, traditional leadership development programs tend to focus on traits, skills, or behaviors that help an individual in a position of authority to enact leadership. Trait-oriented programs attempt to identify and cultivate specific personal characteristics, such as integrity, commitment, intelligence, and trustworthiness, that contribute to a person's ability to assume and successfully function in positions of leadership (Bensimon, Neumann, & Birnbaum, 1989). Behavioral models of leadership development call upon participants to examine the roles, categories of behavior, and tasks associated with leadership, such as planning, fund-raising, or negotiation (Bensimon, Neumann, & Birnbaum). Both the trait and behavioral perspectives of leadership rely solely on individual leaders for understanding leadership—context, culture, and other aspects are generally ignored. Program participants are typically asked to reflect on their traits and abilities and to understand their strengths and weaknesses in order to develop a particular character and set of leadership skills. However, leaders are generally not asked to examine these traits in relation to the culture of an organization. For example, they do not consider what honesty might look like or how this trait might be enacted uniquely within their organization or how different individuals within the organization might interpret or understand honesty.

Another underlying assumption of traditional leadership programs is that leaders are responsible for social control and exercising authority. In recent years, as authoritative power structures have been critiqued, leaders have been taught how to "influence" employees so that they do what positional leaders desire, albeit in a more mutual manner, through notions of a shared vision or planning processes where feedback is obtained from stakeholders. What is important to understand is the ability of leaders to use persuasion to achieve desired organizational outcomes. Many leadership development programs focus on ways to influence others and create change, designing learning activities and resources that target the cultivation of abilities associated with persuasion (e.g., effective communication, creating a vision, and allocating rewards and resources). Finally, programs review decision-making processes and focus on principles of efficiency and effectiveness—the hallmarks of scientific management. Authority figures are not asked to focus on ethical or moral consequences and values are de-emphasized within decision making.

Traditional leadership development assumptions have resulted in skill- and trait-based programs aimed at those in authority (or those who aspire to be in authority) that enact universal, context- and value-free strategies. Although we certainly see the value in fostering important traits and skills among positional leaders, we believe leadership development requires a broader emphasis than is currently included in leadership development programs.

Revolutionary Leadership Assumptions

The civil rights and feminist movements of the 1960s and 1970s, coupled with the rapid rise of the global economy, have fundamentally altered contemporary economic, political, social, and cultural interactions and reshaped our understanding of leadership in the process. The social movements resulted in a questioning of traditional authority, examination of abuses of power, recognition and appreciation of differences among people, the power of a collective, and recognition of movements as important social forces for change, willingness to experiment with new ways to approach social processes, and an awareness of ethical aspects of daily decision making. Globalization resulted in multiple, complex forces, such as changing demographics, technology, faster decisions, and greater competition, that require leaders and organizations to abandon outdated scientific management techniques and enact new leadership processes that emphasize interdependence, awareness of cultural and social differences, and adaptability (Lipman-Blumen, 1996, 2000). The revolutionary leadership concepts described throughout this book reflect this changed context of leadership. The leadership revolution explored in this book is guided by five interdependent assumptions:

1. Leadership is a *process* not the possession of individuals in positions of authority.
2. *Culture and context matter*; leadership is no longer considered a universal or objective phenomenon that transcends context.
3. Leadership is a *collaborative and collective* process that involves individuals working together across organizational and national boundaries.
4. *Mutual power and influence,* not control and coercion, are the focus of revolutionary leadership efforts.
5. The emphasis of revolutionary leadership is *learning, empowerment, and change.*

The adoption of these revolutionary leadership assumptions has upended traditional notions of leadership as an objective, universal reality characterized by preoccupation with predictable behavior and formal authority. The scientific management views of leadership are slowly giving way to perspectives of leadership that emphasize empowerment, context, reflexivity, cross-cultural understanding, collaboration, complexity, and social responsibility for others (DePree, 1992, 2004; Kezar et al., 2006; Palmer, 1990, 2000). In the following, we elaborate on each of these assumptions and highlight their implications for the design of revolutionary leadership development curricula.

Revolutionary frameworks advance the notion of leadership as a socially constructed phenomenon and thus emphasize the influence of perceptions, interpretations, context, culture, subjective experiences, and the processes of meaning making on leadership practices (Grint, 1997; Kezar, 2002a; Parry, 1998; Rhoads & Tierney, 1992; Tierney, 1988; Weick, 1995). Leadership is no longer understood to be a universal truth or individual possession; instead, it is recognized as a highly complex and ambiguous process shaped by interpersonal interactions and the cultural and social norms of particular contexts. In order to account for and address these complexities, organizations should embrace learning as an essential strategy for adapting and thriving in complex environments and implement leadership development programs that foster in organizational members the skills and values associated with learning (e.g., reflection, environmental scanning, collaboration).

Another revolutionary insight associated with the recognition of leadership as a socially constructed process is the acknowledgment that the perspectives of individuals located throughout the leadership setting, not just those individuals in formal positions of authority, play an important role in shaping leadership contexts and outcomes. Thus, power and influence are understood to be distributed throughout the organization rather than centralized in the hands of a few designated leaders.

The assumption that leadership is a process of shared power and mutual influence is of particular relevance to those revolutionary scholars and practitioners who seek to highlight the historic role of leadership as a tool of social control (Ashcroft, Griffiths, & Tiffin, 1995; Blackmore, 1999; Calas & Smircich, 1992; Chliwniak, 1997; Grint, 1997; Kezar, 2000, 2002a, 2002b; Kezar & Moriarty, 2000; Palestini, 1999; Popper, 2001; Rhode, 2003; Skrla, 2000; Tierney, 1993; Young & Skrla, 2003) and work to disrupt this cycle of oppression by helping organizations establish shared power environments that promote social justice and positive social change (Astin & Leland, 1991; Meyerson, 2003; Meyerson & Scully, 1995). Research has shown that leadership processes capable of empowering historically marginalized individuals and transforming organizations are collaborative in nature and framed by a shared vision for a socially just future (Meyerson; Meyerson & Scully). Thus, individuals committed to enacting revolutionary leadership assumptions seek to cultivate teams, partnerships, and networks with individuals who share their view of leadership as a process of resistance and/or a vehicle for social justice. In addition, social change is not likely to be achieved overnight; revolutionary leadership perspectives emphasize sustained commitment to the leadership enterprise.

Inextricably tied to the revolutionary assumption that leadership is a collaborative process focused on empowerment and social change is the realization that leadership can no longer be framed as a values-neutral phenomenon. Instead, revolutionary scholars emphasize the important role values play in shaping the actions and outcomes of leadership. For example, if the empowerment and social change ambitions of revolutionary leadership are to be realized, individual actions as well as organizational processes must reflect the values of equity, reflexivity, collaboration, empathy, and justice.

The revolutionary assumptions described above hold important implications for the design and implementation of higher education leadership development programs. Rather than continuing to sponsor programs that target positional leaders who operate from a values-neutral, top-down, and context-free leadership paradigm, revolutionary leadership educators should expand their target audience and engage individuals from across the organization as a means of fostering leadership environments that value and enact collaboration, empowerment, learning, and social responsibility. Revolutionary leadership programs should incorporate reflective exercises and collaborative activities that shed light on the context-specific dimensions of leadership, and cultivate among participants the skills and commitment necessary to read and negotiate the ever-changing influences of history, culture, social interactions, and subjective experiences on the leadership process. A more detailed discussion of the development implications embedded within the leadership revolution is presented at the end of this chapter, building upon the distinct, yet interdependent, revolutionary leadership concepts described in the next section.

Revolutionary Leadership Development Concepts

In this section we review the core concepts embedded in the leadership revolution. We introduce and define the concept, explain how it relates to the new leadership assumptions, and introduce some main thinkers and resources. We also review a few ways leadership training might be altered to embrace the concept. For more detail on some of these concepts, see Kezar et al. (2006).

Promoting Individual and Organizational Learning

When leadership is assumed to be a mutual power and influence process and involves a collective of individuals who are working to create change, organizational learning becomes critical to fulfilling this new mandate for leadership. It is no longer sufficient for a set of leaders with positions of power to set a vision and to try to force or persuade individuals to follow the vision, one they do not understand or appreciate. Leaders of the future recognize that change within organizations requires collective development of a vision, which typically requires organizational learning. In order to collectively develop a vision, individuals from the organization need to understand external forces, trends in the environment, internal data, and other key information that can help them assess where the organization is and where it needs to go. Margaret Wheatley (1999) is best known for describing this process of self-discovery; successful leaders help individuals throughout the organization participate in a process of organizational self-discovery by providing enough information and opportunities for dialogue, so that organizational learning can occur and eventually a collective vision emerges, a change process develops, or better decisions are made. While Wheatley focuses on the role that leaders play in helping a collective learning process, other authors emphasize the role of leaders in promoting individual development among staff, for example Senge (1990).

Organizational learning is not only important to the development of vision and change (key components of leadership) but is also important for daily decision making and planning. Senge (1990) argues that the most important aspect of leadership is helping people continually expand capabilities and for leaders to be responsible for learning among employees who make meaningful decisions daily. Senge suggests that this places the leader in a fundamentally different role as steward, facilitator, or teacher. Leaders need to focus on asking other people the right questions so that they challenge outdated beliefs and assumptions, support professional development, and create environments that support learning (for example, restructuring hierarchical arrangements that prevent communication and information sharing that support learning).

This fundamental shift in the role of leaders requires new skills and training. Leaders are typically trained to work alone on vision development and often isolate themselves for brainstorming and reflection. Furthermore, leaders perceive that their role is to solve problems rather than to work with others to brainstorm solutions; they alone must have the answers. Instead, leaders need to be trained on facilitation skills for leading brainstorming groups (see Bensimon & Neumann, 1993, for guidance). They also need to be trained to focus on asking questions rather than moving directly to solutions (see Heifetz, 1994, as a resource for facilitation). A helpful case study for understanding how to work with faculty and staff in a collective fashion, asking questions, and providing general design principles for solutions is the Olivet Case study (http://www.kfhet.org/case_studies.html). This case study examines how Olivet College went through transformational change in a 10-year period with the help of a leader who skillfully used principles of organizational learning. Another case study of organizational learning is presented in Kezar et al. (2006) in "Green River Community College: A Different Kind of Leadership," pp. 187–190. In addition to these case studies, Kezar (2006) provides examples of campuses that have leaders who have established mechanisms for creating organizational learning, as well as guidance and advice for other leaders trying to establish similar mechanisms.

Leaders can also play an important role in the promotion of individual development if they see themselves as mentors/role models for the individuals they supervise and familiarize themselves with leadership development opportunities within the professions, such as the Higher Education Resource Services (HERS) Management Institute for Women in Higher Education, the American Council on Education Fellows program, the American Association of Community Colleges leadership conferences, and the National Association of Student Personnel Administrators midlevel managers meeting, also described in chapter 9. Leaders can develop mentoring networks as described in chapter 5 on women in science; in addition, they should try to create as many professional development opportunities within the organization as possible, given budget constraints. Learning needs to be emphasized more as an organizational priority. Part of the role of revolutionary leaders is to realign budgets to support professional development (on and off campus) and organizational development (money for retreats and town meetings with large groups of people).

In sum, promoting individual and organizational learning is certainly common sense but has not historically been emphasized within higher education leadership development programs. Many resources exist for helping leaders become more skilled in this area, but before they can be successful, leaders must be convinced of the value of realigning priorities from their own vision development and problem solving to working more collectively with others to learn and enhance the organization. For many campus leaders, embracing organizational learning will be a fundamental shift in the way they think about leadership, and this needs to be addressed first, as success ultimately rests on shifting institutional priorities and budgets to support such work.

Embracing Complexity and Chaos

In describing the chaotic conditions that surround and define contemporary organizations, Wheatley (1994) asserts, "Stasis, balance, equilibrium—these are temporary states. What endures is process—dynamic, adaptive, creative" (p. 98). Complexity and chaos leadership theorists acknowledge the ambiguous, multiple, and ever-changing realities of organizations operating within modern global societies; they advance leadership frameworks that posit achievement of global, system-level stability necessitating support for autonomy, flexibility, creativity, and adaptability at the local level (Allen & Cherrey, 2000; Cutright, 2001; Heifetz, 1994; Love & Estanek, 2004; Wheatley, 1994). The implementation of strict organizational rules applied without consideration of context, centralized decision-making mechanisms, and the differentiation of tasks associated with organizational hierarchy (all hallmarks of traditional leadership) serve to cement structures and practices incapable of responding to the constant fluctuations and shifting priorities that characterize chaotic and complex organizations. In order to thrive in the midst of chaos, organizations and individuals must abandon outdated hierarchical structures and embrace organizational processes that prioritize collaboration and local decision making. Decentralization and the promotion of local autonomy increase the adaptability of organizations and allow them to creatively and quickly respond to changing environmental conditions (Heifetz, 1994; Wheatley, 1994).

Contemporary chaos and complexity leadership frameworks reflect the revolutionary assumption that leadership is no longer the sole purview of individuals located at the top of the administrative hierarchy. Rather, leadership in chaotic and complex environments is a shared power and mutual influence process defined by the exchange of information and ideas across all levels of the organization. The high priorities placed on collaboration and organizational learning within complex and chaotic organizations also underscore the relevance these frameworks hold for illustrating the contemporary revolution in leadership theory and practice (Heifetz, 1994; Wheatley, 1994).

In addition to reviewing Wheatley's (1999) *Leadership and the New Science: Discovering Order in a Chaotic World,* a key chaos theory resource highlighted in the discussion of organizational learning above, readers are encouraged to read Heifetz's (1994) *Leadership Without Easy Answers* for additional insight on the principles and structures that characterize complex organizational environments capable of thriving in a constant state of flux. Heifetz describes a model of adaptive leadership that embraces ambiguity and actively pursues innovative solutions via organizational learning, creative problem solving, experiments, and collaborations—four constructs that must be addressed in revolutionary leadership development programs.

Birnbaum (1992) and Cooper and Ideta (1994) also serve as valuable resources with respect to designing leadership development curricula that reflect the principles of chaos and complexity theories. Both texts investigate the implications of cognitive complexity in postsecondary decision making. Research in higher education suggests that leaders tend to analyze situations in simplistic ways using only one or two organizational frameworks (Bensimon, 1991) or mental models. However, leadership in complex and chaotic organizations demands cognitive complexity, as the ability to view issues through multiple cognitive lenses is essential for making effective and ethical decisions that reflect the ambiguous realities of postmodern institutions. Two strategies associated with cultivating cognitive complexity include regularly seeking out the perspectives and insights of other organizational members, particularly those individuals historically located on the organizational margins (Cooper & Ideta), and implementing data-gathering and processing systems that allow decision teams to review information collected from multiple sources and perspectives. Both of these strategies underscore the important role organizational learning plays in navigating the leadership challenges of complexity and chaos.

Insights drawn from theories of chaos and complexity hold important implications for higher education leadership development curricula. First, rather than continuing to identify individuals located at the top of the organizational hierarchy as the target audience, leadership development programs need to expand their definitions of leaders and leadership and recruit participants who occupy different rungs of the administrative ladder as well as represent a cross-section of the university's organizational subunits. Creating a more inclusive leadership development roster not only supports the establishment of local autonomy and decentralized decision making—two hallmarks of leadership in complex and chaotic organizations—but this strategy also serves to facilitate the development of boundary-spanning networks that promote the exchange of information and ideas across the organization. These networks are a vital means of promoting organizational learning as well as supporting the adoption of systems-level thinking that helps organizational members recognize the institution-wide implications of local actions.

Leadership development activities must also focus on cultivating the knowledge and skills essential for working in organizational environments characterized by constant change. Specific areas for development include creativity, adaptability, reflexivity, and collaboration. These competencies can be explored and cultivated via the analysis of organizational case studies (for example, see "Case Study One—University of Portsmouth at Doonsbury: Chaos, Complexity, and Change," pp. 179–182, Kezar et al., 2006), artistic and performance exercises that challenge participants to stretch their creative talents, and experiential activities that charge participants with working collaboratively to address pressing campus issues.

Higher education leadership development programs interested in preparing individuals to lead within chaotic and complex organizational environments would also be well served to develop activities that help translate the institution's core mission, values, and priorities into simple organizing rules that participants may use to guide their professional actions and decisions. Wheatley (1994) identifies the establishment and application of simple organizing principles as a vital component of leadership in the midst of chaos, thus campus leadership development programs should make this a priority. One pedagogical strategy for pursuing this learning objective would be to engage participants in a document analysis project that challenges individuals to collect campus documents and distill the key principles and priorities embedded in the texts. Participants could then practice translating these principles into action through individual or collaborative case study analysis.

Teams and Collaborative Leadership

The recognition of leadership as a collective and collaborative process is a central assumption of the leadership revolution. While networks and teams are identified as critical components of organizational learning and leadership in chaotic and complex organizations, the study of teams and collaborative leadership is a distinct strand of the revolution and warrants further discussion. Not all contemporary team and collaboration research can be characterized as revolutionary, however. Some team leadership theories continue to advance scientific management perspectives that emphasize the development of individual skills and the identification of predictable behaviors and outcomes in team leadership contexts (Ilgen, Major, Hollenback, & Sego, 1993; Kelly, 1998; Kinlaw, 1998). In contrast, revolutionary team leadership scholars examine the relationships, shared values, and collaborative processes that frame collective leadership. As with the other revolutionary leadership concepts described above, a process orientation to leadership is at the forefront of team and collaborative leadership research and practice.

Similar to the systems-level perspective advanced in chaos and complexity leadership theories, team and collaborative leadership processes challenge organizations to look beyond individual skills and achievements and instead focus their energy on cultivating environments that emphasize interconnections, a shared vision for the future, and collective accomplishments. O'Conner and Quinn (2004) elaborate, "when leadership is viewed as a property of whole systems, as opposed to solely the property of individuals, effectiveness in leadership becomes more a product of those connections or relationships among parts than the result of any one part of that system (such as the leader)" (p. 420). Thus, team and collaborative leadership models underscore the need for leadership development programs to shift their focus from the identification and cultivation of individual leadership skills to an examination of the organizational structures, relationships, and processes that promote collaboration. These conditions include, among others, a culture of decentralized decision making, open communication, trust, and respect for divergent perspectives (Bensimon & Neumann, 1993; Tierney, 1993; Wheatley, 1994).

One particularly compelling and comprehensive team leadership resource is the Bensimon and Neumann (1993) text, *Redesigning Collegiate Leadership: Teams and Teamwork in Higher Education,* which advances a teams-as-culture model of collective leadership. One of the most important leadership development insights of the Bensimon and Neumann framework is the recognition that differences within the team are vital sources of creativity and innovation. Rather than emphasizing the establishment of harmony, consensus, and coordination within teams (characteristics that may contribute to groupthink and serve to silence individuals who disagree with the collective wisdom), organizers of leadership development programs must seek to cultivate individuals and teams that embrace different perspectives and create avenues for the authentic exchange of information and ideas. One specific strategy for developing teams that recognize the value of multiple perspectives is to provide individuals with opportunities to learn about and practice adopting different team roles. For example, Bensimon and Neumann describe eight different roles within presidential leadership teams (e.g., definer, analyst, emotional monitor, synthesizer). After a brief introduction to each of these eight roles, leadership development participants could then be subdivided into teams and asked to rotate fulfilling team roles during a series of group exercises. This activity not only helps individuals learn how to recognize distinct team roles, but it also challenges participants to step out of their comfort zone and practice adopting team roles they do not usually fulfill. In addition to introducing participants to the notion of team roles, organizers of leadership development programs guided by the team-as-culture framework might also consider integrating conflict resolution and negotiation skill development into the curriculum.

Komives, Lucas, and McMahon's (1998) relational leadership framework also embraces revolutionary collaborative leadership assumptions and serves as an excellent higher education leadership development resource. These authors describe relational leadership as a process in which people work together attempting to accomplish change or make a difference to benefit the common good. Although the Komives et al. text is written primarily for the college student leadership community, the relational leadership principles and leadership development activities shared in the book are of relevance to all individuals interested in cultivating collaborative leadership environments. Of particular value are the reflective activities at the end of each chapter that challenge readers to apply relational leadership principles to specific organizational contexts and identify strategies for cultivating the skills, values, and attitudes (for example, team learning, trust, conflict resolution, developing talent, self- and organizational renewal) essential for realizing the empowering potential of inclusive leadership processes.

Several scholars have explored tangible strategies for promoting collaborative leadership within institutions of higher education, and their findings hold significant implications for the future of higher education leadership development (Allen, Morton, & Li, 2003; Kezar, 2006; Pearce & Conger, 2003). For example, implementing programs and/or structures that provide staff members with opportunities to learn about the unique cultures and missions of other organizational subunits is an important first step toward developing the rapport and trust essential for collaboration. The University of California, Los Angeles (UCLA), Professional Development Program is a great example of this strategy in action. The human resources department sponsors this year-long professional development activity that fosters sustained interaction between staff members from a cross-section of university departments via monthly seminars, field trips to visit participating departments, a mentoring program with senior institutional leaders, team projects, and a buddy program that matches current participants with program alumni. Collectively these activities contribute to the establishment of cross-campus networks that serve as conduits for collaboration and shared leadership.

Engaging leadership development program participants in experiential education activities is also a valuable vehicle for cultivating the abilities and values of team leadership. For example, many campus recreation and/or student affairs departments employ staff who specialize in the facilitation of experiential education programs (often called challenge or low-ropes courses) designed to foster trust, communication, mutual respect, creative problem solving, and conflict resolution abilities within campus teams and work groups. This strategy is particularly appropriate for leadership development programs that invite all members of a team or work group to participate in the professional development opportunity.

Other strategies for fostering team and collaborative leadership include (a) altering institutional mission, vision, and values statements to explicitly identify collaboration as an institutional priority; (b) providing incentives for collaboration in promotion and tenure policies; (c) increasing accountaility for collective action by changing performance review protocols to reflect shared responsibility for organizational outcomes; and (d) offering financial and human resources as incentives for the establishment of collaborative campus projects (e.g., interdisciplinary research centers or crossdepartmental task forces; Allen et al., 2003; Kezar, 2006; Pearce & Conger, 2003). As the nature of these strategies illustrate, collaborative leadership is not a phenomenon that can be cultivated overnight; it requires patience and an extended commitment of time, energy, and resources (Ferren & Stanton, 2004).

Sensitivity to Culture and Context

In a world where leaders are taught that the same behaviors and traits will be successful in any context, cultural sensitivity is not typically emphasized within traditional leadership frameworks. However, we now understand that leadership is context bound and organizationally determined and that good leadership varies by institutional environment (Birnbaum, 1992). In addition, leadership is perceived differently by individuals based on their racial or gender backgrounds (Kezar, 2000, 2002a). With this recognition of the importance of context and culture, new skills are required for leaders. Instead of focusing on action and data, leaders must carefully analyze institutional culture as well as recognize the role of values and history before engaging in a leadership process. Leaders will be more successful if they play the role of organizational anthropologist, getting to know the underlying values, history, and traditions of their campus as well as the key individuals they work with.

Several tools exist for assisting leaders in developing their skills in reading context and culture. For example, Bergquist (1992) provides a detailed description of four cultures—collegial, developmental, political/negotiating, and bureaucratic—that typically characterize entire campuses or subcultures on campuses. This book describes the nature of the cultures and ways that leaders can be successful in working within the four cultures. For example, planning processes within a collegial culture should move at a slower pace, be informal, and try to involve as many people as possible, while planning processes within a political culture should include key constituent leaders and should have transparent and public processes. The role of leaders is to understand these different cultures and work within them but also to challenge them when needed. But it will be difficult to change a culture without understanding it first. Bolman and Deal (1995) also provide information about different organizational contexts and are an additional resource on this concept. Kezar et al. (2006) provide case studies that help leaders to analyze campus culture (see, for example, "Quaker College: Collegiality, Culture and Tradition," pp. 182–187). All of these resources highlight the fact that organizations are dynamic and cultures are always changing and influenced by new people entering the context.

Another important resource is Rhoads and Tierney's (1992) *Cultural Leadership in Higher Education*, which outlines the key principles of culturally responsive leadership. Like Birnbuam (1992) and Berquist (1992), Rhoads and Tierney posit that the most fundamental assumption of leadership is that colleges and universities exist as distinct organizational cultures requiring specific analysis (as outlined in the Berquist resource). Therefore, successful leaders are those who demonstrate the cultural practices (interpreting context, reading history, and determining and appreciating values) necessary to examine and understand the unique dimensions of specific university contexts. Rhoads and Tierney offer tips for such work, including mission analysis, environmental scanning, observation of socialization processes, information patterns, and strategy review. Chaffee & Tierney (1988) describe interpretive strategy, which offers a way for leaders to add values dimensions to planning and which has proven successful. The importance of understanding campus culture suggests that more campuses should consider "growing their own programs" in which leaders can be developed who have great sensitivity to the campus culture because they have been part of it for years. Two additional principles of culturally sensitive leadership advanced by Rhoads and Tierney are putting people/values first rather than strategy or decision making and being aware of diverse perspectives based on race, gender, class, sexual orientation, and other categories.

In the past, leadership development has not focused on helping leaders see how different subgroups within an organization might interpret or understand an issue differently. Since research demonstrates that some women and people of color have different perspectives and definitions of leadership, it is important for leaders to seek out and understand how people on the campus define leadership, creating an environment that is inclusive of multiple perspectives. Kezar (2002a) provides an activity that can be used to help leaders understand their own leadership beliefs as well as improve their skills and abilities to read and understand those they work with. Through the use of case stories, leaders read through a personal reflection by a leader who is attuned to how his or her background, experiences, power dynamics, and context shape the leader's leadership beliefs. A set of guiding questions help leaders to also develop the case story of their own experiences. The article also describes ways the case stories can be used in leadership development courses as part of dramatic readings, role plays, and other simulated activities. Furthermore, campuses and regional and national leadership development programs need to be conscious of ways that different ethnicities think about leadership and not offer a monolithic definition or understanding. Programming supportive of and separate for women and people of color has become a more common practice and is important for supporting these traditionally underrepresented groups.

The importance of being aware of the way context and culture shapes leadership processes will fundamentally improve the leadership on many campuses. Many leadership researchers have found this to be a critical area where leaders fail to be sensitive and results in campuses' losing faith and trust in leaders and leadership processes.

Ethics/Spirituality

As Rhoads and Tierney (1992) note, once leaders understand that leadership is inherently a cultural process, they become attuned to the important place of values within the leadership process. Traditional leadership assumptions often focus on data and strategy rather than values and beliefs. In value-free theories of leadership, leaders' behavior is dictated by the achievement of desired goals, not ethical considerations. Researchers have demonstrated that decision making cannot be value free and that ignoring values has ethical problems, often masking inequities and inhumane processes within organizations (Kezar et al., 2006). However, ethics and spirituality are not necessarily new to understanding the leadership process but rather have regained popularity in recent years; many pre-Enlightenment societies as well as non-Western societies, such as African, Native American, and some Eastern cultures, emphasize ethics and spirituality in relationship to leadership.

In the 20th century, scientific management theories downplayed the importance of ethics, favoring logic-based decision-making and planning processes, attempting to neutralize and downplay the role of values in decision-making processes. So if the leader decided that restructuring a department might improve a product, examining how this might affect people within the organization was not necessary. However, more recent beliefs emphasizing social justice and empowerment focus on the need to examine the underlying values component of decisions (in other words, the implications for loyalty, justice, or equality). Many scholars believe that scientific management has failed to create leadership that is humane or that serves organizations and society well (Bass, 1985; Greenleaf, 1977).

Several leadership frameworks have emerged that have an ethical foundation and embrace notions of character, authenticity, and credibility. Perhaps the most widely known ethical leadership framework is the servant leadership model by Greenleaf (1977). Greenleaf provides guidance, stories, and reflective activities for individuals who want to embrace an ethical framework of leadership. Another framework is provided by Starratt (2004) that outlines a map for leaders based on three ethical systems: care, justice, and critique. Rushworth Kidder (1995) describes how to develop ethical fitness or an examination of core values, right versus right dilemmas, and resolution principles such as ends-based thinking, rules-based thinking, and care-based thinking. It is critical to know that these texts also suggest that ethical climates vary by organizational culture and no one effective ethical leadership culture exists. Leaders strive to develop a culture that people believe is ethical and sustains this environment because it creates organizational effectiveness and health. Any of these three texts provide a helpful foundation for leadership development coordinators. In addition, case studies of campus leaders can also be used to help examine the moral dimensions of the leadership. Nelson (2000) provides case studies of several college presidents and describes moral and ethical dilemmas that they faced. This is an ideal book for helping leaders think about the challenges of academic freedom, institutional mission, shaping students' character, or public service.

In addition to examining specific ethical frameworks that can be introduced to leaders as a means of helping them rethink decision making, revolutionary leadership scholars have also used spirituality as a framework for bringing a values or moral component to leadership. Spirituality is a broader term than religion, which encompasses metaphysical beliefs that are included in formal institutions (such as the Roman Catholic Church) as well as beliefs that are not institutionalized into doctrine. Parker Palmer (1990, 2000) has written extensively on the spiritual dimensions of leadership, describing leadership as a spiritual journey that requires individuals to engage in deep and sustained self-reflection on the motives, intentions, and relationships that guide their decisions and interactions. He recommends that leadership development programs should include activities intentionally designed to cultivate the commitment, values, and abilities essential for engaging in meaningful and sustained reflection on the metaphysical beliefs that guide our actions. Reflective journaling, meditation, creative expression (e.g., writing poetry, painting, reflecting on spiritual and emotional responses to music) are examples of specific pedagogical strategies that may prove effective in facilitating the internal journey called for by revolutionary leadership scholars. While ethics has been much further developed than spirituality, in this book we try to provide specific advice (see chapter 6) on ways that spirituality can be integrated into leadership development.

Ethics and spirituality have often been separated from the workplace and leadership, so this may be difficult for leadership trainers to defend within their curriculum. However, codes of conduct, professional ethical codes, and other such documents provide a foundation for discussing and introducing ethics, prior to deeper discussions. Ethics and spirituality are difficult because there are no ready-made answers and they usually require much longer development than teaching steps and vision creation. Leadership programs can usually only start this journey with the participants.

Emotions

Also directly related to understanding leadership as a cultural process and putting people first (rather than data or strategy) is an appreciation of the role that emotions play in leadership. Traditional scientific management theories denied the importance of emotions just as they denied the importance of values and ethics—these were not to be trusted and they clouded judgment. But more recent theories of leadership emphasize how wisdom, and truly successful decision making, involves the bridging of mind, body, spirit, and emotions. Like spirituality, emotions have always had some relationship to leadership, and even traditional scientific management theories emphasize the importance of charisma. However, emotions are playing a much more prominent role in leadership development than in the past; trainers now see the importance of helping leaders to motivate, persuade, take the emotional pulse of the campus, and to become emotionally intelligent.

A helpful resource for leadership development coordinators is Daniel Goleman's (1995, 1998) books on emotional intelligence and leadership. These books contain several activities to help leaders understand their own emotions, assess other individuals' emotions, help people negotiate different emotional states, and manage emotions effectively so that when interacting with others, they create the right environment. Key missteps and lessons are also emphasized. For example, self-control is paramount to learn because when people get angry and frustrated in stressful situations, they are impulsive and their feelings can negatively affect the outcome. Instead, leaders are trained on how to stay composed and be positive under pressure, using activities that help them to manage difficult emotions.

Emotional development is not just interpersonal, and leadership processes need to examine how collectives of individuals work together and manage emotions. Bensimon and Neumann's (1993) book on leadership teams describes how to foster individuals within leadership teams that play the role of the emotional monitor, helping the team to be successful. Functional leadership teams have individuals who check in on the feelings and emotions of various members of the team and do not allow a cognitive function to overwhelm the relationships of people on the team. These types of collective leadership skills are described and demonstrated in the book.

The spiritual and emotional frameworks of leadership call for more group activities and facilitated role plays that allow program participants to practice working with others in order to apply spiritual insights and the skills of emotional intelligence in a safe environment. In addition, the importance of spirituality and emotions to leadership also challenge the *quick fix* orientation of short-term leadership development programs and, instead, underscore the need for longer-term programs. As noted under spirituality, and reinforced in this section on emotions, development in these areas takes a long time so program length might need to be extended or the nature of program design rethought. In addition to extending the length of formal programs, leadership development educators, committed to addressing the spiritual and emotional dynamics of leadership, should allocate resources (financial as well as personnel) to the development of follow-up activities, communities of practice, and networks designed to offer program alumni guidance and support in the internal journey essential for effective leadership.

Throughout a career, most leaders will have been rewarded for their cognitive abilities, and the suggestion to focus on emotional capacities seems counter to an individual's experience in his or her career. However, the leadership research does suggest that leaders in touch with their emotions are authentic and behave with consistency, can read the emotions of others, and attend to the emotional aspects of the organization. Even if educators can only start the journey, it is better than ignoring this critical area of leadership.

Empowerment/Social Change

In order to successfully create shared leadership environments that enact the revolutionary principles of mutual power and influence, organizational members must find ways to empower individuals historically marginalized because of their social identities, cultural backgrounds, and/or positions within the organizational hierarchy. Empowerment refers to the practice of sharing power and enabling organizational constituents to act on issues they feel are important and relevant. Because organizations have traditionally been designed to reinforce hierarchy, social control, and the concentration of power in positional leaders, empowerment often does not come easy but is an essential step in creating organizational environments that uphold the revolutionary principles of collaborative leadership.

Tightly coupled with the revolutionary notion of empowerment is the idea of fostering leadership for social change. Rather than seeking to implement leadership processes and organizational structures that perpetuate a status quo characterized by self-interest, control, and coercion, leadership for social change is a group process that emphasizes working synergistically toward organizational goals that emphasize equity, social justice, and compassion. These new concepts challenge scientific management leadership models by emphasizing inclusion, interdependence, and shared power. Accordingly, influence is perceived to pass between people instead of passing through formal hierarchical lines; thus the formation of networks and collaborative partnerships are paramount to the pursuit of social change.

Meyerson and Scully's (1995) study of tempered radicals, individuals who patiently and persistently advance social change agendas within their organizations by adopting individual and collective strategies that foster congruence between their actions and values, is an excellent resource for people interested in designing higher education leadership development programs that emphasize empowerment and social change. In *Tempered Radicals: How Everyday Leaders Inspire Change at Work,* Meyerson (2003) builds on her initial collaboration with Scully and identifies five specific social change strategies: (a) resisting quietly and staying true to one's "self," (b) turning personal threats into opportunities, (c) broadening the impact of change efforts through negotiation, (d) leveraging small wins to advance a larger social justice project, and (e) organizing collective action. Meyerson's rich description of each strategy provides valuable guidance to those readers interested in adopting these tactics as the foundation for a higher education leadership development curriculum. First, the program must engage participants in reflective exercises that shed light on the extent to which their personal values and social identities are congruent or at odds with institutional values and priorities. Next, assertive communication and negotiation skill development sessions provide participants with opportunities to foster the interpersonal competencies essential for confronting controversy with civility and maximizing the impact of social change efforts. Finally, the program will include learning objectives centered on developing the resources and skills of collective action (for example, networking, mobilizing, delegation, fund-raising, mentoring, public relations, renewal, and rejuvenation).

Two additional resources of relevance to the development of leadership for social change and empowerment are *Leadership Reconsidered: Engaging Higher Education in Social Change* (Astin & Astin, 2000) and *A Social Change Model of Leadership Development* (Higher Education Research Institute, 1996). Both texts describe the purpose of leadership as the advancement of social change, and offer succinct, although slightly different, descriptions of the core attributes associated with engaging in leadership for social change. The social change model identifies the values of collaboration, consciousness of self, commitment, congruence, common purpose, controversy with civility, and citizenship (these values have come to be known as the 7 Cs of social change leadership) as the hallmarks of leadership for social change. Along similar lines, the authors of *Leadership Reconsidered* describe five individual and five group characteristics essential for cultivating transformative leadership environments: self-knowledge, authenticity/integrity, commitment, empathy/understanding of others, competence, collaboration, shared purpose, disagreement with respect, division of labor, and a learning environment. Although the terms are not identical, there is a tremendous degree of overlap between the two social change frameworks; reflexivity, congruence, collaboration, and respect for different perspectives are essential elements of both models and thus provide the solid foundation for a revolutionary leadership development curriculum focused on advancing the notion of leadership as a vehicle for promoting justice and empowering others. It is important to note that although the social change model guidebook (Higher Education Research Institute, 1996) is predominately used as a curricular resource for student leadership programs (Outcalt, Faris, & McMahon, 2001), the guidebook's utility is not limited to this population. Higher education leadership educators interested in including a social change dimension in their curriculum will find the authors' commentary on each social change value, suggested leadership development activities, as well as the extensive recommended reading list quite useful.

One specific strategy for integrating notions of empowerment and social change in contemporary leadership development programs is to design activities that help participants learn how to identify, acquire, and broadly disseminate information and resources pertaining to pressing campus issues. The development of learning objectives related to the cultivation of institutional assessment and organizational communication competencies contributes to the establishment of a campus environment characterized by open access to information and informed decision making. For example, one leadership development session might focus on helping participants learn how to use the campus's vast technology resources (e.g., e-mail, Listservs, Web page, conference call service) to organize and sustain collective action, while another session might seek to shed light on existing institutional resources and activities of relevance to a particular social issue (e.g., staff diversity, adjunct faculty, academic integrity). The adoption of leadership development strategies that focus on facilitating communication across organizational boundaries is a particularly important vehicle for empowering individuals and groups historically marginalized, given that knowledge is power within contemporary organizations and the open exchange of information and ideas is a critical first step in the establishment of sustained collective action.

Leadership development programs centered on empowerment and social change must also cultivate competencies related to delegation, the implementation of decentralized decision-making processes, and the creation of organizational environments that foster and sustain collaborative networks, teams, and partnerships among individuals from different backgrounds and perspectives. Experiential education activities (i.e., low-ropes and challenge courses) and role-playing simulations can offer meaningful opportunities to practice the art of delegation and collaborative decision making; while involvement in team-based leadership development projects, cross-campus professional development networks (such as the UCLA Professional Development Program), and cross-generational mentoring initiatives can help cultivate the competencies and the relationships associated with empowered leadership.

Finally, to place the notions of social responsibility and social justice at the forefront of campus leadership processes, institutions might consider designing leadership programs centered on pressing social issues (e.g., creating sustainable campuses, recruitment and retention of underrepresented students, employee rights, community partnerships) rather than the development of individual change agents. Guided by the philosophy of learning by doing, campus leadership teams comprising individuals recruited from a cross-section of organizational subunits could be charged with working collaboratively for a year to investigate the issue and develop a campus action plan. Program facilitators might periodically engage the teams in structured leadership development activities designed to cultivate the knowledge and skills associated with collaborative social change efforts. By placing issues, not individuals, at the center of the program, participants gain firsthand experience participating in leadership processes focused on social change.

Globalization

The contemporary era of globalization is characterized by the escalating economic, cultural, and political dominance of multinational corporations; the blurring of nation-state boundaries; the seemingly unchecked expansion of international trade; and the recognition that countries as well as organizations are increasingly interdependent. Unprecedented developments in technology, commerce, and media have created societies defined by the rapid and constant exchange of information, culture, and capital across international borders, leading to a global interdependence that ensures that change in one country affects social and economic conditions on the other side of the globe. Within the context of leadership theory and practice, the concept of globalization sheds light on the unique leadership aims, processes, characteristics, and competencies essential for thriving in an interdependent world. Global leadership is characterized by shared power, rapid decision making, cross-cultural communication, political conflict, complexity, chaos, and constant change.

Similar to the scholarship of teams and collaborative research synthesized above, some studies of leadership in global contexts adopt a more traditional, scientific management orientation. The more traditional strands of global leadership research emphasize the identification of individual leadership competencies and traits associated with the successful navigation of cross-cultural interactions and multinational business transactions. At present, this represents the great majority of the literature and there is a need for more research from a revolutionary perspective. For example, researchers from a more traditional framework have identified the following competencies as particularly relevant for practicing leadership in a world increasingly defined by global capitalism: thinking globally, appreciating cultural diversity, developing technological savvy, building strategic alliances, demonstrating integrity and courage, initiating change, managing uncertainty, negotiating, bargaining, and improvising (Goldsmith, Greenberg, Robertson, & Hu-Chan, 2003; Mendenhall, 2001). Studies that seek to compare and contrast the traits and behaviors of business leaders in diverse cultural and geographic contexts are another prime example of global leadership scholarship informed by the functional assumptions of the scientific management perspective. A prime example of this research is the Global Leadership and Organizational Behavior Effectiveness (GLOBE) Research Project, a network of more than 150 social scientists in 62 countries working collaboratively to identify universally endorsed leadership attributes as well as culturally contingent leadership traits that reflect the unique contexts of specific cultures (House, Hanges, Javidan, Dorfman, & Gupta, 2004). An analysis of the GLOBE leadership data by Den Hartog et al. (1999) confirmed universally endorsed leadership characteristics, including foresight, trustworthiness, and the abilities to encourage, motivate, foster confidence in others, and communicate. Although the GLOBE project seeks to understand the global dimensions of leadership, the research serves to sustain traditional trait and behavior theories of leadership that minimize context in the interest of discovering a set of universal leadership behaviors.

In contrast to the traditional global leadership perspectives described above, revolutionary frameworks place context, culture, and mutual influence at the forefront of global leadership theory and practice. For example, global leadership efforts highlight the importance of reading unique leadership contexts and understanding different cultures given that the expansion of global commerce is inextricably linked to an increase in cross-cultural interactions. Thus, the ability to understand and respectfully navigate different cultural values, goals, and contexts is a critical dimension of global leadership. Revolutionary assumptions regarding the shared power and social justice aims of contemporary leadership processes are also relevant to the study and practice of global leadership. In order to achieve global stability, multinational corporations must embrace decentralized decision-making models and shared-power perspectives of organizational leadership that allow local management teams to demonstrate adaptability and creativity within their unique cultural contexts. One of the major criticisms of globalization, however, is that the rapid growth of multinational corporations and the continued economic and political dominance of certain nation-states such as the United States and China have contributed to the development of unequal power conditions that serve to threaten the delicate balance of shared power vital for sustaining peace and collective prosperity within the global marketplace. Social justice ambitions and the benefits of mutual power and influence processes are easily lost in global dialogues focused on competition and profit maximization. Accordingly, revolutionary global leadership scholars have turned their attention to identifying leadership processes and structures that support shared power and facilitate cross-cultural coordination of goals, activities, and resources in the interest of initiating positive social change (Adler, 2001b; Crosby, 1999; Lipman-Blumen, 1996).

Leadership educators interested in exploring revolutionary global leadership concepts and practices in their program curricula should consider reviewing the work of Nancy Adler (2001a, 2001b), a prominent global leadership scholar who seeks to identify leadership processes that balance the goal of economic prosperity with the values of cross-cultural sensitivity and social responsibility. In "Global Leadership: Women Leaders," Adler (2001b) describes the feminization of global leadership—"the spread of traits and qualities generally associated with women to the process of leading organizations with worldwide influence" (p. 81). This new form of leadership, which best matches the needs of a global world focuses on empathy, interpersonal sensitivity, and a collective orientation, feminine traits that have proven effective in facilitating the interaction of people and ideas across cultural and geographic boundaries. Adler's emphasis on collaboration and cross-cultural networking as essential elements of culturally responsive global leadership is also echoed in the work of Lipman-Blumen (1996). Rather than seeking to cultivate global leaders who prioritize competition, profit, and cultural conformity (principles historically associated with traditional masculine leadership frameworks), Adler's work reinforces the need to develop revolutionary leadership development programs focused on fostering the feminine values and competencies of interdependence. One specific pedagogical strategy for integrating Adler's insights into postsecondary leadership development curricula is to assign and discuss readings that focus on the leadership narratives of women. More specifically, program participants could be asked to review case studies, biographies, and scholarly articles that examine the unique challenges and opportunities encountered by women presidents, prime ministers, and CEOs of global corporations and nonprofit organizations. For example, in *Body and Soul,* Anita Roddick (1991) shares the compelling story of how she founded The Body Shop, an international cosmetics retail chain known for its commitment to natural ingredients and environmental sustainability. Not only did Roddick succeed in launching a highly profitable retail franchise, she also managed to transform the global cosmetics industry in the process by pursuing profits via positive social change. Roddick's narrative is inspirational and informative, detailing specific strategies for enacting revolutionary global leadership. For a comprehensive chronology of global women leaders as well as an extensive list of references on the subject, see Adler (2001b).

In addition to recognizing the interdependent nature of global leadership, Adler (2001a) and Crosby (1999) reaffirm the empowerment and social responsibility dimensions of this revolutionary concept. Specifically, Adler (2001a) asserts, "Given their global influence, which by definition, transcends national borders, global leaders have a responsibility for the well-being of society. . . . Since no government body can regulate companies that span the globe, the social-responsibility function must be internalized by the company and its leaders in ways that have never been needed or seen before"

(p. 259). Similarly, Crosby (1999) describes the qualities of global citizenship (personal leadership; team leadership; visionary leadership; the ability to read and comprehend the social, political, economic, and technological contexts of leadership, among others) and calls upon global leaders to focus their efforts and resources on resolving pressing global concerns. In contrast to more traditional perspectives on global leadership that continue to focus on the identification of individual leadership traits, revolutionary scholars emphasize the moral and ethical dimensions of transnational leadership processes. Within the specific context of higher education leadership development, the global leadership principles of empowerment and social responsibility can be fostered by engaging program participants in activities that shed light on the global implications of policies implemented at the campus, state, or federal level. One specific strategy is to divide program participants into leadership study teams charged with analyzing pressing campus issues (e.g., academic freedom, enrollment management, research productivity) through the lens of globalization. For example, the enrollment management study group might be asked to examine institutional efforts related to the recruitment of international students with a specific aim of understanding how these activities have an impact on economic and political outcomes in a student's home and in the students' host countries. The following questions could guide the project: How does the student's home country benefit from sending students abroad for a college education? What are the social, political, economic, and cultural costs of this global educational transaction? What policies and practices might colleges adopt to ensure that the institution's international enrollment management plan fulfills Adler's vision of global social responsibility? This learning activity not only provides a means for participants to practice the global leadership competencies of shared leadership and collaborative problem solving, it also helps them recognize the global consequences of local actions and empowers them to fulfill the social responsibility expectations of global citizenship.

Building on the ideas and assumptions shared above, it is evident that higher education leadership development programs seeking to incorporate the revolutionary insights and values of globalization should engage participants in curricular activities that foster the values of interdependence, shared power, and global social responsibility as well as cultivate the cross-cultural communication skills needed to read, understand, and navigate the intersection of divergent cultural norms, values, and goals. Leadership exchange programs that provide university faculty and staff with the opportunity to spend significant amounts of time immersed in the culture and leadership processes of an international university is one vehicle for fostering global campus leaders. Campus leadership development programs may also use technology to create virtual exchange programs that allow participants to form networks and regularly collaborate with professional counterparts working in other corners of the world. Whether or not university leadership development programs have the funds to support international travel, the focus of global leadership development efforts should be on helping participants recognize and navigate the escalating influences of global economic, political, and cultural interdependence on contemporary societies in general and institutions of higher education in particular.

Revolutionary Leadership Development Program Design

Reading across the leadership constructs and development practices described in this chapter brings us full circle to our previous discussion of the foundational assumptions that characterize the leadership revolution. Rather than designing programs to emphasize one or two specific revolutionary leadership constructs, program facilitators would be well served to develop curricula that reflect all five revolutionary assumptions, thus preparing individuals to successfully navigate the complex and ever-shifting interpersonal, cultural, and political dynamics that shape higher education leadership processes. To assist readers in the application of these revolutionary leadership principles, we offer the following program design recommendations:

1. **Expand program time frames**: Revolutionary leadership processes are time intensive and require the sustained commitment of time, energy, and resources. One-time seminars and short leadership development courses are certainly not without merit, but the implementation of extended training programs that engage participants in the long-term work of leadership development is an ideal step toward helping individuals cultivate the patience, stamina, and commitment required to practice revolutionary leadership.

2. **Balance reflection with action:** Leadership is often framed as a set of actions, however, the practice of revolutionary leadership necessitates that individuals regularly set aside time to reflect on their emotions, values, experiences, skills, surrounding environments, and goals. As

discussed earlier in this chapter, self-reflection is a critical step in the processes of learning and social change—both essential elements of revolutionary leadership. If individuals wish to contribute to the development of socially just leadership processes, they must first take stock of their own principles and actions, seeking to understand what role they have played in the perpetuation of organizational norms that serve to marginalize, discriminate, and/or inhibit collaboration. Palmer (1990) describes this reflective activity as exploring the "shadow" side of leadership. With respect to facilitating the process of organizational learning, reflection is a critical step in understanding how the past and present might shape the organization's future. Incorporating reflective activities such as journaling and other forms of writing, meditation, or artistic expression in leadership development programs is one strategy for cultivating a commitment to reflection among revolutionary leaders.

3. **Promote interdependence:** Within revolutionary constructs, leadership is no longer viewed as an individual possession but rather a collaborative process characterized by shared power and mutual influence. Higher education leadership development programs must emulate and foster this collaborative perspective via curricular and pedagogical strategies that emphasize interdependence, teamwork, and collective action. Rather than recruiting individual participants, leadership programs might be redesigned to target entire leadership teams or organizational subunits. Team-based programs minimize the role and achievements of designated team leaders and instead place group processes, such as developing a shared vision, conflict resolution, and collaborative decision making, at the forefront of leadership development. In addition, team-based programs underscore the important role cognitive complexity plays in revolutionary leadership environments, providing opportunities for participants to experience difference within teams (whether it be difference as it relates to race, class, gender, education, opinion, etc.) as a team asset, not an obstacle to cohesion and consensus. Programs that emphasize the interdependent nature of leadership will also include activities and/or resources designed to facilitate the development of relationships and networks that will continue well after the formal program has ended.

4. **Situate leadership in context**: Another common thread that connects the revolutionary leadership constructs discussed in this chapter is the recognition that context matters. No longer viewed as a set of universal traits, skills, or behaviors that transcend context, revolutionary leadership processes are understood to be firmly anchored in time and place. Thus, revolutionary leadership development programs must also emphasize the important role local context and culture play in shaping leadership processes and individual experiences. Rather than sending individuals off campus for their leadership training, leaders of institutions might consider increasing support for campus-based leadership development programs that focus on the specific issues, challenges, and opportunities confronting university leadership teams. Local leadership development programs also provide participants with firsthand experience in reading campus culture, especially those programs that encourage interaction among individuals who work in diverse organizational subunits. National leadership development programs can also foster the skills and knowledge essential for the practice of local leadership by including a campus-based project in the curriculum. Participants attending national or international leadership training seminars can be given the opportunity to focus their program activities on a particular project or issue they are grappling with at home.

5. **Focus on values**: Revolutionary leadership processes are not values neutral; indeed, they are far from it. The revolutionary leadership constructs described in this chapter reflect the values of collaboration, reflexivity, social justice, integrity, and change, among others. Through individual reflective exercises and collective dialogue, leadership development participants must be offered opportunities to examine their personal and organizational values as well as receive assistance in the identification of strategies for achieving congruence when dissonance exists. The aims and objectives of revolutionary leadership also demonstrate a strong values orientation, calling upon participants to engage in leadership processes that promote positive social change, civic responsibility, empowerment, and social justice. The well-being of others, not profit and productivity, are at the heart of revolutionary leadership, and this order of priorities must be reflected in leadership development curricula. Placing pressing social

and campus issues, not individual skill building, at the center of leadership development activities is one specific strategy for cultivating individuals committed to leadership for social change.

As detailed in this chapter, revolutionary approaches suggest that leadership is about developing certain habits of mind and heart, not universal truths. Thus, these leadership development program recommendations are intended to offer guidance, not a formula, for designing higher education leadership programs that reflect the foundational principles of the leadership revolution. In order to cultivate individuals, teams, and campus environments capable of thriving in the midst of chaos and complexity, colleges and universities must move beyond traditional scientific management perspectives that reinforce the status quo, top-down leadership. Rather than identifying and training formal leaders to wield authority across presumably universal campus contexts, the adoption of a revolutionary leadership perspective necessitates the development of programs that focus on cultivating leaders throughout the organization who are capable of reading and responding to diverse campus cultures and contexts.

Conclusion

The chapters that follow provide a more detailed vision of how to include these new concepts into leadership development programs.

In chapter 2, Lynn M. Gangone demonstrates how the HERS Institute has always been on the forefront of the leadership revolution and continues to incorporate revolutionary concepts of social change, empowerment, and globalization.

Bridget R. McCurtis, Jerlando F. L. Jackson, and Elizabeth M. O'Callaghan in chapter 3 note specific advice for leaders of color and examine issues of culture as they relate to leadership.

Tricia Bertram Gallant and Cheryl Getz demonstrate in chapter 4 how case-in-point pedagogy can be used to teach leaders to address complexity and chaos and how leaders can navigate a world with greater legal, financial, and cultural challenges.

In chapter 5, Sue V. Rosser details a program that embraces empowerment and collaboration that directly addresses racism, sexism, and other discriminatory practices and abuses of power.

Robert J. Nash and Lara Scott's chapter 6 focuses on spirituality and how it can be infused into leadership development programs.

In chapter 7, Jaime Lester describes the way leaders can help facilitate organizational learning, examine abuses of power, and be sensitive to the cultural context.

In chapter 8, Jeni Hart provides advice for leaders who want to create social change and lead from the bottom up.

In chapter 9, Pamela Eddy identifies how community college leaders can benefit by understanding how to be cultural leaders with a deep understanding of the history and context of their institutions, including its rural or urban focus, the importance of organizational learning, and succession planning.

We hope that the ideas presented in chapter 1 help to provide a foundation for rethinking leadership development and to incorporate revolutionary concepts on your campus or within your organization. Reexamine the underlying assumptions of your program, consider expanding program time frames, balance reflection and action, promote interdependence, situate leadership, and focus on values. Adopting new notions of leadership may not come easy for many participants, particularly for individuals who have been entrenched in traditional systems. It is important for individuals first to acknowledge that they hold traditional notions of leadership, as most of us were socialized to these norms. Next, it is important to consider the values of the revolutionary assumptions. We believe that by introducing and building a case for these new concepts we are helping leadership development professionals and leaders reconsider their practice. Engaging these concepts does require a fundamental shift in thinking. This is also why having individuals/groups attend leadership development programs with representatives from different generations and backgrounds—some of whom are likely to be advocates and allies—can also help the leadership development facilitators in their task of introducing novel concepts.

References

Adler, N. J. (2001a). Conclusion: Future issues in global leadership development. In M. E. Mendenhall, T. M. Kuhlmann, & G. K. Stahl (Eds.), *Developing global business leaders: Policies, processes, and innovations* (pp. 255–271). Westport, CT: Quorum Books.

Adler, N. J. (2001b). Global leadership: Women leaders. In M. E. Mendenhall, T. M. Kuhlmann, & G. K. Stahl (Eds.), *Developing global business leaders: Policies, processes, and innovations* (pp. 73–97).Westport, CT: Quorum Books.

Allen, B., Morton, L. W., & Li, T. (2003). *Shared leadership: Organizational practices* (Report No. 125). Ames: Rural Development Initiative, Iowa State University.

Allen, K. E., & Cherrey, C. (2000). *Systemic leadership: Enriching the meaning of our work.* Lanham, MD: University Press of America.

Ashcroft, B., Griffiths, G., & Tiffin, H. (Eds.). (1995). *The post-colonial studies reader.* New York: Routledge.

Astin, A. W., & Astin, H. S. (Eds.). (2000). *Leadership reconsidered: Engaging higher education in social change.* Battle Creek, MI: W. K. Kellogg Foundation.

Astin, H. S., & Leland, C. (1991). *Women of influence, women of vision.* San Francisco: Jossey-Bass.

Bass, B. M. (1985). *Leadership and performance beyond expectations.* New York: Free Press.

Bensimon, E. M. (1991). An examination of the relationship between academic discipline and cognitive complexity in academic deans' administrative behavior. *Journal of Research in Higher Education, 47*(3), 281–315.

Bensimon, E. M., & Neumann, A. (1993). *Redesigning collegiate leadership: Teams and teamwork in higher education.* Baltimore, MD: Johns Hopkins University Press.

Bensimon, E. M., Neumann, A., & Birnbaum, R. (1989). Making sense of administrative leadership: The "L" word in higher education. *ASHE-ERIC Higher Education Report, 31*(6). Washington, DC: George Washington University.

Bergquist, W. H. (1992). *The four cultures of the academy: Insights and strategies for improving leadership in collegiate organizations.* San Francisco: Jossey-Bass.

Birnbaum, R. (1992). *How academic leadership works: Understanding success and failure in the college presidency.* San Francisco: Jossey-Bass.

Blackmore, J. (1999). *Troubling women: Feminism, leadership, and educational change.* Buckingham, UK: Open University Press.

Bolman, L. G., & Deal, T. E. (1995). *Leading with soul: An uncommon journey of spirit.* San Francisco: Jossey-Bass.

Calas, M. B., & Smircich, L. (1992). Re-writing gender into organizational theorizing: Directions from feminist perspectives. In M. Reed and M. D. Hughes (Eds.), *Rethinking organization: New directions in organizational theory and analysis* (pp. 97–117). Beverly Hills, CA: Sage.

Chaffee, E. E., & Tierney, W. G. (1988). *Collegiate culture and leadership strategies.* Washington, DC: American Council on Education.

Chliwniak, L. (1997). Higher education leadership: Analyzing the gender gap. *ASHE-ERIC Higher Education Report, 25*(4). Washington, DC: Graduate School of Education and Human Development, George Washington University.

Cooper, J. E., & Ideta, L. M. (1994, November). *Dealing with difference: Maps and metaphors of leadership in higher education.* Paper presented at the annual meeting of the Association for the Study of Higher Education, Tucson, AZ.

Crosby, B. C. (1999). *Leadership for global citizenship: Building transnational community.* Thousand Oaks, CA: Sage.

Cutright, M. (Ed.). (2001). *Chaos theory and higher education: Leadership, planning, and policy.* New York: Peter Lang.

Den Hartog, D. N., Weibler, J., House, R., Haynes, P., Ruiz, S., & Dorfman, P. (1999). Culture specific and cross-culturally generalizable implicit leadership theories: Are attributes of charismatic/transformational leadership universally endorsed? *The Leadership Quarterly, 10*(2), 219–256.

DePree, M. (1992). *Leadership jazz.* New York: Dell.

DePree, M. (2004) *Leadership is an art.* New York: Currency.

Ferren, A. S., & Stanton, W. W. (2004). *Leadership through collaboration: The role of the chief academic officer.* Westport, CT: Praeger.

Goldsmith, M., Greenberg, C. L., Robertson, A., & Hu-Chan, M. (2003). *Global leadership: The next generation.* Upper Saddle River, NJ: Prentice Hall.

Goleman, D. (1995). *Emotional intelligence.* New York: Bantam Books.

Goleman, D. (1998). *Working with emotional intelligence.* New York: Bantam Books.

Greenleaf, R. K. (1977). *Servant leadership: A journey into the nature of legitimate power and greatness.* New York: Paulist Press.

Grint, K. (Ed.). (1997). *Leadership: Classical, contemporary, and critical approaches.* New York: Oxford University Press.

Heifetz, R. A. (1994). *Leadership without easy answers.* Cambridge, MA: Belknap Press.

Higher Education Research Institute. (1996). *A social change model of leadership development guidebook version III.* Los Angeles: Higher Education Research Institute.

House, R. J., Hanges, P. J., Javidan, M., Dorfman, P. W., & Gupta, V. (Eds.). (2004). *Culture, leadership, and organizations: The GLOBE study of 62 societies.* Thousand Oaks, CA: Sage.

Ilgen, D. R., Major, D. A., Hollenbeck, J. R., & Sego, D. J. (1993). Team research in the 1990s. In M. M. Chemers & R. Ayman (Eds.), *Leadership theory and research: Perspectives and directions* (pp. 245–271). San Diego, CA: Academic Press.

Kelly, G. (1998). *Team leadership: Five interactive management adventures.* Aldershot, UK: Gower Publishing.

Kezar, A. (2000). Pluralistic leadership: Incorporating diverse voices. *Journal of Higher Education, 71*(6), 722–743.

Kezar, A. (2002a). Expanding notions of leadership to capture pluralistic voices: Positionality theory in practice. *Journal of College Student Development, 43*(4), 558–578.

Kezar, A. (2002b). Overcoming obstacles to change within urban institutions: The mobile framework and engaging institutional culture. *Metropolitan Universities: An International Forum, 13*(2), 95–103.

Kezar, A. (2006). Redesigning for collaboration in learning initiatives: An examination of four highly collaborative campuses. *The Journal of Higher Education, 77*(5), 804–838.

Kezar, A., Carducci, R., & Contreras-McGavin, M. (2006). Rethinking the "L" word in higher education: The revolution of research on leadership. *ASHE-ERIC Higher Education Report, 31*(6). San Francisco: Jossey-Bass.

Kezar, A., & Moriarty, D. (2000). Expanding our understanding of student leadership development: A study exploring gender and ethnicity identity. *The Journal of College Student Development, 41*(1), 55–69.

Kidder, R. M. (1995). *How good people make tough choices: Resolving the dilemmas of ethical living.* New York: William Morrow.

Kinlaw, D. C. (1998). *Superior teams: What they are and how to develop them.* London: Gower.

Komives, S. R., Lucas, N., & McMahon, T. R. (1998). *Exploring leadership: For college students who want to make a difference.* San Francisco: Jossey-Bass.

Lipman-Blumen, J. (1996). *The connective edge: Leading in an interdependent world.* San Francisco: Jossey-Bass.

Lipman-Blumen, J. (2000). *Connective leadership: Managing in a changing world.* Oxford, UK: Oxford University Press.

Love, P. G., & Estanek, S. M. (2004). *Rethinking student affairs practice.* San Francisco: Jossey-Bass.

Mendenhall, M. E. (2001). Introduction: New perspectives on expatriate adjustment and its relationship to global leadership development. In M. E. Mendenhall, T. M. Kuhlmann, & G. K. Stahl (Eds.), *Developing global business leaders: Policies, processes, and innovation* (pp. 1–18). Westport, CT: Quorum Books.

Meyerson, D. E. (2003). *Tempered radicals: How everyday leaders inspire change at work.* Boston: Harvard Business School Press.

Meyerson, D. E., & Scully, M. A. (1995). Tempered radicalism and the politics of ambivalence and change. *Organizational Science, 6*(5), 585–600.

Nelson, S. J. (2000). *Leaders in the crucible: The moral voice of college presidents.* Westport, CT: Bergin & Garvey.

O'Connor, P. M. G., & Quinn, L. (2004). Organizational capacity for leadership. In C. D. McCauley & E. Van Velsor (Eds.), *The Center for Creative Leadership handbook of leadership development* (2nd ed., pp. 417–437). San Francisco: Jossey-Bass.

Outcalt, C. L., Faris, S. K., & McMahon, K. N. (2001). *Developing non-hierarchical leadership on campus: Case studies and best practices in higher education.* Westport, CT: Greenwood Press.

Palestini, R. H. (1999). Leadership tendencies of continuing education administrators. *PAACE Journal of Lifelong Learning, 8,* 31–39.

Palmer, P. J. (1990). *Leading from within: Reflections on spirituality and leadership.* Westfield, IN: Greenleaf Center for Servant-Leadership.

Palmer, P. J. (2000). *Let your life speak: Listening for the voice of vocation.* San Francisco: Jossey-Bass.

Parry, K. W. (1998). Grounded theory and social process: A new direction for leadership research. *The Leadership Quarterly, 9*(1), 85–105.

Pearce, C. L., & Conger, J. A. (Eds.). (2003). *Shared leadership: Reframing the hows and whys of leadership.* Thousand Oaks, CA: Sage.

Popper, M. (2001). *Hypnotic leadership: Leaders, followers, and the loss of self.* Westport, CT: Praeger.

Rhoads, R. A., & Tierney, W. G. (1992). *Cultural leadership in higher education.* University Park, PA: National Center on Postsecondary Teaching, Learning, and Assessment.

Rhode, D. L. (Ed.). (2003). *The difference "difference" makes: Women and leadership.* Stanford, CA: Stanford Law and Politics.

Roddick, A. (1991). *Body and soul: Profits with principles—The amazing success story of Anita Roddick and The Body Shop.* New York: Crown Publishers

Senge, P. M. (1990). *The fifth discipline: The art and practice of the learning organization.* New York: Doubleday.

Skrla, L. (2000). The social construction of gender in the superintendency. *Journal of Education Policy, 15*(3), 293–316.

Starratt, R. J. (2004). *Ethical leadership.* San Francisco: Jossey-Bass.

Tierney, W. G. (1988). *The web of leadership: The presidency in higher education.* Greenwich, CT: JAI Press.

Tierney, W. G. (1993). *Building communities of difference: Higher education in the twenty-first century.* Westport, CT: Bergin & Garvey.

Weick, K. E. (1995). *Sensemaking in organizations.* Thousand Oaks, CA: Sage.

Wheatley, M. J. (1994). *Leadership and the new science: Learning about organization from an orderly universe.* San Francisco: Berrett-Koehler.

Wheatley, M. J. (1999). *Leadership and the new science: Discovering order in a chaotic world* (2nd ed.) San Francisco: Berrett-Koehler Press.

Young, M. D., & Skrla, L. (Eds.). (2003). *Reconsidering feminist research in educational leadership.* Albany, NY: SUNY Press.

2

THE HERS INSTITUTES
Revolutionary Leadership Development for Women

Lynn M. Gangone

T his book is about revolutionary concepts of leadership and the implications of these concepts for leadership development programs in higher education. If any programs have stood out as a model of revolutionary leadership and a model of the application of the revolutionaries' beliefs to leadership development programming, it is the institutes of HERS (Higher Education Resource Services). The five distinctive HERS programs include the original programs, the HERS Bryn Mawr Summer Institute for Women in Higher Education Administration and the HERS Institute for Women in Higher Education Administration at Wellesley College (both begun in 1976). Nearly two decades later HERS collaborated with the National Association of Collegiate Women Athletic Administrators (NACWAA) to create NACWAA/HERS in 1994. With support from the Andrew W. Mellon Foundation the U.S.-based HERS South Africa program began in 2000; subsequently, the HERS-SA Program, based at the University of Cape Town in South Africa, was created and continues to serve African women. The newest HERS program, the Institute for Women in Higher Education Administration at the University of Denver, welcomed its inaugural class in fall 2007.

The HERS institutes have engaged over 3,000 women in their revolutionary programming for nearly 35 years. Standing the test of time, HERS blends the leadership theories of social change and social movements, globalization, and empowerment; adopts staged career development theory that focuses on how careers develop within organizations, with a specific emphasis on women's professional and personal lives; and incorporates artful assessments of need within higher education that results in an ever-evolving curriculum. HERS' nimble programming adjusts to reflect the times as they are changing with the resolute certainty that higher education can only be bettered if a certain group of educators (women) are made ready to accept leadership in higher education at the same level as the predominant leader group (men). Although "none of the [HERS] founders . . . 'thought the Summer Institute would last for fifteen years, because we didn't think there would still be a need'" (Healey as cited in Balukas, 1992, p. 108), the HERS Institutes are now entering their fourth decade of existence, with the advancement of women in careers in higher education administration still the primary goal. These revolutionary leadership development programs for women continue to serve the needs of the academy in the 21st century.

This chapter briefly reviews the origins of the HERS programs, embedded in the feminist movement of the 1970s; provides short descriptions of each institute; uses the HERS Bryn Mawr summer institute to illustrate the themes of social change, globalization, and empowerment that provide the foundations of all HERS institutes; and summarizes the ways in which the HERS programs have had a broad and deep impact on women in higher education administration. This chapter is for those who are interested in developing a better understanding of the HERS institutes, which have contributed significantly to the career advancement of women faculty and administrators in higher education, as well as for administrators and faculty members working to advance women and planning to replicate aspects of the HERS programs' curricula in their work.

The Historical Roots of HERS

Just how revolutionary HERS was may be hard for some readers to grasp without some appreciation for the history of higher education in the United States. However, understanding the history of the times, particularly the impact of feminism within the higher education community, is illustrative of how a social change movement and its resultant theories of leadership affect the practice of leadership. The origins of the HERS programs are imbedded in a time of great change and promise for women in higher education—the 1970s.

The women's movement of the late 1960s and 1970s, sometimes referred to as the "second wave" of feminism in the United States, had as its roots the civil rights movement and the attendant discussions on social justice, equality, and challenging the establishment through events such as the free speech movement and the Vietnam War protests (*Encyclopedia Britannica*, 2006). Encouraged by this second wave of feminism and the increasingly vocal rhetoric of feminists within the academy, women challenged the status quo of higher education; demanded salary and benefits equity; childcare; reforms in the hiring, promotion, and tenure processes; and representation on key campus committees (Glazer, Bensimon, & Townsend, 1993; Glazer-Raymo, 1999). Legislation such as the Equal Pay Act of 1963, Executive Order 11246 (which established the practice of affirmative action), the Equal Credit Opportunity Act (which allowed women to secure their own financial credit), and Title IX of the Education Amendments of 1972 (which guaranteed equal educational opportunity for women) provided the legal backbone for these campus-based efforts.

In the midst of this burgeoning movement of women seeking their rightful place in the academy, pioneering professional development opportunities for women emerged. Because of the pyramidal structure of higher education and the dearth of women in senior leadership positions, projects to advance women in higher education administration, specifically designed to teach women management and leadership skills, were created (Tinsley, Secor, & Kaplan, 1984). Larger foundations, like Ford and the Carnegie Corporation, as well as more modestly endowed foundations like Danforth, William H. Donner, and the Lilly Endowment, invested millions in projects designed to support the administrative advancement of women (Tinsley, 1975).

Chamberlain (1988) traces the origins of HERS to a group called the Committee for the Concerns of Women in New England Colleges and Universities. Convened by women such as Shelia Tobias and Lilli Hornig in 1972, the committee created the HERS organization with a goal of setting "up a central registry, or talent bank, of women qualified for and interested in positions of higher education administration. . . . Funding for the first two years . . . came from the Ford Foundation and office space was provided by Brown University" (Balukas, 1992, p. 64). In 1974 a supplemental grant to Brown University from Ford allowed the work at Brown to continue and established an office at the University of Pennsylvania, which was subsequently called HERS/Mid-Atlantic (Bernstein, 1984). Thus the placement services of the New England group migrated into one of multiple strategies to promote women in higher education in the mid-Atlantic region (Balukas, 1992).

In 1976 the Summer Institute for Women in Higher Education Administration, cosponsored by Bryn Mawr College and HERS/Mid-Atlantic, began with the support of the William H. Donner Foundation; "the goal of its founders was to improve the status of women in the middle and executive levels of higher education administration, areas in which women traditionally have been underrepresented" (Secor, 1984, p. 25). In that same year "HERS/New England reached an agreement with Wellesley College and became an autonomous part of the Wellesley College Center for Research on Women" (Balukas, 1992, p. 65). Several years later, HERS established a third site at the University of Utah. In 1983 HERS/Mid-Atlantic, headed by its founding director (and now president emerita) Cynthia Secor, moved to the University of Denver and became known as HERS/Mid-America (Balukas). Today, the organization is simply known as HERS.

As an early innovator in leadership and management development for women, HERS' foremost goal was "to provide women administrators with skills that can enhance their performance in their present positions and to give them the insights into the institutional structure of higher education that can help them move ahead" (Tinsley, 1984, p. 18). Today, HERS and its programs continue as "the most enduring and visible of the professional development activities pioneered in the mid 1970s" (Secor, 1984, p. 25).

Balukas (1992), Chamberlain (1988), and Bernstein (1984) make the clear connection between the feminist movement and the development of HERS. Academic women, and their male allies, were no longer content with the documented inequalities in women's participation at all levels in higher education. These sentiments, coupled with legislative requirements such as affirmative action, a realization that "other remedies over a longer period of time would be needed to advance women into top administration" (Chamberlain, 1988, p. 318), and a deep belief that women in leadership could transform the academy were the philosophical and pragmatic underpinnings of the convictions of the HERS organizers. It is significant that the focus of HERS was not on changing program participants so that they "fit" into higher education. Rather, according to Secor, HERS was designed around its organizers' belief in "keep[ing] people 'feminist honest' while at the same time moving them up the career ladder so they will be able to handle the structures that will enable feminism to endure" (as cited in Balukas, 1992, p. 70).[1] That HERS began and continues as "a vehicle to create social change by making institutional change" (p. 67) is a result of the organizers' deeply-rooted beliefs in what was necessary to transform higher education. This is surely the reason for HERS' long and successful run on the higher education stage.

The HERS Institutes

This section provides a brief description of each HERS institute, including information on overall curricular format and delivery, participants, and faculty. These descriptions illustrate the many ways the HERS curricula are delivered, as well as the depth and breadth of the HERS institutes in serving national and international participants, as well as women throughout the various sectors of higher education.

HERS Bryn Mawr

The HERS Bryn Mawr Summer Institute for Women in Higher Education Administration is considered the flagship HERS institute and is its best known program. HERS Bryn Mawr is conducted in partnership with Bryn Mawr College, which affixes its official seal to the certificate each woman receives upon the completion of the program. Rooted in the liberal arts, residential college model, HERS Bryn Mawr is offered each summer for three and a half weeks, with participants residing on the Bryn Mawr College campus along with sporadic commuter participants from Philadelphia-area colleges who are not in residence, although many local women have often opted for the fuller residential experience.

Since its inception more than 2,000 women administrators throughout the United States, Canada, South Africa, Saudi Arabia, Nigeria, the Virgin Islands, Bermuda, Sweden, Wales, Iran, Singapore, and the Netherlands have participated (HERS, 2007). With the original Donner Foundation funding contingent on the involvement of U.S. and Canadian women, HERS Bryn Mawr has, from its beginnings, welcomed international participants. Today, on average, 75 women participate; these women are usually at

---

1. Retaining one's identity and characteristics while still fitting in is described ably through the notion of *tempered radicals*, developed by Scully and Meyerson in 1995—people who want to succeed in their organizations yet live by their values or identities, even if they are somehow at odds with the dominant culture of their organizations (Meyerson, 2001).

the midlevel of their career in higher education—recently named department chairs, acting/assistant/associate deans, directors from a variety of administrative areas, and occasionally more senior-level participants at the dean and vice president levels. Generally, the majority of participants come from academic ranks and are from larger, public institutions. In 2006, 74% of the participants were from public institutions, and 76% were faculty or academic affairs administrators, with 40% in their positions for 3–5 years (HERS, 2007). Demographic data are collected on each class, including participants' institutional type, length of tenure in higher education, age, race, position, and so forth. As with all HERS institutes, faculty are current and former senior administrators in higher education and are predominantly women from throughout the United States as well as from other countries.

In the late 1970s, the HERS Bryn Mawr curriculum addressed six areas: professional development, academic governance, human relations skills, finance and budgeting, administrative uses of the computer, and management and leadership (Balukus, 1992). In the late 1980s the curriculum was significantly modified to address the shifts in higher education at the time—growing fiscal constraints rooted in the late 1970s and early 1980s, increasing diversity of the student body and the academic workforce, student consumerism, and the strengthening influence of the external environment and its pressures on higher education (Thelin, 2004). Moving from a curriculum that focused on "the effective and creative use of existing talent and acquisition of new skills" (Bryn Mawr College & HERS, Mid-America, 1986, p. 1) to a curriculum that "prepares participants to work with issues currently facing higher education, with emphasis on the growing diversity of the student body and the workforce" (Bryn Mawr College & HERS, Mid-America, 1989, p. 1), the curriculum encompassed four distinct yet integrated areas: (a) the academic environment, including current issues, strategic planning, curricular reform, assessment of learning outcomes, faculty development, and diversity issues; (b) academic governance, including organization and structure of institutions, issues of concern to specific sectors, decision making, and leadership; (c) the institutional environment, including accounting, budget strategies and politics, state and federal relations, staff development and human resources, and legal issues; and (d) professional development, which addressed the "needs of the individual woman as she functions within the institutional context" (p. 3) with particular attention to leadership skills and "strategies for institutional change with emphasis on women's and minority issues" (p. 3). In 1993 the four units were further refined; professional development remained, and the remaining three units addressed the academic environment, the institutional environment, and a new unit, the external environment, focused on "political, social, and economic trends . . . financial conditions . . . with a special impact on state revenues . . . policies, federal financial aid programs, tuition trends . . . external demands for accountability . . . and the role of the media" (Bryn Mawr College & HERS, Mid-America, 1993, p. 2)—in short, preparing women for the complexities of 21st-century higher education.

In 2006–2007 the HERS Bryn Mawr curriculum was again modified after an extensive review of participant evaluations and interviews with HERS Bryn Mawr faculty and HERS board members; from those discussions it was agreed that the curriculum would focus even more attention on the leadership development of HERS participants (J. White, personal communication, August 31, 2007). To that end, longtime curricular units in the external, academic, and institutional environments were modified to address more directly the topic of challenges and change in higher education, setting a context for the issues participants face on their campuses; the professional development unit, which includes the trademark career mapping work, videotaping, and "fireside chats" with sitting women presidents, was maintained with minor adjustments. The new curricular themes that guide HERS Bryn Mawr are

1. Charting and achieving institutional priorities
   - Academic excellence and institutional distinctiveness
   - Changing trends and emerging opportunities
   - External constituencies and internal stakeholders
2. Developing and maximizing institutional resources
   - Financial planning and resource management
   - Effective recruitment and personnel development
   - Institutional advancement, lobbying, and fund-raising
3. Leading in the academic institution
   - Shared governance and collaborative decision making
   - Strategic change and conflict management
   - Legal issues
4. Mapping a leadership path
   - Career stages and transition planning

- Building professional strengths and network support
- Translating personal values into institutional legacies

These themes are intended to help participants more directly link the content of the curriculum with the real-world leadership challenges participants face on a daily basis. In addition, a new assignment titled the HERS Localized Leadership Project requires participants to bring a work assignment from their campus and use resources from the HERS institute to develop strategies and plans for leading upon their return to their institution. Finally, the curriculum and schedule are shifted to allow more time for participants to work in small groups and to have informal networking time, reinforcing the notion that leaders need supportive teams internal and external to the institution in order to accomplish sustainable change and to sustain their own creative abilities.

HERS Wellesley

At HERS Wellesley, four thematic areas are presented through 5 seminar weekends held throughout the academic year, allowing participants the opportunity to immediately apply concepts and skills acquired through the institute to their work settings and then return several weeks later for reflection and refinement. The thematic areas are

- Trends and challenges for higher education today
  - Leading change in the academic institution
  - Marshalling and managing resources for higher education
  - Launching a leadership plan (HERS, 2007)

The marshalling and managing resources include budget, accounting, and auditing; academic and administrative computing; institutional advancement; missions, markets, and constituencies; federal, state, and community relations; and legal issues. Leading organizational change includes organizational behavior, management strategies, communication, conflict management, and ethics. The leadership plan includes career planning, professional networks, leadership, and advancement strategies, all in the context of understanding and navigating academic organizations. Historically, about 50 participants annually are from the New England region and are from typical midlevel administrative ranks, such as coordinators, directors, registrars, and assistant or associate deans. In recent years the participants have been more senior in rank; additionally, participation of women has expanded from strictly New England–based institutions to colleges and universities throughout the United States, likely because of the weekend structure of the program that is seen as a manageable alternative to HERS Bryn Mawr, which requires nearly 4 consecutive weeks of commitment (J. White, personal communication, June 14, 2007). Like all HERS institutes, the faculty consists of senior leaders, predominantly women from institutions, foundations, and associations, who bring their professional expertise and personal stories to bear on the year-long, weekend program. Historically, these faculty have come predominantly from New England colleges and universities, but that too is changing as HERS Wellesley takes on a more national audience.

NACWAA/HERS

NACWAA/HERS began with a partnership that was formed between NAC-WAA and HERS to address the dearth of senior women athletic administrators. Even as late as 2002, Acosta and Carpenter noted that out of 297 National Collegiate Athletic Association (NCAA) Division I athletic directors, only 27 were female. There were 41 female athletic directors in Division II, and 108 in Division III, the division most likely to have a female head administrator (27.6%), while Division I programs are the least likely (8.4%). The NACWAA/HERS program was created to address this enormous gap between women and men in athletic administration.

The NACWAA/HERS curriculum built on the strengths of the women it was designed to serve, used some traditional HERS components such as the professional development curriculum, and "added a heavier focus on aspects of finance, contracts, vendors—those parts of athletics that are heavily income-driven—selling TV time, packages, looking at corporate sponsorships, all in a legal context" (C. Secor, personal communication, August 25, 2007). The curriculum of this 1-week intensive institute examines athletics culture, including gender equity and Title IX, diversity, and liability and legal issues; leadership skills, including communications styles, team building, and conflict management; professional development, including strategic planning, networking and mentoring, and career mapping; and financial planning, including, fund-raising, marketing/promotions, and finance and operations (NACWAA/HERS, 2007). Not surprisingly, Quarterman,

Dupree, & Willis (2006) in a study of female intercollegiate athletic administrators and directors of women's intercollegiate athletic programs found that
of the NCAA Division I members surveyed, 70.3% of those identified bud-
get/fund-raising, Title IX (gender/pay equity), and inadequate facilities as
major challenges. "This was the most politicized of all the HERS leadership
programs. . . . we always started with Title IX and gender equity. . . . the
senior women wanted to develop and empower the younger women" (C.
Secor, personal communication, August 25, 2007). This focus on leadership
for social change, while empowering women with the skills and expertise
necessary to take on athletic administration, using a core faculty of women
who have themselves survived and advanced, is quintessential HERS. The
NACWAA/HERS faculty are predominantly from the ranks of senior female
athletic administrators, supplemented by higher education specialists outside
athletic administration. Over time, NACWAA has taken full ownership of
NACWAA/HERS, although retaining the explicit affiliation with HERS.
NACWAA now offers NACWAA/HERS on the East and West coasts, and
has created a NACWAA/HERS Level II, the Leadership Enhancement Institute (NACWAA, 2007).

HERS-SA

HERS-SA emerged at the turn of the 21st century from the involvement of
the Mellon Foundation in addressing the postapartheid needs of the South
African university system. In the late 1990s South Africa's higher education
institutions were "being fundamentally reshaped by the post-apartheid transformation of South African society" (Subotzky, 2004, p. 2). As part of this
effort, institutions were preparing to open higher education to all South African populations. Staff of the Mellon Foundation noted the need to engage
women in higher education in the nation's transformation. At the time,
women constituted about 38% of higher education faculty (Subotzky, 2004),
and a 2007 survey noted that 3 of the 23 vice-chancellors and 5 of the 23 registrars were women; and women made up 21% of the deputy vice-chancellors
and 21% of the executive directors (HERS-SA, 2007). Clearly, South Africa
needed all its population engaged in the systemic transformation of higher
education, and women in leadership positions were sorely missing.

In December 1999 HERS/Mid-America received approval of a Mellon-
sponsored program to bring South African women to the United States for

a specifically designed leadership institute. In March 2000 HERS-SA welcomed eight midlevel women administrators and faculty from the University of Cape Town to the Wellesley College campus for a month-long intensive program. The HERS-SA program combined the traditional HERS institute model with immersion in experiential learning, skills-based seminars, and facilitated group work at the beginning and end of the program as bookends to a 2-week intensive, campus-based shadowing experience. The South African participants came to the U.S. institute with a project idea they wished to implement upon their return to their institution; the project framed the context for their experiential learning and was the basis for their final report at the conclusion of the institute. Over the course of the HERS-SA program 73 women have traveled from South Africa to Wellesley College. Participants are paired with women leaders at host institutions that include Bryn Mawr College, Mount Holyoke College, Smith College, Amherst College, Bridgewater State College, and the University of Massachusetts at Amherst (HERS, 2007). The U.S.-based HERS-SA lasted from 2000 to 2004. Additional funding from the Mellon Foundation also supported South African attendance at HERS Bryn Mawr, and by 2004 the South African–based program, HERS-SA, was established and has involved over 450 women from South Africa and other African countries (HERS-SA, 2007).

HERS-SA continues as a HERS affiliate that is a "managed network to improve the status of women in higher education in South Africa" (HERS-SA, 2007, p. 1). HERS-SA aims to develop and offer accessible education and training and development programs for women working in the higher education environment; empower women to take leadership positions in higher education institutions in South Africa, thereby providing much needed leadership role models for women; and challenge institutional culture and facilitate workplace change, thereby addressing gender inequity and enabling women to participate fully in the workforce (HERS-SA, 2007). To meet these stated goals, HERS-SA activities include

- the annual HERS-SA Academy, which is a 7-day interactive professional development opportunity for women employed in higher education throughout Southern Africa. It is aimed at those women in, or aspiring to, senior leadership positions and typically attracts about 80 women.
- the Training of Professional Academic Staff (TOPAS) workshops that are "demand driven" and attract women currently employed at all

levels in higher education institutions. HERS-SA provides experienced facilitators drawn from the higher education sector, who facilitate workshops to groups of 10 to 12 women upon request.

- maintaining a flow of information between women in higher education (Web site and Listserve) and facilitating structured mentoring, circulating information about development opportunities and jobs in higher education, facilitating networking between women in higher education institutions, and research into and advocacy for gender equity in higher education in Africa. (HERS-SA, 2007)

All of these initiatives are guided by the nine core principles that underpin the HERS-SA approach: women-only learning environments, self-nomination, holistic approach of balancing the personal and professional, confidentiality, equality, use of experienced women administrators as facilitators and faculty, participant "ownership of content," practical and participative content, and networking (HERS-SA, 2007). The HERS-SA is coordinated by women who have participated in either the U.S.-based HERS-SA or have attended the HERS Bryn Mawr Institute; alumnae of the U.S.-based HERS programs are deeply involved in the HERS-SA work. Faculty come from HERS alumnae ranks and from other senior-level women in African higher education.

HERS Denver

HERS' newest institute, HERS Denver, is the first national HERS institute to be housed at the University of Denver, HERS' institutional home since 1983. HERS Denver meets a long-standing need for a HERS program based in the western United States; while open to a national audience, women from the mountain west to the West Coast have an easier opportunity, geographically, to access the benefits of HERS in the Denver-based program. The curricular format is similar to the HERS Wellesley program in its overarching programmatic themes and allows participants the opportunity to engage pedagogically in "practice to theory to practice," immediately applying concepts and skills acquired through the institute to their work settings and then returning several weeks later for reflection and refinement. The delivery of HERS Denver differs from HERS Wellesley. Instead of conducting the program on weekends throughout the academic year, HERS Denver is limited to the fall academic semester, beginning with a 1-week intensive session in August, followed by 3 weekends in September, October, and November. In August 2007, 26 women from across the United States constituted the inaugural HERS Denver class. These women have positions that are typically midlevel, from directors of diversity to assistant and associate deans. They spend their first week exploring "the large view of higher education, to larger views of themselves and their potential legacies in higher education" (HERS Denver, 2007, p. 1)—the intersection of the individual with the institution, the backbone of the HERS institutes, coupled with the legacy of social change.

Themes and Commonalities in the HERS Institutes

Kezar, Carducci, and Contreras-McGavin (2006) note that the conceptualization of leadership is shifting from "static, highly structured, and value-neutral" frameworks to "dynamic, globalized, and processed-oriented perspectives of leadership that emphasize cross-cultural understanding, collaboration, and social responsibility for others" (p. 2). These dynamic, globalized, and process-oriented perspectives describe the intentional approaches of all HERS institutes. Philosophically rooted in feminism and social change, recognizing the needs and responsibilities of women to themselves and each other, fostering the development of cross-cultural understanding domestically and internationally, and recognizing that careers are processes that unfold throughout one's career in higher education, the HERS institutes continue in their revolutionary approaches to leadership development. HERS has always focused on women, where they are in the enterprise of higher education, how they can learn to lead from wherever they are in the institutional structure, and what effect their advocacy for themselves and other women administrators can have to transform the academy.

The HERS institutes embody the themes of social change and social movements, globalization, and empowerment through employing staged career development strategies that strategically inform women about themselves and enhance their development as leaders within the organizational structure. These themes are explored through a specific focus on the HERS Bryn Mawr curriculum and its intentional, holistic approach to leadership development. The curriculum facilitates individual skills development and deep knowledge of higher education as a complex, multifaceted, and global enterprise; challenges women to explore the "whole" of who they are in relation to their institution; empowers women to lead from their current position while preparing for senior leadership roles; and pushes individuals and the group to understand the complexity of diversity in higher education through their own experiences negotiating those differences through the institute. Participants return to their campuses empowered from learning more about themselves and their institutions, understanding more fully the opportunities and challenges within their institutions, and uniquely prepared to take on more advanced leadership positions in the academy.

Social Change

From their inception, the HERS leadership development programs were "applied women's studies" (C. Secor, personal communication, July 26, 2007). This "applied women's studies" begins with the experiences of many of the faculty of HERS who are engaged in their own advancement, coupled with their deep knowledge of feminism, social change, skill in negotiating the labyrinth of higher education administration, and determination to create deep and lasting change in the academy that positively affects women's advancement—these sensibilities translate into curricula with a philosophical grounding in social change. HERS staff and faculty combine their expertise in higher education strategies and skills development within a social change framework that emphasizes responsibility to other women and to transforming the academy to facilitate women's positional leadership advancement. Personal narratives of senior women leaders, particularly college presidents, are interspersed throughout the institute; these are stories of career paths and challenges, punctuated by expressed commitments to women's advancement in thought and deed.

Always, the HERS Bryn Mawr institute with its residential, multiweek format, allows participants the space to tackle deep issues around diversity, identity, and social change:

> Judith Katz, Vivian Nix Early, and I talked about psychological techniques like implosion. . . . we consciously designed a curricular model to hit people hard in the first few days, to remove them from their home institutions and to build an ongoing group. . . . we learned how to take a group and let them storm, and then shape the direction of the norming. . . . what I knew could be done developmentally over four weeks [at Bryn Mawr] was

different than what we could do in and out over the course of a year [at Wellesley]. . . . affective change in the individual can make a difference—how she operates, what she is motivated to accomplish—the "aha moments" when she realizes she CAN lead—make a difference . . . it was a four act choreography—storming and norming in the first two weeks, coming together in [the] third week, in the fourth week preparing them to go home—from a curricular perspective, starting with the external environment unit, then immersing in the institution through the academic unit, and then intentionally moving into dual tracks of institutional environment and professional development with its focus on the individual—always allowing for explosions around diversity. . . . this doesn't happen in the other higher education leadership programs. (C. Secor, personal communication, August 26, 2007)

The HERS curricula encourage women to tackle issues of diversity in the academy formally and informally. Participants are encouraged to create their own sessions outside the formal curriculum, so that the gaps participants perceive in the formal program can be addressed. Typically, sessions on racism and on heterosexism and homophobia are most common. Additionally, these informal sessions reflect the specific needs of that particular set of participants, For example, one year, age diversity emerged as an issue, with women creating sessions and lunchtime conversations that allowed participants from particular decades (the 1920s through the 1950s) to address the multitude of personal and professional issues facing women in higher education from their age perspective. At HERS Bryn Mawr, the curriculum carefully allows, and the faculty purposefully encourages, participants to explore their roles as potential social change agents within the academy by providing space in the formal and informal curriculum for participants to "storm," "norm," and return to their campuses with different perspectives—with the understanding that women's leadership in higher education must include a commitment to social change in the academy.

Globalization

Adler's (2001) theory of global leadership, with its emphasis on how people and ideas interact across our cultural and geographic boundaries, particularly notes the role of women in creating the types of leadership necessary for a global society (Kezar et al., 2006). The HERS leadership programs recognize the unique role that women can play to transcend global boundaries and "have responsibility that far exceeds that of their domestic counterparts of yesteryear" (Adler, 2001, p. 97). While the HERS' focus has always been on the U.S. higher education system, consistent involvement of international participants has assisted in an evolving global perspective that has grown, particularly since 2000, with the development of HERS-SA, which significantly affected the Bryn Mawr curriculum, especially through the addition of a deeper, intentional global perspective through small-group work, seminars, and readings (C. Secor, personal communication, August 4, 2007). The involvement of at least six South African women at each HERS Bryn Mawr since 2000, as well as the incorporation of texts such as Cock & Bernstein's (2002), are tangible examples of the ways that globalization has been made an integral part of the HERS leadership model. International participants are encouraged to share their experiences in their higher education systems throughout the curriculum, and the South African women always have a formal panel presentation to the participants specifically focused on the changes in the nation's higher education system and the role women are playing in those changes.

Empowerment + *Leadership*

Always, the focus of the HERS institutes have been on women, where they are in the enterprise of higher education and how they can exercise personal and positional leadership, and empowering participants to create change for themselves and other women in the academy. "The leadership curriculum was clear, although we always marketed the programs as management institutes. . . . we were focused on the individual woman development model and preparing a woman to see herself as capable of leading" (C. Secor, personal communication, August 26, 2007). A key component of this empowerment is to actively engage women in a hallmark HERS strategy: career mapping. Empowerment is also expressed in the curriculum by inviting women to give voice to their experiences throughout the institute in very intentional ways.

Tinsley (1984) provides an extensive review of the HERS Bryn Mawr curriculum, with particular emphasis on the professional development unit as seen through the process of career mapping. It is in career mapping that the intersection between the individual and the institution is most tangibly expressed, and the ways to empower women to move up, beyond, and through where they "sit" in their institution are discovered:

As we gained more experience with the curriculum, we began to see that we could also teach techniques for analysis of institutional structures. An individual's career always unfolds in an institutional setting. A career in higher education unfolds in institutions that have relatively rigid norms and traditions and quite particular histories, behavioral expectations, problems, and ways of solving problems. The more fully an individual can understand the relation between her aspirations and ambitions and her institution's formal and informal agendas the more fully she can understand the relation between her personal values and needs and her institution's organizational structures and political processes, the likelier it becomes she will achieve and will advance. (p. 19)

Career mapping at HERS Bryn Mawr is more than just a linear rendering of one's career trajectory and possible outcomes. Rather, it is a complex process that asks a woman to consider the multitude of opportunities and barriers that exist in her career advancement and leadership development that are personal and institutional. In this, she engages in a self-analysis that provides her with the breadth of information to return to her institution empowered to lead and advance from wherever she is in the institution, or perhaps to seek more formal, positional leadership opportunities.

Career mapping at HERS Bryn Mawr begins with a participant's selection of a triad; groups of three have proved to be beneficial in providing each triad member with a broader peer review of her current circumstances and future path. Participants are not limited at all in their triad choices, with some opting to work with those in similar administrative or faculty areas and others seeking broader perspectives. Triads are given general instructions about the mapping process: individually they develop their own career maps (which may be in any form they choose to express themselves) and collectively, the triads inform one another of their mapping process, as well as choose a senior leader "mapper" from among the HERS faculty. The role of the "mapper" is to serve as a coach and gentle critic, providing the individual triad participants with the realistic assessment that a senior higher education administrator can provide and bringing a full understanding of the complexity of the career mapping process to bear on the coaching work.

Tinsley (1984) outlines the career mapping process used at HERS Bryn Mawr. A first set of questions asks the individual to do a self-assessment to discuss what bars her from achieving her goals. Things like educational attainment, professional experience, geographic mobility, and personal or family responsibilities are reviewed. Next, the individual is asked to do an institutional assessment by asking the question, "What bars my institution from moving me toward my goals?" Here is where the notion of "fit" between the individual and the institution begins to be explored. Questions such as, What are the institutional values, traditions, and structures are explored. Considering the institution's internal and external constraints, be they resource-based or otherwise, are examined. The participant is asked to consider her experience at her home institution—Has it been a positive experience? What type of professional reputation or visibility does she have? What is the institution's informal agenda and how does it affect her? Following this initial self- and institutional assessment, the individual is encouraged to consider how she might get around any barriers and what conflicts she might experience in achieving her goals. In all of this, she considers herself, the people in her life, any internal conflicts such as personal value conflicts and time and energy commitments, as well as any institutional conflicts with people (colleagues, superiors, people who work for her, people in other departments), institutional structures, or external forces. Key questions at this stage include whether any conflicts could be resolved or harmonized, and are those potential resolutions worth their effort? The individual is also challenged to consider what resources she brings to achieve her goals, such as education, experience, mobility, ambition, and drive; the resources that come from others in her life, including key personal and professional relationships; and resources the institution can bring to bear, including support from colleagues, subordinates, superiors, as well as financial resources that the institution can invest in the individual. Ultimately, in career mapping the task is to articulate personal values and career goals in an institutional context and from an institutional perspective, with the goal being empowerment to make informed career advancement decisions.

According to Cynthia Secor, career mapping is the "backbone of the curriculum" (personal communication, August 25, 2007). Career mapping allows for individual empowerment through developing an understanding of self and one's self in relation to the institution, fostering an understanding of one's personal values and professional ambitions, helping women identify the barriers that exist to advancement, assisting them in recognizing systemic rigidity and even systemic discrimination, and ultimately, at its best, career mapping fosters the development of individual strategies. A woman may chose to stay and change herself or the institution she serves, or perhaps at some point she will make a decision to leave—"she will be able to take the normal accident and chance of daily personal and professional life and shape it in a way that is consonant with what she most genuinely desires" (Tinsley, 1984, p. 24). It is intentional that the professional development piece is a key component of every HERS institute.

Empowerment extends beyond career mapping to other aspects of the institute. Women are invited to actively participate in their learning at HERS Bryn Mawr through a series of intentional activities throughout the institute, such as topical sessions that are supplemented by participant panels where women are invited to speak and relate their own experience to the material being presented. These panels are specifically created in areas that have traditionally been more challenging to the newly minted academic administrator. For example, an intentional activity within the session on planning and budget is the participant panel titled "Being a Budget Advocate," where women from various positions within the academic structure volunteer to discuss the ways they are able to advocate for their students, programs, or specific unit using the planning and budget process. This demystifies the abstract concept of budget and planning, often a challenging administrative responsibility for new administrators to embrace, by having participants relate real-life experiences to their peers, and in the process illustrate how one applies planning and budget theory to practice. Another panel highlights participants who have actively engaged in government relations and advancement work. Not only do these panels provide important, concrete examples of how one applies theory to practice, but they also empower the women panel participants as "experts" in critical administrative areas. Another intentional way that the curriculum allows for individual empowerment is through the invitation to cocreate the informal curriculum. Each year, participants identify perceived gaps in the formal curriculum and remedy those gaps through creating and implementing an informal curriculum that runs throughout the institute. As mentioned earlier, the informal curriculum often is an opportunity for participants to probe more deeply into issues of diversity, however, the informal curriculum can include sessions as utilitarian as Careers in Higher Education Associations. These opportunities to exercise leadership within the curricular framework, whether as expert panel participants or as creators and facilitators within the informal curriculum, empower HERS participants in deep and meaningful ways.

Ultimately, the career mapping, panels, and deliberate participation in the informal curriculum provide essential opportunities for women to empower themselves and each other. Increased self-knowledge, greater understanding of the institutional context in which one works, identification of areas of expertise, and the invitation to be an active participant in one's own learning all serve to facilitate greater learning during the institute, and aids participants in developing bonds of collaborative learning that extend through the institute and beyond.

Reflections on the HERS Institutes and Their Impact

Ahead of their time in assumptions about what constitutes management and leadership, as well as who should be the leaders in higher education administration, the founders of the HERS leadership development programs drew from the radical social and political changes of the 1960s and 1970s. Then "many of the democratic, collaborative, and nonhierarchical trends in leadership . . . (such as) collaboration, empowerment, multiculturalism, and leadership as a collective process" emerged (Kezar et al., 2006, p. 3). The HERS programs have, over time, balanced the realism of negotiating the pyramidal, hierarchical enterprise of higher education (Tinsley, 1984) with the beliefs of empowering women to lead from wherever they are in the institution, imbuing in its participants an understanding that social change in the academy is not a luxury but an imperative. Furthermore, facilitating an understanding of globalization, and the role women can play in creating the leadership that is increasingly necessary in a global society, move women beyond the confines of their campus to a broader, more powerful perspective on their role as social change agents and leaders.

This chapter addressed the historical and philosophical foundations of HERS and its institutes, provided brief descriptions of each institute, and highlighted the themes embedded in the HERS model, such as empowerment, globalization, and social change. While HERS has existed to educate and empower women to move into senior leadership positions, expanding women's leadership from the middle to the top levels with intentionality, it is a model that has always recognized that one can lead from wherever one is in the institution and that leadership for social change in the academy is not a luxury but an imperative. While all the HERS programs were described, there was a specific emphasis on the flagship program, HERS Bryn Mawr, and its foundational themes of social change, globalization, and empowerment.

What has made HERS so distinctive in the arena of leadership programs for faculty and administrators and important to include in this book on new horizons for leadership development? The following are some of the attributes of the HERS institutes that illustrate the unique and enduring contributions these institutes make:

- The HERS curricula are rooted in certain sets of principles and revolutionary leadership theories—commitment to fostering diversity in the academy, empowering women to lead from anywhere in the institution, fostering a global perspective, and instilling an obligation to social change—which are delivered to adult women through the use of seasoned, senior higher education scholar-practitioners as faculty. While the content of the HERS institutes have evolved and changed as higher education has evolved and changed, the core principles and revolutionary leadership approaches have not, which allows the HERS institutes to retain their integrity of purpose while meeting the needs of contemporary higher education professionals and the institutions they serve.
- HERS is a place that nurtures individuals committed to change within higher education. Also, HERS curricula are taught by women and men who are committed to higher education as an enterprise but understand that the academy and its systems require continual challenge to make institutions more welcoming of women and people of color through systemic and attitudinal change. Those who have taught in the HERS institutes understand what we are about—to paraphrase Cynthia Secor, keeping ourselves and our participants "feminist honest" while also moving participants up the higher education career ladder so that they can succeed *and* effect change for others within higher education. This, in and of itself, is revolutionary leadership theory in action.
- The HERS institutes, embedded always in their fundamental principles and revolutionary leadership development theories, are implemented in four distinctive pedagogical formats in the United States—4-week intensive, 1-week intensive, weekends throughout an academic year, and a 1-week intensive plus 3 weekends in an academic semester. In South Africa, HERS-SA is implemented in a week-long (7-day) format. The delivery of the institutes through these multiple

formats shows the elasticity and replicability of the HERS program and provides a model for those committed to women's advancement to emulate. NACWAA/HERS is an example of the replicability of the HERS core for a specific professional group—athletic administrators—while HERS-SA is illustrative of its replicability in an entirely different national context. These are two tangible examples of the depth and strength of the HERS model.

- The grounding of each institute in career mapping methodologies— the intentional exploration of the individual (individual development) and what the institution is (processes and politics), truthful assessment of compatibility/incompatibility between the individual and the institution, and determining how the individual moves forward through her career (career stages and leadership from an institutional perspective)—as a framework empowers women with a fuller understanding of themselves and their institutions. Armed with this knowledge, these women return to their campuses grounded in expressing leadership regardless of their place in the institutional hierarchy, because this self-knowledge ultimately makes them more effective leaders. Effective HERS career mappers have worked with hundreds of women and watched this empowering transformation occur during the institute and beyond. A HERS graduate said, "I'm finding that I am still learning from my experience at the Summer Institute, and that the impact is deepening over time. One of your suggestions for me [during the career mapping process] was to think about coaching high-level candidates who are negotiating if and when to "come out" in the search process. . . . I have been thinking about it and have decided I want to do this" (E. Hornsby, personal communication, August 29, 2007). This is typical—women come away from the career mapping exercise invigorated to take on new challenges or empowered with renewed intent, often with a deeper commitment to social change within the academy.

- Each institute creates an immediate professional network for its participants, and each institute fosters a sense of connection to the greater HERS network of over 2,000 alumnae, as well as the hundreds of faculty and invited speakers. Each class has its own Listserv, where participants share their triumphs and tragedies as the years progress, and alumnae within and outside each class support one another in their professional advancement and personal growth. Job announcements, family changes, triumphs of achieving the next position—all these and more are shared on the class Listserves. This participant networking extends to HERS faculty as well. As someone who has been a HERS Bryn Mawr faculty member since 1996, taught in the U.S.-based HERS-SA, and on the faculty of HERS Denver, I am continually contacted by alumnae from all HERS programs for career coaching, job recommendations, and just generally staying in touch; my experience is the same with each and every HERS faculty member. My move to the University of Denver means that I am enriched by the investment it has made in sending women to the HERS institutes, which resulted in a ready-made network of women colleagues. This type of social capital is nurtured through the HERS institutes and their subsequent networks and is an invaluable resource for alumnae and their advancement.

- HERS women do move up within higher education institutions, because what is taught at the HERS institutes adds value to their skills portfolio and, perhaps more importantly, because of what women think of themselves once they leave a HERS institute. A core of senior leaders—presidents, vice presidents, and deans—who have been through the HERS institutes now exists. These women are in all sectors of the academy and in all academic and professional disciplines. Many of these women would not have considered senior leadership positions without the HERS experience. Midlevel women faculty and administrators are similarly affected; faculty chairs return to campus as more effective leaders and are encouraged to seek administrative advancement, many complete successful chairships and move on to assistant and associate dean/vice president positions, knowing they are leaders.

The distinctiveness of the HERS institutes is their intentional, holistic approach to leadership development. The curriculum facilitates individual skills development and deep knowledge of higher education as a complex, multifaceted, and global enterprise; challenges women to explore the whole of who they are in relation to their institution; empowers women to engage in their own learning and purposeful career advancement; and pushes individual women and the group to understand the complexity of diversity in higher education through their own experiences negotiating those differences. Participants return to their campuses empowered from learning more about themselves and their institutions, understanding more fully the opportunities and challenges within their individual institutions, and uniquely prepared to take on more advanced leadership positions in the academy. HERS institutes provide women with skills that can enhance their performance and the opportunity to gain insights into the institutional structure that can help them move ahead, to develop an understanding of executing leadership from wherever one sits in the institutional hierarchy, to recognize that a commitment to social change is part of leadership, and to move women into more senior leadership roles able to handle the structures that will enable feminism to endure and institutional transformation to occur.

Until women achieve true parity in the academy, programs like HERS continue to serve a dual purpose—to move, with intentionality, women into positional leadership roles, and to empower all women, as tempered radicals, to lead from wherever they are in the institution, understanding that social change is not a luxury but an imperative. Higher education is indeed fortunate to have the HERS programs continuing to support the advancement of women in the academy.

References

Acosta, R. V., & Carpenter, L. J. (2002, June/July). Acosta-Carpenter study shows decline in female ADs. *Athletic Management, 14*(4). Retrieved September 23, 2007, from http://www.momentummedia.com/articles/am/am1404/bbstudy.htm

Adler, N. J. (2001). Global leadership: Women leaders. In M. E. Mendenhall, T. M. Kuhlman, & G. K. Stahl (Eds.), *Developing global business leaders: Policies, processes, and innovations* (pp. 73–97). Westport, CT: Quorum Books.

Balukas, J. V. (1992). *The perception of participants as an aspect of management training program assessment: A study of the HERS/Bryn Mawr Summer Institute for Women.* Unpublished doctoral dissertation, Widener University, West Chester, PA.

Bernstein, A. (1984). Foundation support for administrative advancement: A mixed record. In A. Tinsley, C. Secor, & S. Kaplan (Eds.), *Women in higher education administration* (pp. 77–84). San Francisco: Jossey-Bass.

Bryn Mawr College & HERS, Mid-America. (1986). *Summer Institute for Women in Higher Education Administration* [Brochure]. Bryn Mawr, PA: Bryn Mawr College & HERS, Mid-America.

Bryn Mawr College & HERS, Mid-America. (1989). *Summer Institute for Women in Higher Education Administration* [Brochure]. Bryn Mawr, PA: Bryn Mawr College & HERS, Mid-America.

Bryn Mawr College & HERS, Mid-America. (1993). *Summer Institute for Women in Higher Education Administration* [Brochure]. Bryn Mawr, PA: Bryn Mawr College & HERS, Mid-America.

Chamberlain, M. K. (Ed.) (1988). *Women in academe: Progress and prospects.* New York: Russell Sage Foundation.

Cock, J., & Bernstein, A. (2002). *Melting pots & rainbow nations: Conversations about difference in the United States and South Africa.* Urbana: University of Illinois Press.

Encyclopedia Britannica. (2006). Contemporary feminism in the West: The "second wave" of feminism. Retrieved August 31, 2007, from http://www.britannica.com/eb/article-216010/feminism

Glazer, J., Bensimon, E. M., & Townsend, B. (Ed.). (1993). *ASHE Reader: Women in higher education.* Nedham Heights, MA: Ginn Press.

Glazer-Raymo, J. (1999). *Shattering the myths: Women in academe.* Baltimore, MD: Johns Hopkins University Press.

HERS. (2007). *HERS Institutes.* Retrieved September 10, 2007, from http://www.hersnet.org/Archives.asp

HERS-SA. (2007). *Professional development.* Retrieved September 10, 2007, from http://www.hers-sa.org.za/development.htm

Kezar, A., Carducci, R., & Contreras-McGavin, M. (Eds.) (2006). Rethinking the "L" word in higher education: The revolution of research on leadership. *ASHE-ERIC Higher Education Report, 31*(6). San Francisco: Jossey-Bass.

Myerson, D. E. (2001). *Tempered radicals: How people use difference to inspire change at work.* Boston: Harvard Business School Press.

National Association of Collegiate Women Athletic Administrators. (2007). *NACWAA/HERS Institute for Administrative Advancement.* Retrieved August 31, 2007, from http://www.nacwaa.org/pe/pe_hers_main.php

Quarterman, J., Dupree, A. D., & Willis, K. P. (2006). Challenges confronting female intercollegiate athletic directors of NCAA member institutions by division. *College Student Journal 40*(3), 528–545.

Secor, C. S. (1984). Preparing the individual for institutional leadership: The Summer Institute. In A. Tinsley, C. Secor, & S. Kaplan (Eds.), *Women in higher education administration* (pp. 25–33). San Francisco: Jossey-Bass.

Subotzky, G. (2004). *Country higher education profiles: South Africa.* Retrieved August 31, 2007, from http://www.bc.edu/bc_org/avp/soe/cihe/inhea/profiles/South_Africa.htm

Thelin, J. R. (2004). *A history of American higher education.* Baltimore, MD: Johns Hopkins University Press.

Tinsley, A. (1975). *Academic women, sex discrimination and the law: An action handbook* [Rev. ed.]. Middletown, CT: Commission on the Status of Women, Modern Language Association.

Tinsley, A. (1984). Career mapping and the professional development process. In A. Tinsley, C. Secor, & S. Kaplan (Eds.), *Women in higher education administration* (pp. 17–24). San Francisco: Jossey-Bass.

Tinsley, A., Secor, C., & Kaplan, S. (Eds.). (1984). *Women in higher education administration.* San Francisco: Jossey-Bass.

3

DEVELOPING LEADERS OF COLOR IN HIGHER EDUCATION

Can Contemporary Programs Address Historical Employment Trends?

Bridget R. McCurtis, Jerlando F. L. Jackson,
and Elizabeth M. O'Callaghan

While the number of college students from diverse ethnic/racial backgrounds has steadily increased, the same level of diversity has not been achieved for those holding leadership roles in higher education (Harvey & Anderson, 2005), and certainly not for positions that traditionally lead to the college presidency (Jackson, 2004a). Bensimon and Tierney (1993) note that the "absence of diversity in the upper administrative echelon works against the creation of a multicultural campus" (p. 67). For instance, while there has been an overall decrease in participation in leadership positions for African Americans (Jackson, 2004a); interestingly, there has been a slight increase in African Americans' participation in executive-level positions (i.e., department chair and provost) at particular types of institutions (i.e., 2-year institutions). This growth in leadership diversity among certain institution types creates a unique opportunity for these campuses to realize the benefits of creating a multicultural environment.

In order to thrive in an increasingly competitive and diverse global market, institutions of higher education cannot leave leadership development for people of color to chance (León, 2005). Developing leaders of color requires special attention and focus because racism and inequities in the workplace are still a prevalent issue in the United States. In turn, discriminatory practices are often embedded in the social norms, structures, and practices of universities (Bensimon & Tierney, 1993; Coleman, 1998; Howard-Hamilton & Williams, 1996). Leadership development for people of color is an important and sometimes missing component of efforts to diversify the higher education workforce (Jackson, 2004b; Jackson & Daniels, 2007). However, recognizing the importance of a diverse workforce and focusing on specific cultural differences and needs is a hallmark of the leadership revolution.

This chapter seeks to move beyond the published literature on leadership within higher education and focus on leaders of color who make daily contributions to our campuses yet whose development is often ignored. In order to set the context for this chapter, we review national employment trends for leaders of color in higher education and summarize the literature on leaders of color. The main focus of this chapter is the identification and review of professional associations and leadership programs to develop current and future leaders of color, demonstrating how many are limited in their ability to appropriately prepare leaders of color. The chapter concludes by proposing a new model of leadership development for people of color, informed by an analysis of the literature and guided by the revolutionary leadership concepts such as context, culture, and collaboration.

National Employment Trends for Leaders of Color in Higher Education

National-level data highlight differences between people of color and their counterparts at various points in time.[1] The trends that emerge from the data help to form the core need for development of specific programs targeted for leaders of color as they increasingly become part of the leadership ranks. Data show that while advancements are discernible for these groups, they lag behind in terms of sufficient percentage growth to meet equitable levels in relation to their total percentage of the higher education leadership workforce.

---

1. Discussion of leadership positions included full-time administrators and college and university presidents. Data for this section were computed using two national data sets/sources: (a) the Integrated Postsecondary Educational Data Systems (IPEDS) and (b) the American Council on Education database on college and university presidents.

Full-Time Administrators in Higher Education

Employment opportunities for full-time administrators in higher education increased significantly during the past two decades (see Table 3.1). Over a 20-year period (1983 to 2003), the number of full-time administrative positions in higher education increased 51%. Therefore, any ethnic/racial group with a percent change of less than 51% did not keep pace with the growth in the academic job market. Interestingly, while Whites remain the largest number of full-time higher education administrators, their numbers (40%) did not keep pace with the academic job market. Therefore, the majority of the new positions appear to have been filled with people of color. Among people of color, Asian Americans realized the largest percent increase (290%), more than doubling that of African Americans/Blacks who had the lowest percent increase (106%). It must be noted that while African Americans/Blacks had the lowest percent increase, they still are the largest group of color numerically. Next, Hispanics experienced a 243% increase in full-time higher education administrative positions, followed by American Indians with a 147% increase.

College and University Presidents

Employment opportunities for college and university presidents in higher education increased modestly during the past 10 years (see Table 3.2). Between 1995 and 2005, the number of college and university president positions in higher education increased 12%. Therefore, any ethnic/racial group

TABLE 3.1
Distribution of Full-Time Administrators in Higher Education

Race/Ethnicity	1983	1993	2003	% Change
African Americans/Blacks	8,362	12,232	17,228	106%
Hispanics	2,040	3,580	7,006	243%
Asian American[a]	1,234	2,243	4,813	290%
American Indians[b]	430	726	1,064	147%
Whites	105,420	118,651	147,613	40%
Total	**117,486**	**137,432**	**177,724**	**51%**

Note. [a]Asian American includes Pacific Islanders. [b]American Indian includes Alaska Natives. Calculations are based on data from the U.S. Department of Education, National Center for Educational Statistics, Integrated Postsecondary Education Data System (IPEDS), Fall Staff Surveys.

TABLE 3.2
College and University Presidents

Race/Ethnicity	1995	2000	2005	% Change
African Americans/Blacks	171	175	211	23%
Hispanics	59	80	91	54%
Asian American[a]	35	37	45	29%
American Indians[b]	31	22	24	−23%
Whites	2,475	2,500	2,728	10%
Total	**l2,771**	**2,814**	**3,099**	**12%**

Note. [a]Asian American includes Pacific Islanders. [b]American Indian includes Alaska Natives. Figures include presidents of regionally accredited, degree-granting institutions in the United States or its outlying areas (e.g., Puerto Rico). The term *president* is defined within the American Council on Education's Corporate Database as the president, chancellor, superintendent, executive director, campus dean, and so forth, including interim/acting president heading regionally accredited institutions, branches, and affiliates. From American Council on Education database. Data compiled in June 2006.

with a percent change of less then 12% did not keep pace with the growth in the academic job market. Again, as with full-time higher education administrators, Whites remain the largest number of college and university presidents despite the fact that their increase (10%) did not keep pace with the academic job market. Therefore, the majority of the new positions appear to have been filled with people of color. Among people of color, Hispanics realized the largest percent increase (54%), more than doubling that of African Americans/Blacks who had the lowest percent increase (23%). Again, it must be noted that while African Americans/Blacks had the lowest percent increase, they still are the largest single group of people of color. Next, Asian Americans experienced a 29% increase in college and university president positions, and American Indians was the only group to experience a decrease (−23%).

These data present encouragement and cause for concern with regard to diversifying higher education leadership. The encouraging news is that people of color are increasingly assuming a share of the leadership positions in higher education. For example, the number of Asian American and Hispanic leaders shows great promise to continues growing at a rapid pace. These trends are particularly encouraging for full-time administrative staff, and less so for college and university presidents. A significant concern is that while the growth in leaders of color is encouraging, the pace would have to intensify in order to reduce their numerical distance from Whites. The slow steady growth and sometimes setbacks (decline for American Indians) for people of color in college and university president positions is another area of major concern.

Literature on Leaders of Color in Higher Education

To date, there is nascent literature that focuses specifically on leadership development for people of color in higher education. The most comprehensive volume is León's (2005) *Lessons in Leadership: Executive Leadership Programs for Advancing Diversity in Higher Education.* Considering that research on leaders of color in higher education is minimal, it is no surprise that there is a dearth of literature regarding people of color in leadership development programs (Jackson, 2000). Much of the literature on leaders of color focuses on recruitment and retention (e.g., Jackson, 2001) but not on the actual preparation of leaders. Nevertheless, professional growth and development have been conceptualized as a key component of retention and as a benchmark for campus diversity (Davis, 1994; Jackson, 2003; Jackson, 2004b). Of the research that has been identified, it is important to note that it tends to center predominantly on African Americans (women in particular), with little research on Hispanics/Latinos (Esquibel, 1992; Gorena, 1996; Haro, 1990; Martinez, 2005), Asian Americans (Fujimoto, 1996; Montez, 1998; Nakanishi, 1993), and American Indians (Kern-Foxworth, 2000; Lynch & Charleston, 1990; Swisher, 2001; Warner, 1995).

Research narratives from the qualitative tradition have demonstrated that people of color who have successfully risen to leadership positions have participated in leadership development programs at some point during their careers (Cavanaugh, 2007; Holmes, 2004; Jenifer, 2005; Thomas, 2005). The literature highlights the need for targeted leadership development but suggests many connections between racial/ethnic classification, gender, and institution type. Beyond identification of success stories from specific individuals, two distinct features emerged: (a) there is a specific focus on *women of color* in leadership, and (b) the presence of diverse leaders is predominantly at *2-year institutions and minority-serving institutions, primarily*

Historically Black Colleges and Universities (HBCUs). Each of these features is discussed in greater depth below.

Women Leaders of Color

The literature surrounding people of color focused mostly on women of color in leadership roles (e.g., Holmes, 2004; Watson 2001). It has been speculated that this is because of the overwhelming historical underrepresentation of women in leadership positions in higher education, and the volume of literature with this focus is evidence of early efforts to remedy this fact (Jackson, 2001, 2006). For example, women in general tend to be concentrated in lower-level leadership positions, with women of color holding a small percentage of these positions (Berryman-Fink, Lemaster, & Nelson, 2003). While the role of leadership development programs for women of color must be stressed, it cannot be discussed outside of the context of other social obstacles, such as racism and sexism. The "dual burden" (Singh, Robinson & Williams-Greene, 1995), also known as a "double bind" of discrimination (Montez, 1998; Warner, 1995), illustrates the continued struggles that women of color face as they pursue and prepare for executive-level leadership roles in higher education (Wilson, 1989).

It should be noted that through program initiatives that provide targeted skill development and mentoring, some women have been successful in assuming leadership positions (Berryman-Fink et al., 2003) and navigating the pitfalls of sexism and racism. In addition to skill development, female participants in leadership development programs have reported increased self-esteem, self-worth, and self-confidence (Ebbers, Gallisath, Rockel, & Coyan, 2000). However, lest the picture for women of color in leadership be painted as rosy, it should be noted that increases in representation in senior-level leadership have not been consistent across all types of institutions, and the increase for women of color who take on executive leadership roles has been largely at 2-year institutions (Opp & Gosetti, 2000). This trend, which runs parallel to the overall increases in diversity at the upper level, highlights a fundamental distinction in the practice of leadership selection based on institutional type. The next section discusses this dynamic in detail.

Specific Institutional Types: Community Colleges and HBCUs

Institutional types have distinct cultures and practices that influence the kinds of leaders who are attracted to them and the scope of support provided

to leaders by the institution. Community colleges and Minority-Serving Institutions (MSIs; Vaughan, 1996) particularly HBCUs, have traditionally enrolled large numbers of students of color and have been known to nurture
people of color (Nichols, 2004). Literature points to HBCUs as the training
ground for Black leaders, and select research has focused on creating leadership programs for Black administrators (Lauth, 2005; Zolner, 2005), and students (Glenn, 1997). In addition, research highlights leadership challenges
(Manzo, 1996; Pluviose, 2006) and at times offers suggestions for success
by examining the historical significance of HBCUs (Cheek, 1988) and the
important social and societal implications (Jean-Marie, 2006).

Community colleges have been particularly focused on developing leaders of color and women compared to 4-year institutions (Pierce, Mahoney, & Kee, 1996). However, these institutions are still underprepared to
facilitate the succession of diverse candidates to leadership roles because few
individuals are prepared to step into those leadership roles (Zamani, 2003).
Community colleges have focused on leadership development through professional associations dedicated to community college concerns, such as the
American Association of Community Colleges (AACC), which serves as the
primary advocacy group, and through programs connected to doctoral-
granting institutions such as the community college leadership program at
the University of Texas, Austin (Manzo, 1996; Phelan, 2005). Higher education would benefit greatly from a more robust understanding of the specific
ways that community colleges and HBCUs cultivate and support leaders of
color, as they may influence practice and help set leadership agendas for
higher education at large. Consistent themes in the literature on leaders of
color surrounding race, gender, and institutional type highlight the importance of considering culture and context in developing leaders of color. This
is further underscored in the review of professional associations and leadership development programs.

Select Professional Associations and Higher Education Leadership Development Programs

At least two entities have played and continue to play a significant role in
leadership development in higher education: (a) professional associations and
(b) leadership development programs. Higher education professional associations have collectively defined core missions, visions, and values for higher

education in general, as well as governing practices for various subspecialties. These associations have been proactive in setting standards for the field, as well as reactive in offering new and emerging efforts as higher education continues to change and diversify. Leadership development programs address the need to develop and train potential leaders who can most appropriately address the needs of students, administrators, and society today. This section begins with a discussion of various professional associations and leadership development programs. Next, a general discussion for each approach will be provided, followed by specific initiatives for people of color.

Professional Associations

Professional associations provide their prospective fields and professions with a governing body, guidelines, and most offer some form of targeted approach to advance the leadership capabilities of their members (Pierce et al., 1996). A multitude of associations and councils focus on higher education (see http://www.acenet.edu/Content/NavigationMenu/ProgramsServices/Leadership/Leadership_ACE.htm). However, often missing from general lists are several professional associations that pay particular attention to increasingly diverse needs of higher education constituents (see Table 3.3). Some focus on the needs of specialty subfields or professions within higher education, such as the American Association of Collegiate Registrars and Admissions Officers (AACRAO) and the American Association of University Professors (AAUP). While others focus by institutional type, such as liberal education (Association of American Colleges and Universities [AAC&U]); community colleges (American Association of Community Colleges [AACC]); and state colleges and universities (American Association of State Colleges and Universities [AASCU]). Still others focus on scholarly pursuits and research, such as the American Educational Research Association (AERA) and the Association for the Study of Higher Education (ASHE).

With the changing climate of higher education and the increase of diverse participants, it is important to have organizations that focus on special racial and ethnic populations, such as the American Association of Hispanics in Higher Education (AAHHE) and the Hispanic Association of Colleges and Universities (HACU), both committed to providing access and strengthening the understanding of Hispanics in college; those committed to HBCUs and predominantly Black institutions, such as the National Association for

TABLE 3.3

Higher Education Organizations Focusing on Ethnic Minority Groups

Name	URL	Purpose
American Association of Blacks in Higher Education (AABHE)	http://www.blacksinhighered.org	Focus on leadership development for various constituents and collaborate with other ethnic minority groups to achieve this.
American Association of Hispanics in Higher Education (AAHHE)	http://aahhe.org/	Highlight achievements of Hispanics in the academy; identify professional opportunities to increase Hispanic faculty and focus on issues surrounding Hispanics in higher education.
American Indian Higher Education Consortium (AIHEC)	http://www.aihec.org/	Support tribal colleges to enhance American Indian education and to develop and maintain consistent standards for these colleges.
Hispanic Association of Colleges and Universities (HACU)	http://www.hacu.net	Provide Hispanic Serving Institutions (HSIs) with the necessary resources, professional development and legislative power to serve Hispanic students.
National Association for Student Affairs Professionals (NASAP)	http://www.nasap.net	Provide professional development, promote scholarly inquiry and foster a sense of unity among student affairs professionals devoted to the needs of minority students.
National Association for Equal Opportunity in Higher Education (NAFEO)	http://www.nafeo.org/	Provide a unifying voice to issues pertinent to Historically Black Colleges and Universities (HBCUs) and Predominantly Black Institutions (PBIs) and to provide support through advocacy for these organizations.

Equal Opportunity in Higher Education (NAFEO) and the National Association of Student Affairs Professionals (NASAP); as well as those committed to the American Indian experience, such as the American Indian Higher Education Consortium (AIHEC). Two in particular continue to focus on professional development for student affairs administrators: the National Association of Student Personnel Administrators (NASPA) and the American College Personnel Association (ACPA). Last, the American Council on Education (ACE) provides a unifying voice of all higher education public policy. Though not an exhaustive list, the aforementioned are representative of the varying types of organizations that share a common theme for the advancement of higher education. These organizations guide the field, are charged with developing leaders, and are most often associated with administering leadership programs.

Participation in professional associations is particularly beneficial for people of color because (a) participants have access to standard practices and are able to stay abreast of current topics and trends in higher education; (b) participation provides an opportunity for professionals to reenergize, retool, and receive recognition for their efforts; and (c) there is an opportunity to focus on a specialized area of the field. For example, NASPA offers knowledge communities that disseminate information to targeted populations —African Americans, Hispanics, Latinos/Latinas, and Asian Pacific Islanders—and seminars such as the Multicultural Institute, which focuses on addressing critical concerns of multicultural professionals and the constituents they serve (see www.naspa.org). These opportunities allow leaders of color to focus on issues that may be important to them professionally or personally while engaging in professional development. Though some leaders of color may not be part of the good old boy network on their campus, participation in professional organizations provides them with access to a national network.

Leadership Development Programs

Leadership development programs were traditionally formed to address pertinent higher education issues and to provide training opportunities for current and future leaders (Green, 1990; Montez, 1998). Perhaps the most well-known and comprehensive leadership development program that focuses on training college- and university-level leaders is the fellows program administered through ACE (Smith & Ross, 2005). An ACE fellows report stated that its participants preferred the specific leadership development and internship components of the program compared to other professional development and leader development programs (Cavanaugh, 2007). The finding that the internship is a significant benefit relates to the importance of skill development, observation, and exposure to new responsibilities happening through on-the-job-experience and is valuable in the leadership development process (Green, 1990).

ACE notwithstanding, an examination of six national leadership development programs, at various stages of a career trajectory in higher education (preentry, midlevel, and senior level), revealed various parallels within the group (see Table 3.4). Each program, though different in focus and time commitment, includes an intensive learning/seminar experience ranging from 2 days to 1 year, provides access to a national network of colleagues, stresses the importance of using formal or informal mentors, and provides a

TABLE 3.4
Comprehensive Leadership Development Programs for Pre- Entry, Mid and Senior Level Professionals

Name	Organization	Participants	Purpose	Length	Key Features	Cost
Pre-Entry						
NASPA Undergraduate Fellows (NUFP)	National Association of Student Personnel Administrators (NASPA)	Undergraduates interested in student affairs careers	To expose diverse undergraduates to careers in higher education	4 day summer institute–ongoing mentoring	Mentoring Internship Seminars Summer Institute National Network	Cost absorbed by NASPA and home institution
Mid-Level						
Donna M. Bourassa Mid-level Management Institute	American College Personnel Association (ACPA)	Mid level career—with 5 + years experience	Focus is on understanding the changing campus climate to further develop skills	5 days	Seminars National Network Mentoring	$525 for members/$625 for non-members with early registration
Higher Education Resource Services (HERS) Institutes	HERS Institute for Women in Higher Educ. Administration at the University of Denver	Mid and upper level female administrators	To enhance governance and management skills	6 day residential & 3 weekends	Mentoring Seminars National Network	$4675 for residents/$4175 for weekend commuters
	HERS Institute for Women in Higher Educ. Administration at Wellesley College	Mid and upper level female administrators	To enhance governance and management skills	5 inter-related weekends	Mentoring Seminars National Network	$3475 covers materials and meals
	Summer Institute for Women in Higher Educ. at Bryn Mawr College	Mid and upper level female administrators	To enhance governance and management skills	Approx. 4 weeks	Mentoring Seminars National Network	$6950 residential/$5950 commuter covers room & board and materials
Senior-Level						
ACE Fellows Program	American Council on Education (ACE)	Faculty or Admin. with institutional wide responsibilities	To prepare individuals with min. of 5 years experience with tools to become Admin. Leaders, i.e. Assist. Deans	up to 1 year	Mentoring Internship Seminars National Network	Split cost between nominating and host institution up to $10,000 each
Kellogg MSI Leadership Program (Consists of 3 separate programs)	AIHEC, HACU , and NAFEO Kellogg Leadership Fellows Program	Those interested in senior level and presidential posts in MSIs.	To prepare leaders of MSIs with the skills to become college leaders-Presidents	1 week institute, conference attendance	Mentoring Seminars National Network Conference	No cost to participants or mentors
Millennium Leadership Initiative (MLI)	American Association of State Colleges and Universities (AASCU)	State colleges and universities Senior admin.	To prepare underrepresented individuals for leadership in higher education	4 days	Mentoring Seminars National Network	$2500 members /$3500 non-member for room & board and materials

comprehensive and ongoing experience even after the completion of the program (Institute for Higher Education Policy, 2004; León, 2005; Thomas, 2005). What follows is a brief description of six leadership development programs by level.

Preentry Career

The NASPA Undergraduate Fellows Program (NUFP) is the only program of the six that focuses on development prior to beginning a professional career. NUFP, formerly known as the Minority Undergraduate Fellows Program (MUFP), was started in 1989 with the intent to increase the number of ethnic minority students interested in pursuing student affairs careers. In 2003 the participant population was expanded to continue to address increasing diversity on campus and to be more inclusive of other traditionally underrepresented students such as disabled, and lesbian, gay, bisexual, and transgender students. The NASPA fellows participate in a structured internship, a 4-day summer institute, and at least one conference coupled with a formal mentoring relationship. To gain admission, applicants must be supported by a mentor and have support of a senior-level administrator at the university. Financial and other professional support resources are provided by the program and the senior-level supporter at the host university (see http://www.naspa.org).

Midlevel Career

The Donna M. Bourassa Mid-Level Management Institute administered through the ACPA prepares midlevel professionals with 5 or more years of experience with the necessary skills to better understand increasingly complex and changing campus communities. The institute enhances development through a week-long curriculum of group seminars and discussions as well as promotes future discussions through a Listserv. This program serves to provide midlevel student affairs leaders with necessary professional development and does not focus on targeted populations. The application focuses solely on support documents from the applicant and does not require a recommendation and institutional support. Up to 50 applicants may compete for two scholarships of $245 to offset program costs (excluding transportation and travel). Early registration costs $525 for ACPA members or $645 for nonmembers (see http://www.myacpa.org).

The Higher Education Resource Services (HERS) Institutes for Women in Higher Education supports three residential programs that prepare mid-

and senior-level female professionals to successfully deal with increasing diversity on campus and globalization by training more women administrators and faculty in management and governance. The Summer Institute for Women in Higher Education, sponsored by HERS and Bryn Mawr College offers 4 weeks of intense seminars and activities 6 days a week; the HERS Institute for Women in Higher Education Administration at Wellesley College offers 5 weekends of comprehensive seminars and activities; and the HERS Institute for Women in Higher Education Administration at the University of Denver offers a 6-day, full-time program followed by 2-day seminars during 3 separate weekends. The programs stress intensive seminars, a national network, and mentoring, including a connection to alumnae. To gain admission, applicants must submit an application and have support from a senior-level executive (specifically for the summer institute). Although the three programs operate at separate locations, have an individualized curriculum, and varied timeframes and costs, they all focus on preparing participants for institutional leadership and addressing diverse administrative needs in higher education (see http://www.hersnet.org).

Senior-Level Career

The ACE Fellows Program prepares emerging leaders for institution-wide leadership roles through a year-long experience that includes seminars, mentoring, and on-the-job training through an internship. The ACE Fellows Program also stresses the national network and participation in national associations. This program is for all emerging leaders and does not have a specific focus on targeted populations. In addition to the application, participants must submit a recommendation from the chief administrative officer at the university, participate in an interview, and agree to participate in an internship up to 1 year in length. Fellows are responsible only for their living expenses during the internship, while the host and nominating institution split the cost of the $6,000 program fee and the additional professional development budget up to $14,000. In addition, the nominating institution agrees to maintain the participant's salary and benefits during the fellowship year (see http://www.acenet.edu).

The Kellogg MSI Leadership Fellows Program administers three separate programs: the American Indian Higher Education Consortium (AIHEC) Leadership Fellows Program, the Hispanic Association of Colleges and Universities (HACU) Leadership Fellows Program, and the National Association for Equal Opportunity (NAFEO) Kellogg Leadership Fellows Program. All of them are overseen by the Institute for Higher Education Policy, the Alliance for Equity in Higher Education, and supported by a 4-year grant of $6 million from the W. K. Kellogg Foundation. The collaborative programs provide week-long intensive seminars, mentoring, and other professional development elements to prepare a cohort of senior-level leaders for institution-wide leadership, with a particular focus on MSIs. All expenses for participation for mentors and fellows in the Kellogg MSI Leadership Fellows Program are covered by the program (see http://www.hacu.net).

The Millennium Leadership Project prepares senior-level administrators of color at state colleges and universities for the chief executive role through a 4-day professional institute and a year-long mentoring relationship with a president or chancellor. Universities identify participants and nominate them for participation. Member institutions have raised funds to support participation in the program. However, the cost of the program is $2,500 for member institutions and $3,500 for nonmember institutions and includes meals, housing, and materials (see http://www.aascu.org).

Only one of these programs provides exposure and prepares potential college student leaders for careers in higher education, two others primarily support midlevel professionals, and three more provide opportunities for seasoned individuals with institution-wide responsibilities. These programs are further distinguished by one program focusing on women administrators (midsenior level) and three focusing on ethnic minority populations. All but one of the programs for underrepresented populations focus on training senior-level leaders of color, while one is a preentry undergraduate exposure program. This is particularly interesting because Taliaferro and Montoya (1995) found that many leaders of color set their sights on positions as coordinators, directors, and vice presidents, but there do not seem to be targeted efforts to help individuals advance to or achieve midlevel positions.

Leadership programs for people of color have primarily been reactive responses to the growing number of students of color on campus (Harvey & Anderson, 2005) and an attempt to provide higher education with prepared and diverse leadership to address the increasingly complex political and social climate on campus (Thomas, 2005). For example, the Kellogg MSI fellows program was a pilot effort supported with a 4-year grant from the Kellogg

Foundation in conjunction with the Alliance for Equity in Higher Education, HACU, AIHEC, and NAFEO, with the intent to address the needs of MSIs (Merisotis & Aveilhe, 2005). Of the leadership programs specifically designed to help leaders of color prepare for institution-wide responsibilities at MSIs, this is the one that concentrates on success at MSIs. This program has the explicit purpose of preparing leaders who work at MSIs, which have a distinct culture and face a unique set of challenges different from those at Predominantly White Institutions (PWIs). Considering that the majority of college presidents of color lead MSIs, it would seem reasonable for at least one of the three leadership programs to focus on those types of institutions (Jackson, 2004c). However, the experience for leaders of color at PWIs should not be minimized. It is important to note that all discussed mainstream national programs (i.e., ACE, HERS, and Donna M. Bourassa Management Institute) do address racial/ethnic diversity in the curriculum as a seminar, but it is not a driving objective of the program.

Discussion and Conclusion

There is great opportunity to diversify the higher education administrative workforce by providing exposure, experience, and support to an increasingly diverse group of higher education leaders. If we are to see diversity among those at the presidents' and vice presidents' ranks, it is crucial to provide developmental opportunities at various levels of the career trajectory. This development should include specific targeted efforts that focus on skill development, mentoring, and participation in a national network. A body of knowledge is emerging regarding leadership development for leaders of color, especially as it relates to their participation in leadership development programs and professional associations. As discussed in this chapter and elsewhere, affiliation with and participation in these programs has been beneficial for many people of color. Additionally, literature on leadership development has focused primarily on community colleges and gender. For the most part, leadership development options for people of color focus primarily on preparation for top-level positions (e.g., vice president and president). Therefore, in turn, support for leaders of color for entry to midlevel positions seems to be absent. Giving full consideration to all of this, there is clearly a need for more research on leadership development of leaders of color.

New Directions for Inquiry on Leaders of Color

When discussing leadership programs for people of color, researchers have generally asked: What are the different needs of senior-level people of color in the leadership role? (Lauth, 2005; León, 2005). One question that has gone unanswered is: Are the needs of senior-level leaders of color different from their majority counterparts? From the current review of the research, the answer appears to be yes and no. Based on the paucity of research on the experiences of those in leadership development programs the needs are not different as they relate to the diverse curricula that address such topics as financial management, strategy and planning, and the need for mentors. However, the needs are different when it comes to addressing specific issues that are associated with certain institution types or climates, and these are the needs that the people of color-centered programs tend to focus on (Merisotis & Aveilhe, 2005). The lack of leadership programs through the career life span leads to another unanswered question: How do leadership needs change for people of color at different stages of the *career trajectory?* Clearly, existing institutional, cultural, social, and political dynamics in the U.S. higher education system continue to be perpetuated through organizational structures that highlight multiple factors that have an impact on success for leaders of color (Chesler & Crowfoot, 2000).

Though some recognizable efforts exist through a few programs (e.g., the Kellogg MSI Leadership Fellows Program and the Millennium Leadership Project) that primarily focus on leaders of MSIs, there is a clear need for further consideration to be given to leaders of color who serve at PWIs. These individuals face a unique challenge on campuses where they are the minority within the campus community but especially in the upper-level leadership positions. Furthermore, a long-term comprehensive study on leaders of color in executive leadership positions who have participated in leadership programs is absent. There is an opportunity to use evaluation and research data to improve upon the implementation of existing leadership development programs at various career stages (e.g., preentry level, entry, and midlevel). A clear opportunity exists to provide leadership development at the preentry, entry, and midlevel stages where the bulk of leaders reside in the professional ranks and may never ascend to the senior-level position without appropriate guidance, development, and mentoring.

Barriers to Participation in Leadership Programs for Leaders of Color

Participation in leadership development programs is not as straightforward as identifying individuals who have the capacity for leadership. The pipeline is sometimes riddled with challenges as individuals try to ascend to leadership. As Jackson (2007) indicates, the pipeline is sometimes clogged by personal or professional attainment, cracked because of poor perceptions, leaky because of an inability to persist, noisy because internal and outside influences interfere with the goal, and frozen because of an inability to navigate through the circumstances of the institution. These metaphors emphasize the many internal and external impediments that exist as individuals move through their career. In addition to barriers in the structure of higher education, such as racial tension and feelings of tokenism and isolation, there are very real barriers and/or obstacles within the structure of these leadership programs that impede participation: lack of financial resources, support from senior-level executives, and time.

For those who do have access to and understand the value of participating in a structured leadership experience, financial constraints remain a significant reason why more individuals do not participate. Costs associated with the majority of the programs may prove to be a financial burden to the leader or the nominating institution. Most programs are costly for individuals to participate in and offer limited financial aid. One such example is the Summer Institute for Women in Higher Education at Bryn Mawr College at $6,950. The exception is the Kellogg MSI Leadership Fellows Program, which absorbs all costs of participation. Although the institution may assume some or all of the costs, the participant will inevitably incur some general living expenses from being away from home for an extended period of time.

Second, leadership programs expect the participants to have the support and buy-in from their universities. Many of the programs require the application to be accompanied by a recommendation from the chief executive officer, provost, president, or another senior-level leader. This requirement assumes that participants have a certain amount of cultural capital and exposure to these university leaders. This may be problematic for people of color who may not have had the opportunity to interface with senior-level leadership on campus, particularly because people of color tend to work in areas that are more student focused and take on such roles as advisor for a student organization and committee member for diversity issues. Additionally, leadership development may be perceived as an individual priority versus an institutional opportunity (Green, 1990).

Finally, time is a factor for the individual and the institution when determining if an employee is able to participate in a 2-day program or a more intense 26-day program. Personal priorities such as raising a family or serving as a caregiver for an elderly relative make attending a residential program virtually impossible for some. Since participants are considered leaders, their absences are surely to be felt on their campuses, and a short or long absence may adversely affect the day-to-day work schedule, particularly for smaller institutions. Therefore, personal circumstance can influence professional attainment. Ideally, leadership programs are valuable rigorous experiences that continue to help shape higher education and successful leaders. However, sometimes realistically they are difficult to partake in because of the concentrated amount of time required to participate.

Thus far, this chapter has provided insights into current employment and research trends on leaders of color, existing levels of intervention through leadership programs, noted gaps in career development efforts, and described some of the barriers to participation in these programs. As previously revealed, several key leadership programs have indicated that participation in mentor-mentee relationships, seminars, and a national network are crucial components to a successful leadership experience. An examination of the collective efforts and landscape of professional development for leaders of color indicates there is an opportunity to develop a program that will successfully prepare those individuals for leadership roles in higher education and address some of the barriers of financial resources, executive-level support, and time. A model of a leadership development program that can be implemented at various stages of the career trajectory and facilitated by associations that guide the profession follows.

Toward a Comprehensive Approach to Leadership Development for People of Color

To consider a true comprehensive approach to leadership, a few assumptions guide this program development. These assumptions are derived from the previous review of the literature, demonstrated success from existing leadership programs, an examination of what is missing from current leadership development efforts, and includes revolutionary leadership characteristics. First, and arguably most important, culture and context guide the leadership development process. In the model program, race, sex, institution type, and geographic cultural realities are considered throughout all key components of the program. Second, it is beneficial for leaders of color to interact with their White counterparts as part of a comprehensive approach to leadership development, but it is crucial that they interact with other leaders of color. Third, leadership development requires individual motivation, group support, and collaboration throughout each of the key components. Fourth, the most effective leadership development efforts involve buying in from the participant's home institution and support from a national professional association. Fifth, development of a leadership program should go beyond on-site programming and in-person interactions to include creative programming that includes the implementation of technology and flexible time schedules. These assumptions were used to establish a model for a comprehensive leadership development program designed for leaders of color. In order to provide a heuristic tool, this model is referred to as the Comprehensive Approach to Leadership Development for People of Color (CALD-PC). We must warn readers, CALD-PC is a dream leadership program that is national in scope. The following are its key components:

Program Curriculum/Seminars

All participants in CALD-PC will take part in a standard curriculum appropriate to the career level that covers general information and skills. For example, those at the midcareer level will engage in seminars that focus on managing a unit, gaining senior-level support, fiscal responsibility, and effecting change. In addition to participating in the standard curriculum, participants will choose educational tracks that focus specifically on the type of institution and institutional climate they are presently in or desire to work in. Therefore a participant from a midwestern PWI will participate in seminars that address some of the cultural, political, and racial themes particular to those types of environments. There will be opportunities to address some institutional climate idiosyncrasies through mentoring. Options for participating in content-focused components include a week-long residential experience, weekend and evening seminars, Web and video conferencing, and live online discussions. Because this is a national-level program, the on-site options will be duplicated in various regions of the country. Collectively, these experiences purposely stress collaboration with other CALD-PC peers but will include some individual activities. Attendees have the option to choose how they will fully participate in the experience but will have to complete a specific set of experiential requirements.

Though participants may choose components that meet their individual needs and lifestyle, they do not have the option to experience the program in isolation. CALD-PC is a national-level program, administered at various stages of the career trajectory, and therefore seminars and projects are designed to be interactive and require work with participants in various educational units, not just their own functional area. The CALD-PC programs at different career levels will run simultaneously or overlap to allow participants to engage in at least one seminar with a different career-level class. For example, senior-level and entry-level CALD-PC participants may take a seminar together on technology and its impact on university management/leadership. This encourages participants to see beyond the individual cohort they begin the program with, expand their perspective by interfacing with leaders at different career levels, and cultivate membership in a larger community of CALD-PC participants. Along with the curriculum, individuals will be expected to develop an individualized leadership development career plan they can reference and revise during and after the formalized leadership development program.

Mentoring

CALD-PC mentoring is seen as an ongoing exchange of ideas and experience with individuals and groups. Often we think of mentoring as only a one-on-one process. However, mentoring takes place in many forms, and attendees will have the opportunity to participate in one-on-one and group mentoring. One-on-one mentoring matches participants to leaders of color. It is not just important that leaders of color interface with other leaders of color but, specifically, leaders of color who work in similar institutional settings. For example, an aspiring dean at a Hispanic-Serving Institution (HSI) on the West Coast will be matched with or have access to a dean of color at a western HSI. This mentoring match complements the educational track the participant has chosen and provides real-life examples of experiences in that setting. However, group mentoring incorporates majority leaders into the process who are invested in developing leaders of color for their particular institutions. This is beneficial for the mentors, because they are able to share the mentoring load and have an opportunity to identify potential future talent for their institutions.

National Network

CALD-PC has built-in structural mechanisms that facilitate a national connection. This national network is composed of a consortium of national professional organizations that work together to create context and culturally relevant professional development experiences for leaders of color that meet the needs of an increasingly diverse field of higher education. This true national network reiterates shared purpose, ensures a diversity of resources, provides a preexisting support system, and places the responsibility of developing leaders of color on the field and not on one particular association. For CALD-PC the national network will facilitate a programmatic network that includes a shared database for participants, instructors, mentors, and those who desire to support but may have less of a formal role (e.g., a retired college president who may not take on a formal program role but is open to being listed as a resource); optional quarterly conference calls hosted by institutions of past participants; yearly skill refreshers or new information seminars; and 5-year reunions. Relationship building is ingrained in the culture of CALD-PC and facilitated through seminars and mentoring that provide individual attention as well as group development. To regenerate the experience and continue to develop future leaders, past participants are encouraged to stay involved through evolving roles, such as seminar instructor and mentor.

Administrative Components

Several administrative components that affect participation include the application process, funding, and program administration. These are discussed last because the greater focus for developing leaders of color appropriately lies in the curriculum, mentoring, and establishing a career-long network. However, these issues require equal attention by administrators and institutions because, as established previously, the administrative processes associated with participation in leadership programs can create barriers to participation for people of color.

An ideal CALD-PC application packet would include a minimum of three items. The first is two professional recommendation letters—one from a professional in a more senior position than the applicant to help establish work abilities and work ethic, and one from a professional peer to help establish the applicant's ability to work with others and the desire to participate in a peer-supported environment. While it is important to express leadership capabilities outside one's own self-description, this is best demonstrated by those who know the applicant well. The second is a demonstrated interest in leadership development determined through participation in other informal or formal leadership experiences, projects taken on, and positions held professionally or in a volunteer capacity. The third item is an essay that details the applicant's leadership and career goals. Though the application requires support from others through references, the focus for acceptance is individual merit and abilities.

One of the most crucial administrative aspects of successfully facilitating CALD-PC is funding. CALD-PC requires funding and support from a consortium of national-level professional associations, educational institutes, or foundations to administer the program and to offset the costs of participation, because ultimately the goal is for CALD-PC to offer full-experience scholarships to participants. However, CALD-PC will also offer other funding options to increase the diversity of participants and reduce finance as a barrier. Some of those options include a sliding pay scale based on need, or fund-raising opportunities for individuals and institutions. A new, unexplored option for funding might include an educational loan provided from a partner institution that will be forgiven based on the number of years a participant decides to work at that particular institution. While not currently in use in the leadership development setting, it is successful in other areas of advanced educational opportunity (e.g., AmeriCorps). In addition, CALD-PC works to lower the cost of administration through donations and in-kind gifts. For example, CALD-PC works with CALD-PC–friendly institutions that may or may not have employees participating in the program but have an expressed interest in developing leaders of color. Accordingly, it might be possible for CALD-PC to tap into resources of CALD-PC institutions (e.g., space to conduct seminars) to help run the program. This serves as a mutually rewarding relationship, because not only do the CALD-PC institutions become part of the national network, they are able to highlight their campuses while providing much needed resources.

To help visualize this proposed model, participation in a CALD-PC leadership development program resembles a wheel that moves the process of professional development forward (see Figure 3.1). The national and institutional supporters provide the structure and overall direction of the CALD-PC process. These organizations also provide financial resources, such as scholarships and forgivable loans, to help students participate, and in-kind

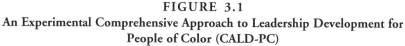

FIGURE 3.1
An Experimental Comprehensive Approach to Leadership Development for People of Color (CALD-PC)

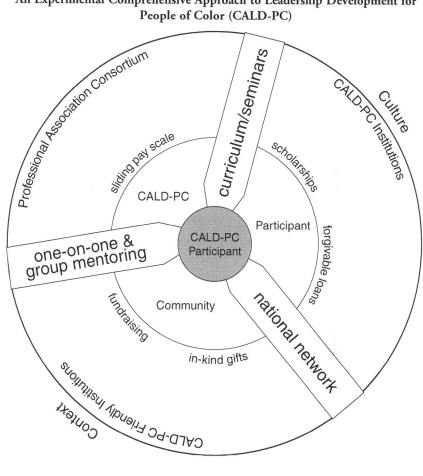

donations, such as meeting space and materials, to help with the administration of the CALD-PC experience. The key program components of mentoring, curriculum/seminars, and national network provide the content and ongoing link to other participants. In essence, these key components are the core of the program and allow for participants to remain connected with CALD-PC after graduation in evolving roles (e.g., those who have participated in mentoring may one day become a mentor or may facilitate a seminar). As with any wheel, if there is a deficiency in it (e.g., a flat) or the resources are not fully employed, the wheel may continue to move forward, but it makes getting to the destination of leadership development more difficult. Therefore, participation in a leadership development program is not the only part but may play a significant role in the career development process. However, a true comprehensive approach to leadership development focuses not just on skill development but fully integrates into the curriculum the context and culture of institutions individuals lead (Kezar & Carducci, 2007).

In closing, institutions of higher education can no longer be silent about race within these unique organizations (Nkomo, 2000). With the increasing number for people of color joining the ranks of higher education, we must reconsider how, when, and why we engage in leadership development. Institutions of higher education that claim to embrace the value of diversity must put forth a sincere, pointed effort to increase the number of people of color in leadership positions. As well, key decision makers must work to acknowledge and affirm racial differences, and work to break down the misconceptions and stereotypes that impede productive developmental experiences and the inclusion of diverse groups. The higher education community has recognized through the efforts of leadership development programs that mentoring, networking, and skill development work. Now we have an opportunity to take a major step in this regard by developing more programs that meet the unique needs for leaders of color in various institutional settings, cultural climates, and geographic regions, while simultaneously recognizing the historical and cultural discriminatory practices that exist in society. Additionally, institutions that currently provide leadership programming would benefit from a firm understanding of the barriers and challenges that remain with regard to participation based on a traditional format. The future development and promotion for leaders of color demand that these barriers be removed or minimized in order to maximize participation from a more diverse participant pool.

References

Bensimon, E., & Tierney, W. (1993). Shaping the multicultural college campus. *Education Digest, 59*(3), 67.

Berryman-Fink, C., Lemaster, B., & Nelson, K. (2003). The women's leadership program: A case study. *Liberal Education, 89*(1), 59–63.

Cavanaugh, C. (2007). *The ACE fellows program: The benefits and values to ACE fellows.* Pensacola, FL: American Council on Education.

Cheek, J. (1988). A leadership blueprint for equity and excellence in Black higher education. *Urban League Review, 11*(1/2), 18–27.

Chesler, M. A., & Crowfoot, J. (2000). An organizational analysis of racism in higher education. In M. C. Brown II (Ed.), *Organization and governance in higher education* (5th ed.; pp. 436–469). Boston, MA: Pearson.

Coleman, J. (1998, April). *Barriers to career advancement by African-American and Caucasian female administrators in Minnesota organizations: A perception or reality?* Paper presented at the annual meeting of the American Educational Research Association, San Diego, CA.

Davis, J. D. (Ed.). (1994). *Coloring the halls of ivy: Leadership & diversity in the academy.* Bolton, MA: Anker.

Ebbers, L. H., Gallisath, G., Rockel, V., & Coyan, M. (2000). The leadership institute for a new century: LINCing women and minorities into tomorrow's community college leadership roles. *Community College Journal of Research & Practice, 24*(5), 375–382.

Esquibel, A. (1992). *The career mobility of Chicano administrators in higher education: A fifty year replication study.* Boulder, CO: Western Interstate Commission for Higher Education.

Fujimoto, M. J. (1996). The community college presidency: An Asian Pacific American perspective. *New Directions for Community Colleges, 1996* (94), 47–56.

Glenn, G. (1997). Following the leaders: The establishment of leadership development centers in historically Black colleges and universities. *Black Issues in Higher Education, 14*(1), 22–25.

Gorena, M. (1996, April). *Hispanic women in higher education administration: Factors that positively influence or hinder advancement to leadership positions.* Paper presented at the annual meeting of the American Educational Research Association, New York.

Green, M. (1990). Investing in leadership. *Liberal Education, 76*(1), 6.

Haro, R. (1990). Latino and executive positions in higher education. *The Educational Record, 71*(3), p. 39–42.

Harvey, W. B., & Anderson, E. L. (2005, February). *Minorities in higher education twenty-first annual status report.* Washington, DC: American Council on Education.

Holmes, S. L. (2004). An overview of African American college presidents: A game of two steps forward, one step backward, and standing still. *The Journal of Negro Education, 73*(1), 21–39.

Howard-Hamilton, M. F., & Williams, V. A. (1996). *Assessing the environment for women of color in student affairs.* Paper prepared for Office of Affirmative Action, Florida University, Gainesville.

Institute for Higher Education Policy. (2004, August). *Leading the way to America's future: A monograph about the launch and implementation of the Kellogg MSI leadership fellows program, 2002–2004.* Washington, DC: Institute for Higher Education Policy.

Jackson, J. F. L. (2000). Administrators of color at predominantly White institutions. In L. Jones (Ed.), *Brothers of the academy: Up and coming African Americans earning our way in higher education!* (pp. 42–52). Sterling, VA: Stylus.

Jackson, J. F. L. (2001). A new test for diversity: Retaining African American administrators at predominantly White institutions. In L. Jones (Ed.), *Retaining African Americans in higher education: Challenging paradigms for retaining students, faculty, and administrators* (pp. 93–109). Sterling, VA: Stylus.

Jackson, J. F. L. (2003). Engaging, retaining and advancing African Americans in student affairs administration: An analysis of employment status. *NASAP Journal, 6*(1), 9–24.

Jackson, J. F. L. (2004a). Engaging, retaining, and advancing African Americans to executive-level positions: A descriptive and trend analysis of academic administrators in higher and postsecondary education. *Journal of Negro Education, 73*(1), 4–20.

Jackson, J. F. L. (2004b). An emerging engagement, retention, and advancement model for African American administrators at predominantly White institutions: The results of two delphi studies. In D. Cleveland (Ed.), *A long way to go: Conversations about race by African American faculty and graduate students in higher education* (pp. 211–222). New York: Peter Lang.

Jackson, J. F. L. (2004c). A crisis at the top: A national perspective [Editor's introduction]. In J. F. L. Jackson (Ed.), Top line: A status report on African American leadership in higher and postsecondary education [Special focused section]. *Journal of Negro Education, 73*(1), 1–3.

Jackson, J. F. L. (2006). Hiring practices of African American males in academic leadership positions at American colleges and universities: An employment trends and disparate impact analysis. *Teachers College Record, 108*(2), 316–338.

Jackson, J. F. L. (2007). Reconceptualizing the African American educational pipeline. In J. F. L. Jackson (Ed.), *Strengthening the African American pipeline: Informing research, policy and practice* (pp. 197–209). Albany, NY: SUNY Press.

Jackson, J. F. L., & Daniels, B. D. (2007). A national progress report of African Americans in the administrative workforce in higher education. In J. F. L. Jackson (Ed.), *Strengthening the educational pipeline for African Americans: Informing policy and practice* (pp. 115–137). Albany, NY: SUNY Press.

Jean-Marie, G. (2006). Welcoming the unwelcomed: A social justice imperative of African-American female leaders at historically Black colleges and universities. *Educational Foundations, 20*(1/2), 85–104.

Jenifer, F. G. (2005). *Minorities and women in higher education and the role mentoring plays in their advancement.* Austin, TX: Office of Academic Affairs, University of Texas System.

Kern-Foxworth, M. (2000). Beyond gender: The experience of women of color. In D. M. Smith (Ed.), *Women at work: Leadership for the next century.* (pp. 80–100). Upper Saddle River, NJ: Prentice Hall.

Kezar, A., & Carducci, R. (2007). Cultivating revolutionary educational leaders: Translating emerging theories into action. *Journal of Research on Leadership Education, 2*(1), 1–46.

Lauth, R. (2005). Handing one another along: The creation of AASCU's millennium leadership initiative. In D. J. León (Ed.), *Lessons in leadership: Executive leadership programs for advancing diversity in higher education* (pp. 151–171). New York: Elsevier/JAI Press.

León, D. J. (2005). Why leadership programs matter. In D. J. León (Ed.), *Lessons in leadership: Executive leadership programs for advancing diversity in higher education* (pp. 85–105). New York: Elsevier/JAI Press.

Lynch, P. D., & Charleston, M. (1990). The emergence of American Indian leadership in education. *Journal of American Indian Education, 29*(2), 1-10.

Manzo, K. (1996). Building leaders. Leadership development program important step for community college presidents. *Black Issues in Higher Education, 13*(17), 18.

Martinez, R. O. (2005). Latino demographic and institutional issues in higher education: Implications for leadership development. In D. J. León (Ed.), *Lessons in leadership: Executive leadership programs for advancing diversity in higher education* (pp. 85–105). New York: Elsevier/JAI Press.

Merisotis, J. P., & Aveilhe, K. (2005). The Kellogg MSI Leadership Fellows Program. In D. J. León (Ed.), *Lessons in leadership: Executive leadership programs for advancing diversity in higher education* (pp. 207–222). New York: Elsevier/JAI Press.

Montez, J. (1998). Asian/Pacific American women in higher education administration: Doubly bound, doubly scarce. *Issues in Policy, 9.* Pullman, WA: Washington State University.

Nakanishi, D. T. (1993). Asian Pacific Americans in higher education: Faculty and administrative representation and tenure. *New Directions for Teaching and Learning, 1993* (53), 51–59.

Nichols, J. (2004). Unique characteristics, leadership styles, and management of historically Black colleges and universities. *Innovative Higher Education, 28*(3), 219–229.

Nkomo, S. M. (2000). Race in organizations. In M. C. Brown II (Ed.), *Organization and governance in higher education* (5th ed., pp. 417–431). Boston, MA: Pearson.

Opp, R., & Gosetti, P. (2000). Equity for women administrators of color in two-year colleges: Progress and prospects. *Community College Journal of Research and Practice, 2,* 591–608.

Phelan, D. (2005). Crossing the generations: Learning to lead across the leadership life cycle. *Community College Journal of Research and Practice,* 29(9/10), 783–792.

Pierce, D. R., Mahoney, J. R., & Kee, A. M. (1996). Professional development resources for minority administrators. *New Directions for Community Colleges, 1996* (94), 81–92.

Pluviose, D. (2006). Hung out to dry. *Diverse: Issues in Higher Education,* 23(14), 22–25.

Singh, K., Robinson, A., & Williams-Greene, J. (1995). Differences in perceptions of African American women and men faculty and administrators. *The Journal of Negro Education,* 64(4), 401–408.

Smith, G. A., & Ross, M. (2005). American Council on Education Fellows Program: Celebrating 40 years of leadership development in higher education. In D. J. León (Ed.), *Lessons in leadership: Executive leadership programs for advancing diversity in higher education* (pp. 109–126). New York: Elsevier/JAI Press.

Swisher, K. G. (2001). Solid ground: Comment on "Shifting Sands: Reflections from the Field of Higher Education." *Anthropology & Education Quarterly,* 32(4), 502–506.

Taliaferro, B., & Montoya, A. (1995). *Faculty and administrators of color in the Pennsylvania state system of higher education: A status report.* (ERIC Document Reproduction Service No. ED381504).

Thomas, J. (2005). African American leadership in higher education. In D. J. León (Ed.), *Lessons in leadership: Executive leadership programs for advancing diversity in higher education* (pp. 85–105). New York: Elsevier/JAI Press.

Vaughan, G. B. (1996). Paradox and promise: Leadership and the neglected minority. *New Directions for Community Colleges, 1996* (94), 5–12.

Warner, L. S. (1995). A study of American Indian females in higher education administration. *Initiatives,* 56(4), pp. 11–17.

Watson, L. W. (2001). In their voices: A glimpse of African-American women administrators in higher education. *NASPA Journal, 4,* 7–16.

Wilson, R. (1989). Women of color in academic administration: Trends, progress, and barriers. *Sex Roles: A Journal of Research, 21,* 85–97.

Zamani, E. M. (2003). African American student affairs professionals in community college settings: A commentary for future research. *NASAP Journal,* 6(1), 91–103.

Zolner, J. P. (2005). The Harvard institutes for higher education. In D. J. León (Ed.), *Lessons in leadership: Executive leadership programs for advancing diversity in higher education* (pp. 127–147). New York: Elsevier/JAI Press.

4

FACING ORGANIZATIONAL COMPLEXITY AND CHANGE

A Case-in-Point Approach to Leadership Development

Tricia Bertram Gallant and Cheryl Getz

Higher education organizations are faced with unprecedented challenges in the 21st century: increasing diversity of students and faculty and enhancing environments where that diversity can thrive, responding to federal calls for greater accountability, creating cultures where academic integrity is the norm and academic misconduct is minimized, harnessing the beneficial power of technology while not diminishing the power of interpersonal relationships, and maintaining a strong teaching and learning environment in the face of increasing pressures to do more research and admit more students.

These are all common and quite complex challenges facing higher education organizations in the 21st century, challenges that may not be easily resolved through the application of known technologies, instruments, tools, or schemas. Rather, such challenges often create tensions between the existing practices of the organization and demands for new ways, demands that extend deep within the organization beyond the external barrier of admissions to the interior life of the classroom and faculty member (Altbach, 2001). The tensions created from these demands cannot be ignored, but must be acknowledged and creatively managed in a way that honors core institutional integrity while adapting to new ways (Selznick, 1957; Senge, 1990). A notable example is the tension created between protecting academic freedom while responding to public demands for greater accountability (for example, see Jaschik, 2005, on the Ward Churchill debate at University of Colorado).

Higher education organizations, like most, cannot ignore changing surrounding environments or the external pressures exerting force on the institution because higher education is an open system and its boundaries are permeable (Birnbaum, 1988). There is a constant exchange between higher education organizations and society—through admissions and graduations, service and outreach, research collaboration, and routine transactional (i.e., economic) processes. Colleges and universities survive and thrive based on these relationships with the public and by upholding the implicit (and sometimes explicit) social and economic contracts under which higher education organizations are expected to serve society's needs and interests (Altbach, 2001). However, society's needs and interests and those of the institution do not always align, creating an ever present necessity for tackling these conflicts.

If creatively managing values conflicts between higher education organizations and the external world is not in itself difficult, which we suggest it is, higher education organizations themselves are complex with multiple coexisting, and sometimes conflicting, goals, aims, values, and purposes (Birnbaum, 1988; Duderstadt, 2000). Take, for example, many institutions' interests in effectively engaging in teaching and research and the delicate balance between the two that most institutions struggle with. Or, for another example, take the difficulty in meeting the interests of the social and the economic good when they more often seem in direct conflict (Longanecker, 2005). These are just two of the numerous examples of the tensions within, and complexity of, the modern higher education organization.

Understanding and appreciating the complexity of organizational dynamics and developing the capacity to deal with prevailing uncertainties in higher education is a great challenge (Gabelnick, 2004). Unfortunately, the majority of faculty and administrators are not provided opportunities to develop such leadership capacity, and if they receive any training, it tends to be in the development of management skills disguised as leadership development. For example, faculty moving into administrative positions may receive training in managing (people and budgets), delegating, and strategic planning. An increasing number of administrators, especially in student affairs, are earning higher education doctorates in which they also typically receive training in management-type tasks and responsibilities. While not unimportant, of course, the development of management skills in those reaching for positions of formal authority may not be sufficient for responding to the complex problems facing the 21st-century college or university:

> There must be institutional change that responds to the changing nature of the broader system of higher education. To achieve this requires a different and more effective leadership, not just at the top but throughout the institution, leadership with the ability to draw the whole organization into the process of change, assessment, and constant and unremitting improvement. (Newman, Couturier, & Scurry, 2004, p. 7).

Thus, we propose here that faculty and administrators who hope to creatively respond to organizational tensions and mobilize organizational members to tackle difficult problems desperately require engagement in revolutionary approaches to leadership development. In this chapter, we present one such approach, case-in-point pedagogy (Parks, 2005), that develops in participants the "knowledge and skills to manage the complexity of issues that dominate everyday life" (Getz & Gelb, 2007, p. 1). Before describing case-in-point, however, we review some basic assumptions of leadership, problems, groups, and organizations that inform the pedagogy. Then after case-in-point is illustrated, we offer some common lessons that are learned by participants and end with recommendations for readers who are intrigued by this approach.

Underlying Assumptions

In this section, we discuss the three basic assumptions underlying our argument for a different kind of leadership development: (a) complex organizations present a range of problems to be resolved, from routine (also known as technical) to adaptive (also known as generative); (b) in response to such problems, a range of actions from management to leadership (complementary but not synonymous activities) is required; and (c) leadership is distinct from, but shaped by, authority (Heifetz, 1994).

The Complexity Continuum: Routine to Adaptive Problems

Although higher education organizations are complex, routine problems still arise and require resolution on a daily basis. Routine problems are easily definable, have known remedies, and can be resolved by our knowledge, skills, or technologies (Heifetz, 1994; Selznick, 1957; Senge, 1990). Routine problems are not unimportant and in fact, their resolution is critical to the successful operation of a college or university. At the same time, however, routine problems do not present significant challenges because their resolution is possible using existing expertise.

For example, a common routine problem in colleges and universities is overenrollment—the miscalculation of the *take ratio* of admissions to enrollment, which subsequently requires the college to increase its capacity. Although an effective resolution is extremely important to ensure that all students feel welcome and receive required services, the problem can be easily handled with known solutions. It may require someone with authority to coordinate efforts, usually through the formation of a committee of experts, but the local experts will know how to respond. For example, the residential life staff will house three students in each double room to ensure that students have a place to live, academic departments will hire adjunct faculty to cover the additional classes that will be needed, and administrators will coordinate class schedules so the increase in classes can be accommodated on campus.

Problems become adaptive when they present challenges that have no known or effective resolutions (Heifetz, 1994). These problems require new ways of thinking and doing as they typically challenge existing or dominant norms, prevailing views, or underlying values and assumptions. Take, for example, the routine problem presented previously. What if the increased enrollment became a pattern? Diagnosed as still a routine problem, residential life experts ask for more residence halls to be built and an increase in funding for community programming, academic departments ask for increased funding to hire additional full-time tenure-track appointments, and facilities request that new classrooms be built. To be sure, if the college decides to permanently increase its student population these are all necessary technical responses to ensure that basic services are provided to enrolled students. But what of the conflicts that emerge out of such growth and corresponding decisions?

For example, suppose the new growth results in larger rather than additional classes and the institution that once prided itself on a low faculty-student ratio and its dedication to teaching now faces a very different future? What if during the 4 years it takes to build residence halls, staff are forced to restrict housing to 1st-year students or keep students in cramped triple or quad rooms? What if the larger student population ushers in a fundamentally different type of student, one that is more interested in the professional programs and less in the liberal arts education held sacrosanct in the college? The conflicts that emerge all require a different type of action that addresses values conflicts and potential threats to institutional integrity. These types of adaptive challenges require leadership, not management.

A Range of Actions: Management to Leadership

We suggest a range of actions exist from management to leadership and that the appropriate action is connected to the problem presented. In response to a routine problem, such as temporary overenrollment, we suggest the more traditional notion of leadership is required, one that we would call management—responsiveness, organization, coordination, delegation, and responsible decision making. In other words, the skills covered in traditional leadership programs normally followed by faculty and administrators. Effective management is extremely important in successful organizations, so we certainly are not advocating for its abandonment. We are advocating, however, that it is different from the leadership required when facing adaptive problems.[1] Adaptive problems, such as those caused by persistent overenrollment, challenge people's values and normal ways of thinking. They disturb people, organizations, and systems, creating tensions where otherwise there were none. In the face of these adaptive challenges, higher education organizations need leadership—the mobilization of people to tackle difficult issues (Heifetz, 1994). Leadership does not necessarily mean solving problems but does mean creating the environment and facilitating the processes that enable the community to tackle the issues facing it.

Distinguishing Authority and Leadership

The distinction between leadership and authority is critical to mention here as the two are traditionally conflated. Because leadership is a process and not a position, we assume that leadership can be exercised by anyone within the organization, not just by those in positions of power. Although we submit that leadership is not positional, we do acknowledge that it is shaped by the rules of authority—whether informal or formal. Informal authority is

---

1. It is important here to acknowledge that the same situation can present technical and adaptive problems, and that management and leadership may be required at the same time.

granted to a particular person by others based on implicit promises to fulfill people's expectations, desires, or needs. People grant this authority informally usually based on a perception of referent (e.g., likeability, attractiveness) or expert (e.g., knowledge, intelligence) power. For example, although faculty often have little formal power within higher education organizations, individual faculty or faculty as a group may have tremendous informal authority to be able to sway public opinion and influence those with the formal authority to make changes.

Formal authority, on the other hand, is conferred upon people based on their position or title within the organization and the power they have to reward others or to make changes to the organization's structures or functions. In the college or university setting, the president has much formal authority, whose reach is often moderated by the governing board or faculty senate. The president's ability to exercise leadership, to help people tackle adaptive challenges, then, can be hindered and enhanced by informal or formal authority (Heifetz, 1994). For example, the ability of a president to brainstorm with the community to generate alternative responses to the adaptive problems caused by persistent overenrollment may be hampered by his or her authority; staff may resist the brainstorming experience because of their implicit expectations that it is the president's or leader's job to make the decision for the rest of the organization.

In summary, there is a difference between routine and adaptive problems, the first of which can easily be resolved by management or through the delegation of authority, because the definition of the problem is clear, the solutions are known, and expertise is available. Adaptive problems are more difficult because they are not easily understandable, solutions are unknown, and/or they require people to change norms, values, and assumptions. These types of problems, especially in today's complex educational organizations, require a new understanding of leadership, one that is not tied directly to authority, as referential, expert, positional, or reward power may make such leadership difficult. We suggest then that this new type of leadership requires a different way of learning, learning in *real time* in temporary social systems that reflect those found in colleges and universities across the country.

Case-in-Point Pedagogy for Leadership Development

One pedagogy that has been largely untapped in mainstream leadership development, especially for those employed in higher education, is called case-in-point (Parks, 2005). When viewing leadership development pedagogies on a continuum from traditional and didactic to learner-centered and interactive, lectures would be situated at one end with case-in-point pedagogy at the other. In between are other strategies such as debates, storytelling, small-group dialogue circles, case studies, simulations, reflection and journaling, role playing, problem-based learning, and internships, to name a few. These experiential methods have been found to greatly enhance the capacity of participants to increase their learning edge and also to improve practice over more traditional pedagogies. Case-in point methodology, however, is distinctive from other experiential methods because of its potential to develop in people the ability to exercise adaptive leadership. It has this potential because it positions participants in an environment where a sense of order and routine, and thus comfort, is replaced by a perception of chaos. The chaos is initially created by simply not meeting participants' expectations of a traditional learning experience in which someone in authority directs every event, movement, and task. When those in formal authority do not take up the roles expected of them or enforce the boundaries that organizational members expect, a sense of chaos is experienced by membership. This creates the space for a very different learning experience from that offered in traditional leadership development programs. In this created space, with expectations unrealized, participants begin to experiment with roles and boundaries and then eventually with their own capacity for exercising leadership and authority. In this environment, the complexity of groups and organizations is heightened and participants have to learn their way through unfamiliar situations and challenges. Faculty assist in the work by drawing participants' attention to the dynamics unfolding in the group and intervening in ways to keep the participants engaged in, rather than avoiding, the complexity and chaos.

While case-in-point pedagogy may not be the only way to develop leadership, we believe its relative obscurity among higher education faculty and staff, and yet its powerful potential for developing adaptive leadership, warrants special consideration in a book on revolutionary leadership development. The case-in-point pedagogy, unlike any other leadership learning experience we know, best harnesses the power of experiential learning, introspection, sophisticated analysis, and group dynamics simultaneously. In the remainder of this section, we describe three main aspects of case-in-point pedagogy that enable such an experience: (a) it asks the participants to study group and organizational dynamics in the moment as they act and interact in the temporary organization of the class, (b) the study the students are engaged in requires analysis at four levels (intrapersonal, interpersonal, group, and system as a whole), and (c) the experience and analysis can develop in people the capacity to exercise leadership in the face of organizational complexity and adaptive challenges.

The Group as Temporary Organization

The key difference of the case-in-point pedagogy is that the class is seen not as a collection of disconnected individuals but as a temporary organization or system that, in its very act of functioning, creates dynamics or data that can be studied in the here and now (see box on p. 101)—a form of learning in action (Gillette, 1995). This is not a simulation but rather a real experience of a system, complete with implicit and explicit boundaries, roles, authority, and tasks. Thus, leadership development programs using the case-in-point method usually involve a large number of participants (anywhere from 50 to 100) so that characteristics similar to most organizations can emerge. The size of the group creates just enough anxiety and complexity for participants to negotiate the confusion that often ensues. The dynamics that emerge provide experiences for learning about authority and leadership, as well as the unconscious forces that are normally ignored or buried for the sake of the task or a sense of everyone "just getting along" (Hayden & Molenkamp, 2004, p. 141). These dynamics are manifested in the actions and voices of individuals, which, in fact, represent the group's desires, fears, and needs. The faculty (the formal authority figures of the organization) are there to help participants navigate and learn from these dynamics.

Unlike rote learning situations where the answer is supplied, though paced by the teacher, adaptive learning situations demand that people discover, invent, and take responsibility. "Leadership is a special sort of educating in which the teacher raises problems, questions, options, interpretations, and perspectives, often without answers, gauging all the while when to push through and when to hold steady" (Heifetz, 1994, p. 244)

In effect, case-in-point pedagogy offers participants the opportunity to learn how to do adaptive work because the structure of the conference (the organization) requires participants to function within unfamiliar territory where they have to define the issues, determine the appropriate tasks, and then act. This guided adaptive challenge experience can develop in higher

---

Here and Now

Often, organizations and leadership are studied in a there-and-then format (such as case studies)—students examine what other people in other organizations have done that led either to successes or failures. The here-and-now format, however, requires participants to look within the group—the temporary organization—for data to learn from. Participants are asked to reflect in the moment, in action, to consider what is going on in the group (here) and in the moment (now). So, for example, illustrations of leadership are drawn not from outside but directly from within the group and the actions of the participants themselves.

---

education faculty and administrators the capacity to tackle adaptive challenges in their day-to-day, complex organizations.

Engaging the Levels of Analysis

Although the primary levels of analysis in case-in-point pedagogy are the group or organization (system), participants become skilled in two additional levels: intrapersonal and interpersonal (Wells, 1990). The intrapersonal level is the study of one's own actions and behaviors in the context of the group(s) and the organization. Intrapersonal analysis in case-in-point pedagogy moves beyond self-awareness of one's skills, emotional intelligence, beliefs, or values, to the way in which one is pulled and pushed within systems, and develops in participants the capacity to hold steady in the face of anxiety so that adaptive work can continue: "the person can resolve his internal conflicts, mobilize his resources, and take intelligent action only if anxiety does not interfere with his ability to profit from his experience, to analyze, discriminate, and foresee" (Bennis & Shepard, 1956, p. 415).

Although such intrapersonal analysis can be facilitated by many different pedagogical methods, case-in-point invites participants to study their own actions and behaviors within the moment. Participants may, for example, study how they respond to formal authority, informal authority, organizational chaos, and organizational change. To be sure, the intrapersonal analysis can extend long after the course is over, but the in-class experience can

---

Intrapersonal

Adaptive challenges require one to hold steady with personal anxieties and not rush into problem definition and solution implementation. Many leadership development programs provide participants with opportunities to learn about themselves, but case-in-point pedagogy provides the space and opportunity for the participant to experiment with this in the midst of adaptive challenges. These opportunities replicate those offered in our daily organizations without replicating the consequences that might occur if we were to experiment in professional or personal groups.

---

offer the participant an opportunity to try different actions within the temporary (yet safe) organization simply for the purposes of learning about self and self in relation to others.

This leads to the last level of analysis—interpersonal or the interaction between and among individuals. This type of interaction is a standard occurrence (in meetings, passing in the hallway, or even through e-mail) that most of us do not think about very much. (Or we think about them and how angry they make us feel.) The value of case-in-point pedagogy is that participants have the opportunity to learn how even the slightest interaction with a colleague can on the surface mean one thing but understood in the context of the other levels of analysis, could mean something very different. To make matters worse, hidden agendas (that are often unconscious) can often derail important work to be accomplished in a group. These often exist and rarely become apparent because most people do not have the awareness or the skill to call attention to them.

In its entirety, case-in-point pedagogy asks participants to engage in all four levels of analysis (intrapersonal, interpersonal, group, and system as a whole) simultaneously, although developing the ability to conduct such a complex analysis develops slowly over time and with practice. The skill includes understanding that observable actions and behaviors of individuals, dyads, and triads often speak not just for the people performing in those roles but for the larger group or organization and perhaps even the system. The "dances" people are engaged in provide information about the adaptive

Interpersonal

In complex organizations, unknown interpersonal dynamics can hinder or facilitate the tackling of adaptive challenges. In case-in-point pedagogy, participants have the opportunity to learn about the impact these interactions have on the capacity of groups and organizations to tackle adaptive challenges. Dyads and triads form within the class and can hijack the group in one particular direction or another. Faculty and others can call attention to this dynamic for the benefit of the group's learning.

challenges being faced by and within the organization because their behaviors are manifestations of the anxieties and fears being surfaced by the challenge. By developing the ability to analyze at all four levels, higher education faculty and administrators can engage in adaptive learning.

Adaptive Learning

It is imperative in the 21st century that individuals and groups have the ability to tackle adaptive challenges and mobilize organizational transformation. Change and transformation cause anxiety, however, so 21st-century leadership requires in people the capacity to hold steady and work with the anxiety and resistance that often arises (Obholzer, 1999). This type of learning is possible in case-in-point precisely because of its real-time, real-life focus; participants learn that they cannot easily solve the adaptive problems that evolve within the class experience using routine methods or normal levels of analysis. This pedagogy awakens in its participants the awareness necessary to begin to see the intrapersonal, interpersonal, group, and organizational levels of system dynamics, and the interactions between and among them. It is in this way that faculty and administrators can be trained to see and grapple with the complexity of the college and university and its problems; "understanding the group processes may provide [participants] with heightened awareness and the ability to make previously unavailable choices about their roles and functioning in a group setting" (Hayden & Molenkamp, 2004, p. 141).

This pedagogy and the awareness (or consciousness) it surfaces challenges peoples' basic assumptions that organizations are naturally and unavoidably fragmented and disconnected, assumptions that are manifested by the division of colleges and universities into several subsections such as schools, departments, programs, disciplines, part-time faculty, full-time faculty, and tenure status (Long, 2004). This fragmentation is actually counterproductive to the leadership needed in complex organizations because it encourages the blaming (or scapegoating) of individuals for problems and contributes to the tendency to seek technical fixes to adaptive challenges. Case-in-point provides an experience (pedagogical tool) to develop the ability to see inside and outside the system at the same time, in other words developing the skill to see the whole and the parts simultaneously.

A useful metaphor is that of a photo mosaic, which is a picture or photo made up of many (sometimes hundreds) of much smaller pictures or photos. On close inspection, each individual picture becomes visible and each has a story of its own. Stepping back from the photo one sees a whole new picture that conveys one story that is made up of hundreds of smaller pictures that tell different stories. Within each story are the people and the systems and subsystems they live and work in. Each person attempts to negotiate tensions and make sense of the systems they participate in. For example, tensions often arise as a result of unclear boundaries or roles that are not clearly defined or articulated to the group. Boundaries (spatial, psychological, emotional, etc.) around individuals, groups, organizations, and systems can be seen that guide negotiations but also potentially inhibit the resolution of problems and necessary systemic changes. Roles, whether taken on or assigned to individuals within the organization, greatly influence negotiations as they implicitly and explicitly restrict people's actions.

As discussed at the beginning of this chapter, the complexity of the 21st-century higher education organization begets numerous tensions faculty and administrators have to grapple with. Although numerous other leadership development programs may help to develop intrapersonal skills for management of these tensions, case-in-point pedagogy provides participants with the opportunity to develop this capacity in the midst of adaptive challenges arising within a complex (albeit temporary) organization. Beyond intrapersonal and interpersonal dynamics many might be at least familiar with, participants become more familiar and comfortable with analyzing situations and organizations from four levels of analysis, and competent at noticing and giving voice to dynamics normally left unarticulated. In the next section, we describe how higher education faculty and administrators can begin to use case-in-point analysis to understand their own organizations by using the concepts of boundaries and roles. We do this in an attempt to illustrate how, over time, such practice can enhance one's own leadership development and the capacity to function and exercise leadership within complex organizations.

Case-in-Point in Action

The capacity of case-in-point participants to exercise leadership in the face of organizational complexity can be greatly enhanced over time. The ability to use all four levels of analysis while in the midst of the action, for example, does not come easily or early. More novice participants tend to get stuck at the intrapersonal level of analysis because this level is easier to notice and identify; after all, people and their actions are visible. However, because case-in-point pedagogy violates the "normal" roles and boundaries expected in the traditional classroom or learning environment, awareness of these aspects is heightened, and participants are often able to extend their analysis and learning beyond the intrapersonal and interpersonal levels. In this section, we describe in further detail the notions of boundaries and roles in order to provide the reader with some concrete illustrations and to strengthen our case for the applicability of case-in-point pedagogy for the leadership development of higher education faculty and administrators.

Boundaries

When thinking about our institutions, the complexity, number, and types of boundaries and their impact on our work can be overwhelming. Boundaries provide the glue that holds the group together, as they encompass the shared values, traditions, and modes of operating (Monroe, 2004). Boundaries are present everywhere; they are physical and spatial or nonspatial (thoughts and perceptions), they can be rigid and impermeable or less impermeable, they can separate or connect us. Physical boundaries are important when deciding where to hold a meeting, how the room will be set up, where people will sit, and so on. Boundaries of time are also an important element in any analysis, because groups can be distracted from their task if boundaries related to time are too rigid or loose depending on the context. Lack of clarity or sudden changes in the way the boundary is managed often sets the system into chaos.

Higher education organizations that are typically fragmented and disconnected into departments, divisions, schools, and so on, are heavily boundary dependent. Faculty and administrators often define themselves or experience their identity by their place in the organization; we know, for example, that the boundary between faculty and administration is itself often perceived as very divisive in many colleges and universities. Difficult leadership challenges often come into play in higher education organizations when they revolve around or transcend boundaries—establishing new or dismantling old academic programs, developing programs that require academic-student affairs collaboration, creating institution-wide efforts that transcend school or academic department boundaries. Case-in-point pedagogy focuses on developing in people the capacity to recognize and manage the tensions around boundaries and the impact that boundaries can have on organizational change.

Picture yourself in a meeting of a university-wide committee that is dealing with the overenrollment of undergraduates for the upcoming academic year. You notice that the housing people seem resistant to any changes in the residence halls to accommodate the new students, and those in the college of arts and sciences are refusing to offer the large general education courses that will be required. Their resistance seems unreasonable and counterproductive to institutional interests, but no matter how often the admissions director pleads with them to comply, the resistance sticks (and even grows). You, however, pick up on some of their words and actions that reflect a concern about boundaries. Although the housing and college faculty are not included in admissions planning or enrollment management, they are expected to alter their normal course of functioning to deal with what they perceive as the *errors* of the admissions department. They resent the fact that they are asked to be saviors but not contributors. When you call attention to that boundary dynamic, and suggest possible solutions in the future, the tenor of the committee changes. And, because they are no longer caught up in the dynamic, the committee is able to move on with recommending the necessary steps, including housing and college representation on admissions and enrollment committees in the future.

Roles

We each occupy a variety of roles every day in every situation. Just like authority, there are two types of roles: formal and informal. Formal roles are those that we occupy in our professional and personal lives, such as president, provost, director, professor, coach, student, and so on. Essentially these are roles that have often been designated to us by outside authorities, and thus they give us some formal (albeit positional) authority. All too often it is unclear to many what the responsibilities of a given position actually are (we have all heard the adage, *responsibility with no authority*). In this case it is important to have clarity about the role functions. When there is a discrepancy (gap) between how we see ourselves in a particular role and the perception of others, it is important that this gap be addressed in order for the person with a formal position of authority to be taken seriously.

One of the most important lessons to learn is how to differentiate between *self* and *role*. Anyone who has been in a formal position of authority has experienced the pain and frustration of being challenged, berated or scoffed at, often in a public forum. When this occurs, it is helpful to understand what one represents for the group and the individual members, whose previous experiences with authority shape the ways in which they interact with people in positions of authority. The challenges that come our way have very little to do with who we are, they have much more to do with the roles we are taking up at any given time. The capacity to distinguish role from self is one of the gifts of developing a critical, systemic perspective and can yield a useful analysis of what is really going on (Parks, 2005, p. 87). Thus, holding steady in these situations is easier if we are able to separate our role from who we are as individuals.

Informal roles are those we take up in a group that are not necessarily tied to any formal position. These roles can be explicit, for example, sometimes when we do group work we assign the role of facilitator, time keeper, and so forth, or the roles are implicit. Implicit roles are often invisible, below

---

Scapegoat

If you often find yourself at the receiving end of dissatisfaction no matter your job performance, you may represent something unwanted by the group. Rather than dealing with the unwanted (feelings, conflict, tension, etc.), the group will undermine or assassinate you as a proxy. Sometimes the scapegoat is attached to a position rather than a specific person, but in either case, the group often loads up their dissatisfaction onto one person.

Optimist

How often in a group do you find yourself saying, "Let's look at the bright side?" Perhaps you make this comment at times when the stress level in the group has risen or when a particular conflict is escalating. You might perceive that it is better to stay positive than to engage in difficult conversations. If this is a pattern, then try to understand why you are the one who seems always to bring this voice to the table, and ask yourself: Is this the best way to move the group forward?

the surface (Stapley, 2006), or unconscious. We can become more aware of getting stuck by examining how the group (as a unit of analysis) is using us in a specific role to represent a hidden issue for the group or a larger system issue (see the boxes on pp. 107–109).

We often take on these roles without being fully aware, and sometimes we find ourselves *stuck* in the same role over and over again. This is because we bring with us to any group predispositions based on our history, factors such as social identity, and previous experiences with authority (this includes relationships with our family, friends, and coworkers). Many of our vulnerabilities are based on these past experiences, and every member of any group brings with him or her a full set of expectations about how the group (or organization) *ought* to be managed. Hence individuals within the organization are often drawn to other members who share similar histories (or stories), and this creates factions in the group that often impede any progress or opportunities for adaptive work. Those in positions of leadership are successful when they are able to manage the many factions and forces at play in any

Peacekeeper

Do you routinely find yourself taking on positions within dysfunctional or conflict-laden groups and then performing in ways that help to regulate or manage the dynamics within a peaceful range? Your valence may be to avoid conflict—groups will tap into that and make peacekeeper your informal role, whether you want it or not.

group or system. This is fundamental to developing the capacity to exercise leadership in a complex system such as higher education.

Picture yourself back in that overenrollment committee meeting, now as the admissions director. You are feeling personally beat up and attacked. You have heard rumors outside the committee, coming from all parts of campus that you are being blamed for the overenrollment and people are questioning your effectiveness as an administrator. Faculty are complaining that they are not provided with sufficient input and decision-making power in the admissions/enrollment process, and other staff are angry at you for causing challenges in their departments as they deal with the fallout of overenrollment. You go home every night, exhausted, emotionally drained, and feeling like a failure. You are beginning to doubt your abilities and wonder if it is not time for a career change.

However, in the middle of all this, you attend your third leadership conference based on the case-in-point pedagogy and you become aware that during your first conference you experienced some of the same reactions that your staff are now exhibiting. You had been angry at the conference authority figures for not being leaders, that is, for not better managing the learning experience and for causing the chaos that had ensued when participants' expectations were not met. During that week-long conference, you began to develop the capacity to manage the anxiety associated with the chaos and employ analysis at the group and organizational levels. With the help of the conference faculty, you experimented by taking up some different roles, from silent observer to instigator, throughout the conference. After attending your

Antagonist

Every group has an antagonist! If you notice that you are always at odds with the majority, consistently accused of impeding the progress of the group, or if you are often angry and dissatisfied after meetings, then you may be the group's stand-in. Unable to cope with their own anxiety, especially around change, the group will often project their fears onto one member. You can choose not to be used in this way by becoming more aware of how the group is putting you in this role: don't accept it.

third conference, you began to better understand how complex organizational dynamics can be and how one has to recognize the adaptive challenges and fight the urge to reduce complexity by applying technical solutions. As you recall your learning experiences, you realize that your current institution is trying to apply technical solutions to what is now an adaptive challenge, and your staff is less frustrated with you than they are anxious in the face of the complexity of the issue and their changing roles and boundaries. In becoming aware of these new organizational dynamics, you are able to readjust your actions and interactions with others and begin to help faculty and staff move forward.

Recommendations for Leadership Development

We end this chapter with some leadership development recommendations for those who are intrigued by the power of the case-in-point pedagogy to develop the adaptive leadership needed in the face of complex and chaotic times. Although the recommendations we provide next are certainly not the only methods or opportunities for revolutionary leadership development, we feel that they are particularly relevant to the topic of this chapter and are important to mention because they are not normally addressed in the mainstream leadership literature.

Attend Training

The foundation of the case-in-point pedagogy can be found in the group relations tradition, and numerous training opportunities are thus available (see the A. K. Rice Institute for the Study of Social Systems for information, http://www.akriceinstitute.org/). We suggest that anyone interested in developing a capacity to exercise leadership in the face of adaptive challenges and within complex higher education organizations consider attending a group relations event. Several universities in the United States sponsor seminars, academic courses, opportunities for research and training, and weekend group relations conferences. Among these are the University of San Diego School of Leadership and Education Sciences; Harvard University, Kennedy School of Government; University of Chicago, Department of Psychology and Psychiatry; New York University, Department of Applied Psychology; and Teachers College, Columbia University, Department of Organization and Leadership, to name a few. The Web site http://www.grouprelations.com is a good resource for training and events, as is http://www.akriceinstitute.org/

Read Related Resources

An abundance of useful resources can be helpful in beginning one's exploration into this revolutionary model of leadership development. For more information on the way we describe leadership, we highly recommend Heifetz's (1994) *Leadership Without Easy Answers* as well as Heifetz and Linsky's (2002) *Leadership on the Line*. The first text is somewhat denser with theory but full of illustrative examples; the second text is a more practical, easy-to-grasp review of techniques and skills. For specific information about the case-in-point methodology, Parks's (2005) *Leadership Can Be Taught* is an excellent text that describes the method in detail using examples from people who have been transformed by participating in leadership development programs at Harvard. For more information on group relations, the four levels of analysis, boundaries and roles, we recommend Hayden & Molenkamp's (2004) "Tavistock Primer"; various chapters from Gillette and McCollom's (1995) *Groups in Context*, specifically chapters 1–3; Lionel Stapley's (2006) *Individuals, Groups, and Organizations Beneath the Surface*; and *Experiential Learning in Organizations: Applications of the Tavistock Group Relations Approach* by Gould, Stapley, and Stein (2004).

Readers may also consider works that can supplement the case-in-point approach and conceptions of leadership, such as Goleman's (2006) book on social intelligence, which points to our innate drive for connection with others, despite daily challenges that prevent us from engaging in these positive relationships. We concur with many others who believe that understanding ourselves and others in the context of groups and organizations is essential for effective leadership. Initial reactions to the case-in-point method would suggest that it is antithetical to developing positive relations and rapport with others because participants become angry and frustrated, particularly with the faculty and staff who represent *all* the authority figures in their lives to that point. Adaptive learning requires a deeper introspection and reflection about one's social intelligence and the destructive patterns that often emerge preventing us from exercising effective leadership.

Enhance Self-Awareness

A good way to begin developing your capacity for adaptive leadership is to simply pay more attention to yourself and the way you are in relation to others, specifically in groups and organizations. All of us have particular pre-dispositions (or valences), ways in which we are "used" by others to achieve desired ends. Heifetz and Linsky (2002) refer to these valences as "hungers" or "expressions of our normal human needs . . . [that can] disrupt our capac-ity to act wisely or purposefully" (p. 164). These hungers can include power/control, affirmation/importance, and intimacy. Others refer to these valences as dependencies within groups, such as the need for identity, involvement, independence, and dependence. If you begin to pay attention to yourself in group situations, you can begin to identify your own valences. For example, notice how you get pulled into situations you do not want to be in. Do you crave affirmation, the power you'll receive, the feeling of being needed? Although it is difficult to do, you should try to avoid attaching value judg-ments to these inquiries. The point is not to blame yourself for group dy-namics but to acknowledge the roles you consistently play in different groups and how the roles you take up (on behalf of the group) may at times hinder or facilitate the movement of the group and leadership toward organizational change.

Apply Theory in Daily Life

In addition to developing a greater awareness of yourself in relation to the group, you can also fairly easily begin to apply this learning to your daily activities and work. For example, begin to notice the most impermeable and protected boundaries on campus. Are the more protected boundaries the vir-tual ones, like those between faculty and staff, student and academic affairs, faculty senate and upper administration? Or are they the more physical boundaries, such as the street that divides the medical school from the cen-tral campus or the separation of the administrative offices from faculty of-fices? As you encounter difficult challenges or issues where there is organizational paralysis, look at the boundaries being protected for hints on what fears or desires may be impeding organizational progress.

In committee meetings, as described in the earlier scenarios, you can apply your knowledge of boundaries, roles, and authority to understand the dynamics of any group. Notice who speaks the most or to whom other peo-ple defer. Is it the high-level administrator, the tenured faculty member, or the longtime employee? At what points or during what topics of discussion do people defer to that authority? Who (i.e., what role) retreats or attacks and during what topic or point in the discussion? Who (i.e., what role) is consistently silent throughout the committee meetings and what might that person represent (unwanted or wanted) to the group? How are you being pushed or pulled by the group (i.e., notice when you feel angry or overly self-satisfied)?

Heifetz (1994) refers to this *analysis-in-action* (i.e., being in the task at the same time you are observing the group dynamics) as analogous to being simultaneously in the dance and on the balcony. In learning how to dance, a novice dancer may stay on the dance floor in the midst of the action, but then he or she will not be able to see the dance as a whole and understand the dynamics of the entire dance floor. Another novice dancer may choose to stay on the balcony in order to come to understand the dance patterns and dynamics, but that dancer will not be part of the action and thus may become a better dance critic than a dancer. The skill in dancing, that is, exercising leadership in the face of complex, adaptive challenges, is being able to see the larger dynamics, patterns, and challenges while being in the middle of the action, to be able to move between the dance and the balcony in the moment so one is both analyzing and applying the analysis for the benefit of the organization.

One way to practice this difficult movement between the dance and the balcony is to first notice the physical clues of your own heightened anxiety. Does your heart start racing? Do your palms become sweaty? Then find some way to check in with yourself and to understand why you are reacting that way. For beginners, an easy way to do this is in meetings—when you notice your own anxiety, slightly push yourself away from the table. This physical separation from the group (sufficient but not noticeable enough to interfere with the group's task) helps with the mental break out of the chaos of the dance. With time, this movement can be accomplished more organically and with less effort.

Final Thoughts

Our objective in writing this chapter is twofold: first, to help others consider the usefulness of case-in-point pedagogy for leadership development, and second, to respond to the call for more effective and transformational leadership in our institutions of higher education. Given the complexity of this task it is not surprising that many people rely on traditional or known methods instead of exploring other methods and strategies that might (at first) shake up the status quo. We view this as a journey, and certainly not the final destination, as it is the exploration of the process of getting there that will ultimately transform our institutions.

References

Altbach, P. G. (2001). The American academic model in comparative perspective. In P. G. Altbach, P. J. Gumport, & D. B. Jonstone (Eds.), *In defense of American higher education* (pp. 11–37). Baltimore, MD: John Hopkins University Press.

Bennis, W., & Shepard, H. (1956). A theory of group development. *Human Relations, 9*(4), 415–437.

Birnbaum, R. (1988). *How colleges work: The cybernetics of academic organization and leadership.* San Francisco: Jossey-Bass.

Duderstadt, J. (2000). *A university for the twenty-first century.* Ann Arbor: University of Michigan Press.

Gabelnick, F. (2004). Leading institutional transformation: The architecture of change. In S. Cytrynbaum & D. Noumair (Eds.), *Group dynamics, organizational irrationality, and social complexity: Group relations reader 3* (pp. 267–288). Washington: A. K. Rice Institute.

Getz, C., & Gelb, S. (2007). An integral approach to the teaching of leadership studies at the University of San Diego School of Leadership and Education Sciences. *Integral Leadership Review, 7*(1). Retrieved April 21, 2007, from http://integralleadershipreview.com/archives/2007-01/2007-01-getz-gelb.html

Gillette, J. (1995). Toward a practice of learning. In J. Gillette & M. McCollom (Eds.), *Groups in context* (pp. 15–33). New York: University Press of America.

Gillette, J., & McCollom, M. (1995). *Groups in context.* New York: University Press of America.

Goleman, D. (2006). *Social intelligence.* New York: Bantam Books.

Gould, L. J., Stapley, L., & Stein, M. (2004). *Experiential learning in organizations: Applications of the Tavistock group relations approach.* London: Karnac.

Hayden, C., & Molenkamp, R. J. (2004). Tavistock primer II. In S. Cytrynbaum & D. Noumair (Eds.), *Group dynamics, organizational irrationality, and social complexity: Group relations reader 3* (pp. 135–158). Washington, DC: A. K. Rice Institute.

Heifetz, R. A. (1994). *Leadership without easy answers.* Cambridge, MA: Belknap Press.

Heifetz, R. A., & Linsky, M. (2002). *Leadership on the line: Staying alive through the dangers of leading.* Boston: Harvard Business School Press.

Jaschik, S. (2005, February 4). A step toward dismissal. *Inside Higher Education.* Retrieved from www.insidehighered.com on February 4, 2005.

Long, S. (2004) Building an institution for experiential learning. In L. J. Gould, L. F. Stapley, & M. Stein (Eds.), *Experiential learning in organizations: Applications of the Tavistock group relations approach* (pp. 101–136). London: Karnac.

Longanecker, D. (2005). State governance and the public good. In A. J. Kezar, T. C. Chambers, & J. C. Burkhardt (Eds.), *Higher education for the public good: Emerging voices from a national movement* (pp. 57–70). San Francisco: Jossey-Bass.

Monroe, T. (2004). Boundaries and authority. In G. Goethals, G. Sorenson, & J. MacGregor Burns (Eds.), *Encyclopedia of leadership* (pp. 112–117). Thousand Oaks, CA: Sage.

Newman, F., Couturier, L., & Scurry, J. (2004). *The future of higher education: Rhetoric, reality, and the risks of the market.* San Francisco: Jossey-Bass.

Obholzer, A. (1999). Managing the unconscious at work. In R. French & R. Vinc (Eds.), *Group relations, management, and organizations* (pp. 87–97). Oxford, UK: Oxford University Press.

Parks, S. D. (2005). *Leadership can be taught.* Boston, MA: Harvard Business School Press.

Selznick, P. (1957). *Leadership in administration: A sociological interpretation.* New York: Harper & Row.

Senge, P. M. (1990). The leader's new work: Building learning organizations. *Sloan Management Review, 32*(1), 7–23.

Stapley, L. F. (2006). *Individuals, groups, and organizations beneath the surface.* London: Karnac.

Wells, L. (1990). The group as a whole: A systematic socioanalytic perspective on group relations. In J. Gillette & M. McCollom (Eds.), *Groups in context* (pp. 49–85). Reading, MA: Addison-Wesley.

5

CREATING A NEW BREED OF ACADEMIC LEADERS FROM STEM WOMEN FACULTY

The National Science Foundation's ADVANCE Program

Sue V. Rosser

Today higher education relies increasingly on federal and foundation funding to close the gap caused by the decrease in funding of public institutions from state legislatures and shrinking tuition dollars at private institutions. Cutting-edge research for science and technology becomes a primary means for institutions of higher education to obtain substantial federal and corporate dollars, as well as to advance the institution's reputation, nationally and internationally. This holds true particularly for elite Research I and comprehensive institutions, private and public.

This reliance on science and technology research has created a demand for leaders from the science, technology, engineering, and mathematics (STEM) disciplines. Particularly on the academic side of the institution, and especially in certain positions such as chairs of science departments, dean of letters and sciences, vice provost/president for research, provost, and even president, a scientific background becomes a requirement (chairs of science departments and vice provost/president for research), strong desideratum (dean of letters and sciences and provost), or a strongly positive attribute, depending on the type of institution and background of the other members of the top academic administrative team. Knowledge of future directions for research, of patenting, technology transfer, and licensing, as well as experience in negotiating conditions for multimillion dollar centers and start-up packages constitute requirements for chairs of science departments, the vice president/provost for research, and at least one person in the dean's and provost's office, unless the dean or provost handles these areas.

Because of the nature of the scientific enterprise, STEM faculty have exposure to, or training in, some of the building blocks for the new revolution in leadership described in the preface of this volume. *Context specific, globalized, process oriented, collaborative,* and *dealing with cognitive complexity* are characteristics of the new revolution in leadership and of science and technology. For example, the experimental nature of most scientific research is extremely context specific. Water boils at a certain temperature under specific atmospheric and other conditions. A parasite survives in a specific host and in that host only.

Long before economic globalization and the "flattening of the world" because of the Internet as described by Thomas Friedman (2006), science was global and international. Unlike the social sciences that tend to analyze data and describe conditions specific to a particular society or culture, and unlike most humanities where language prescribes parameters, scientific findings are universal for all societies and cultures. In fact, most STEM graduate students in U.S. science and engineering departments currently come from other countries.

The scientific method exemplifies a process-oriented approach to the physical, natural world. Reliability and verifiability stand as cornerstones of the scientific method, meaning others should be able to replicate the results of the experiment by following the same method or process.

Scientists and engineers use theoretical and empirical information to make sense of the physical, natural world. This involves a cognitively complex process, including observation, hypothesizing, gathering of data, often using complex tools or machinery, analysis of data, and drawing theories and conclusions based upon the analysis.

Because of the increasingly complex problems that most scientists attempt to solve today, most require teams of individuals with different skills and backgrounds working together. Collaboration, sometimes with very large teams of more than 100 individuals, rather than working in isolation characterizes modern science and scientists. In short, because of the nature of STEM today, most scientists and engineers have experiences and training in some of the aspects of the revolutionary new leadership, although the scientific paradigm for modern science reflects conservative and masculine elements.

This chapter explores how the National Science Foundation's (NSF's) ADVANCE initiative may facilitate development of a source of new leadership for higher education. ADVANCE seeks to retain and promote women in tenure-track positions in STEM to leadership positions, such as full professor, department chair, dean, and higher administrative positions in the academy.

Statistics on Women in STEM

STEM has a dearth of women; most individuals with a scientific or technical background who rise to leadership positions are men. In the United States, women currently earn more of the bachelor and master's degrees than men. In 2004 women earned 57.6% of the bachelor's degrees in all fields (Commission on Professionals in Science and Technology [CPST], 2006, Table 3-15) and 59.1% of all master's degrees (CPST, 2006, Table 3-22). Beginning in 2000, women also earned more of the bachelor degrees in science and engineering (S&E; 50.4% in 2004) (CPST, 2006, Table 3-14), although they earned only 43.6% of the master's degrees in S&E (CPST, 2006, Table 3-22). In 2004 women earned almost 60% of the PhDs in non-S&E fields, but only 44% of the PhDs in S&E among U.S. citizens and permanent residents (CPST, 2006, Table 3-28).

The major gender differences occur in distribution of the genders across the disciplines. Overall, at the bachelor level, women earn the majority (61.1%) of the degrees in the non-S&E fields, such as humanities, education, and fine arts, and in the S&E fields of psychology (77.8%), the social sciences (54.2%), and agricultural (52.2%) and biological sciences (62.5%). Men earn most of the degrees in the physical sciences (57.9%); earth, atmospheric, and ocean sciences (57.8%); mathematics and statistics (54.1%); computer sciences (74.9%); and engineering (79.5%) (CPST, 2006, Table 3-15).

At the level of the master's degree, women earned the majority of degrees in 2004 not only in non-S&E fields, but also in agricultural sciences (53.5%), biological sciences (58.6%), psychology (78.1%), and the social sciences (55.9%). Women earned less than half of the master's degrees in earth, atmospheric, and ocean sciences (44.6%); mathematics and statistics (45.4%);

physical sciences (37.5%); computer sciences (31.2%); and engineering (21.1%) (CPST, 2006, Table 3-22).

Women still earned less than half of the S&E PhD degrees in 2004 in all fields except psychology (67.3%) and a few social sciences, such as anthropology (55.1%), history of science (58.9%), and sociology (58.7%). Women earned 38.0% of the PhDs in the agricultural sciences, 46.3% of those in biological sciences; 20.5% in computer sciences; 33.9% in earth, atmospheric, and ocean sciences; 28.4% in mathematics and statistics; 25.9% in physical sciences; and 17.6% in engineering (CPST, 2006, Table 3-28).

These increasing numbers of women science PhDs translate slowly into women in STEM faculty positions. At 4-year institutions in 2004, women made up 34.2% of assistant professors, 25.8% of associate professors, and 11.8% of full professors. At the top 50 PhD-granting institutions, women accounted for 21% of assistant professors, 22% of associate professors, and only 10% of full professors (Marasco, 2006). Since women constitute only 10% of full professors in STEM, very few candidates for science department chair, dean of letters and science, vice provost/president for research, provost, and president can emerge from their ranks.

What Attracts Men to STEM

What impact does having men as the overwhelming majority of individuals in these positions have on leadership and institutions of higher education? The "old style" of leadership was based on a male model. The hierarchical, authority-based, context-free, highly structured, and values-neutral leadership that Adrianna Kezar describes in the preface of this book as the "heroic, controlling and distant leader of the past" (p. xii) exemplifies male leadership. Several historians and philosophers of science (Keller, 1985; Merchant, 1979; Noble, 1993) have described the extent to which science represents a masculine domain. Dinnerstein (1977) and Chodorow (1978) have used an aspect of psychoanalytic theory known as *object relations theory* to examine the construction of gender and sexuality during the Oedipal stage of psychosexual development, which usually results in male dominance. They conclude that the gender differences resulting in male dominance can be traced to the fact that in our society, women are the primary caretakers for most infants and children.

Keller (1983, 1985), in particular, applied the work of Chodorow and Dinnerstein to suggest how science, populated mostly by men, has become a masculine province in its choice of experimental topics, use of male subjects for experimentation, interpretation and theorizing from data, as well as the practice and applications of science undertaken by the scientists. Keller (1983, 1985) suggests that since the scientific method stresses objectivity, rationality, distance, and autonomy of the observer from the object of study (i.e., the positivist neutral observer), individuals who feel comfortable with independence, autonomy, and distance will be more likely to become scientists. This objectivity and rationality of science have become synonymous with a male approach to the physical, natural world.

Historians of technology have explored the conjoining of masculinity with technology (Wajcman, 1991), particularly via the military and engineering (Cockburn, 1983). These studies suggest that the men attracted to becoming scientists and engineers tend to be distant, separate, and autonomous. The science and technology they create in turn reflects these same characteristics, which may also be reflected in their leadership style.

What Attracts Women to STEM

In contrast, a considerable body of research (Eccles, 1994; Rosser, 1990, Seymour & Hewitt, 1994; 2004) suggests that women scientists have somewhat different motivations from those that attract men to STEM. An overwhelming attractant for women to STEM is its social usefulness, especially to help people. My book, *Re-engineering Female Friendly Science*, presented 20 ways the teaching of science needed to be changed to attract and retain women, based upon different questions, approaches, and conclusions drawn by women scientists from their research (Rosser, 1997, p.9).

The emphasis upon seeing new things, inclusion, interactive methods, collaboration over competition, social concern, communication, and placing science in its social context overlap with the characteristics of revolutionary leadership. Because of their STEM background, women scientists and engineers have the characteristics held by men scientists—context specific, globalized, process oriented, collaborative, and dealing with cognitive complexity; women also demonstrate the characteristics of revolutionary leadership. Women scientists particularly seek to study the physical, natural world using nonhierarchical, socially responsible, context-specific methods in teams of diverse individuals to find solutions to complex, interdisciplinary, global problems to help people and save the planet.

In short, one way to increase the pool of individuals with revolutionary leadership lies in increasing the number of women scientists and providing them with the training for advancement to leadership positions such as chair, dean, vice provost for research, provost, and president. Simultaneously, increasing the numbers of women in STEM and incorporating their values and interests may change traditional views of leadership and science.

The NSF ADVANCE Program

In fiscal year 2001 NSF launched the ADVANCE initiative. Funded initially at $19 million, ADVANCE's two categories—Institutional Transformation Awards and Leadership Awards—include institutional, rather than only individual, solutions to empower women to participate fully in science and technology. NSF encouraged institutional solutions, in addition to the individual solution permitted under the category of Fellows Awards, because of "increasing recognition that the lack of women's full participation at the senior level of academe is often a systemic consequence of academic culture" (NSF, 2001a, p. 2). Under ADVANCE, Institutional Transformation Awards, ranging up to $750,000 per year for up to 5 years, promote the increased participation and advancement of women; Leadership Awards recognize the work of outstanding organizations of individuals and enable them to sustain, intensify, and initiate new activity (NSF, 2001a). ADVANCE promises to go beyond individual research projects of women scientists and engineers that earlier NSF initiatives for women supported to solve problems with broader systemic and institutional roots such as balancing career and family.

Summary of Georgia Tech's ADVANCE Initiative

A brief synopsis of the five major threads of Georgia Tech's (GT) ADVANCE project illustrates the approach one institution is taking to retain women faculty in STEM and facilitate their advancement to leadership positions as full professor, chair, dean, and above to empower them as revolutionary leaders.

Thread 1: Termed Professorships to Form a Mentoring Network

Because mentoring networks facilitate retention in STEM as well as the organizational learning needed for leadership, they became the centerpiece of the GT ADVANCE project. One tenured woman full professor in each of four colleges with disciplines funded by NSF became the designated ADVANCE professor. The title and the funds of $60,000 per year for 5 years associated with the ADVANCE professorship conferred the prestige and funds equivalent to those accrued by other endowed chairs at the institution. This sum also meant that $1.2 million of the $3.7 million grant went directly to support the ADVANCE professors, consonant with the NSF notion that the ADVANCE grants should be substantial to recognize the importance of activities to build workforce infrastructure. Because GT is a research university, the principal investigators (PIs) of the grant particularly recognized the necessity for ADVANCE professors to sustain their research productivity while undertaking this mentoring role. ADVANCE professors often used funds to pay for graduate students or postdocs to support their research.

Each ADVANCE professor developed and nurtured mentoring networks for the women faculty in her college. The focus of the mentoring activities varied among the colleges, depending upon the numbers, ranks, and needs of the women. In the College of Engineering, a large college with about 42 women out of 400 tenure-track faculty, isolation constituted a primary issue in many units. The lunches arranged by the ADVANCE professor with women faculty from the college provided an opportunity for them to meet women in other departments and develop social and professional networks. A popular professional networking opportunity included evaluation of the curriculum vitae of junior faculty by senior colleagues to assess their readiness for promotion and tenure and/or gaps that must be addressed for successful promotion to the higher rank.

The ADVANCE professor often helps to explain and mediate problematic issues in some schools with the chair and dean. In the smaller College of Computing, with 8 of 60 women as tenure-track faculty, many of the women had young children, so many of the lunches and activities focused on explication of family-friendly policies and strategies to balance career and family. In the College of Science, lunches and activities centered on grant-writing workshops and other means to establish successful laboratory research. In Ivan Allen College, where 40% of the tenure-track faculty are women, the ADVANCE professor chose luncheon themes on publication and scholarly productivity. Although all four ADVANCE professors held luncheons and mentored individual women faculty, each focused the initial activities upon those issues she perceived as most problematic and/or critical for achieving tenure, promotion, and advancement to career success for the women in her particular college. By the fourth year of the grant, the professors evolved more cross-college activities, expanding programs and initiatives particularly successful in one college to women from all colleges on campus. Through this process, the women faculty created a network within their college and across the entire institution. In the future this network will help them with contacts and building skills to become a better collaborative leader.

Thread 2: Collection of MIT-Report-Like Data Indicators

Because success as a leader depends partially on the context, knowledge of the data becomes crucial. To assess whether advancement of women really occurs during and after the institutional transformation undertaken through ADVANCE, data must be collected on indicators for comparison with baseline data upon grant initiation for several indicators. GT proposed in its grant to collect data on 11 of the following 12 indicators that NSF eventually required all ADVANCE institutions to collect by gender: faculty appointment type, rank, tenure, promotion, years in rank, time at institution, administrative positions, professorships and chairs, tenure and promotion committee members, salaries, space, and start-up packages.

Start-up packages exemplify one area where gender differences often emerge. In some fields of S&E, the start-up package for a laboratory and equipment may be in the hundreds of thousands, if not millions, of dollars. Failure to negotiate properly for the appropriate space, equipment, and personnel needed to carry out the research retards not only the initiation of the candidate's research at the new institution, but it may also affect promotion and tenure, given the 6-year tenure clock. Research (Babcock & Laschever, 2003) documents the fact that on average, women scientists ask for less in start-up funds than their male peers in the same area of research. This gender difference may result from inadequate mentoring, fear they won't get the position, or reluctance to ask for too much. One male department chair, after attending a workshop that made him aware of these gender differences, used his leadership position to coach new women hires. If a woman candidate he was negotiating with asked for a start-up package that was less than that from a man he had just hired in the same area, the chair told her that he would give her a start-up package that equaled that of the recently hired man and explained why. This male chair demonstrated leadership to transform institutional practices in a manner to attract and retain women scientists.

Thread 3: Family-Friendly Policies and Practices

Good leaders must be sensitive to cultural factors that impede or facilitate advancement of particular groups within their organization. Recent studies document that balancing career and family constitutes the major difficulty for tenure-track women faculty in general (Mason & Goulden, 2004) and women S&E faculty in particular (Rosser, 2004; Xie & Shauman, 2003). Competition between the biological clock and the tenure clock becomes a significant obstacle for women faculty who have delayed childbearing until they receive a tenure-track position. For women faculty in S&E, significant time away from their research makes it less likely they can successfully achieve tenure in a research institution. The dual career situation becomes an additional complicating factor for women scientists and engineers, 62% of whom are married to men scientists and engineers (Sonnert & Holton, 1995). Given the dearth of women scientists and engineers, the reverse situation does not hold as that would mean few men scientists and engineers would be married. To facilitate the balancing of career and family, perceived overwhelmingly by women scientists and engineers particularly those of younger ages, as the major issues (Rosser, 2004), GT instituted the following family-friendly policies and practices: stop the tenure clock, active service, modified duties, lactation stations, and day care. The specific details of these policies can be accessed at http://www.advance.gatech.edu/family.html

Thread 4: Miniretreats to Facilitate Access to Decision Makers and Provide Informal Conversations and Discussion on Topics Important to Women Faculty

Research has demonstrated that women faculty tend to have less access and opportunities than their male colleagues to speak with the decision makers and institutional leaders (Rosser, 2004). Often this unintended discrimination and lack of access result from women's absence from informal and social gatherings. To ensure access of tenure-track women faculty to the senior leadership of chairs, deans, provost, vice presidents, and president, the GT ADVANCE grant organized 2-day miniretreats during each year of the grant. Focused on topics of interest and concern to all faculty, such as case studies of promotion and tenure, training to remove subtle gender and racial bias in promotion and tenure decisions, and effective strategies in hiring dual career couples, these retreats have provided opportunities for the tenure-track women faculty to interact with the institutional leadership and express their opinions/views on matters of mutual interest.

Thread 5: Removal of Subtle Gender, Racial, and Other Biases in Promotion and Tenure

Understanding processes, including the subtleties of their cognitive complexity, that have an impact on the advancement of particular groups within the organization stands as a hallmark of a good leader. Close involvement with the promotion and tenure process provides insight into subtle ways unintended, barely perceptible biases might influence decisions on promotion and tenure. For example, I observed that in some cases when the tenure clock has stopped for a year for a valid reason such as childbirth, the clock appears not to have stopped in the heads of colleagues, as they considered the individual for promotion and tenure. Colleagues seem simply to expect an additional year's worth of papers, talk, and productivity to be added.

To address this issue, the PI, who was also the provost, appointed the Promotion and Tenure ADVANCE Committee (PTAC) to assess existing promotion and tenure processes; explore potential forms of bias, providing recommendations to mitigate them and to elevate awareness of candidates and committees for expectations and best practices in tenure and promotion. After 1 year of studying the research documenting possible biases because of gender, race/ethnicity, ability status, as well as interdisciplinarity, the committee developed nine case studies with accompanying sample curricula vitae. Each illustrated one or more issues or areas where possible bias might affect the promotion and tenure decision. After discussion of these case studies at a miniretreat, the refined versions served as the basis for an interactive Web-based instrument, Awareness of Decision in Evaluation of Promotion and Tenure (ADEPT), designed by colleagues in the College of Computing. Individuals can use ADEPT to participate in a virtual promotion and tenure meeting where, depending upon their response, the meeting takes different directions and generates different outcomes in promotion and tenure. The Web-based instrument, along with best practices from PTAC and resources on bias can be accessed at http://www.adept.gatech.edu.

Results of ADVANCE Leadership Building

The NSF funding for GT's ADVANCE project ended March 31, 2007. The dynamic changes resulting from the grant in the quality of mentoring, new understanding of promotion and tenure, numbers of women retained and given endowed chairs, and emergence of new family-friendly policies gave me hope for genuine diversification of leadership in science and technology. As the grant funding ended, the absence of NSF prestige and monitoring, coupled with a change in academic leadership at the top, provided new challenges for institutionalization, recruitment, and advancement of women into leadership positions in S&E.

Assessment of the long-term results of a multiyear, multimillion dollar effort at institutional transformation to advance women to leadership positions would be premature. Data from the project and the report of the external evaluators do reveal evidence of some movement of women into positions of institutional leadership. The number and share of women faculty increased; the number and share of senior women faculty, including those tenured and those in high administrative positions, rose; and faculty recruitment rates, salaries, and other resources reflected more gender equity.

As the substantial literature on institutionalization of reforms in higher education documents, effective institutionalization must include the top leadership (Eckel & Kezar, 2003; Heifetz & Laurie, 1997), middle administrators (Meyerson, 2003), and the faculty (Merton, Froyd, Clark, & Richardson, 2004; Woodbury & Gess-Newsome, 2002). Changes diffuse throughout the organization (Rogers, 2003; Strang & Soule, 1998) at different rates but must ultimately penetrate the structure, procedures, and cultural levels (Braxton, Luckey, & Helland, 2002) of the university for genuine institutionalization.

If the institution, and particularly the upper levels of institutional leadership, have not been informed, do not understand, and/or have not committed to sustaining the trajectory and impacts of advancing women to senior faculty and leadership positions after the grant funding ends, then the project will not succeed in maintaining this institutional transformation in the long run. Although the NSF grants carry considerable prestige, the institutional investment in terms of human and capital resources and the commitment to establish, change, and implement policies and practices to support AD-VANCE serve as the real keys to success. This investment is as critical as the NSF support, even during the short term of foundation funding.

Institutional transformation remains difficult, even when the environment is ripe for change (Seel, 2000), and institutional leaders (Eckel & Kezar, 2002) and grassroots support (Woodbury & Gess-Newsome, 2002) for the transformation exist. In the absence of such environments, leadership, and support, and in situations where the goals of the project do not mesh with the objectives of the institution (Tierney, 1988), the transformation will certainly fail.

In the United States women now serve as president of four of the eight Ivy League Schools and of many of the Big Ten or University of California institutions. These include the following, all but two of whom are scientists or engineers:

Mary Sue Coleman, president, University of Michigan
France Cordova, president, Purdue University, formerly chancellor, University of California–Riverside
Drew G. Faust, president, Harvard University
Mary Anne Fox, chancellor, University of California, San Diego
Amy Gutmann, president, University of Pennsylvania
Susan Hockfield, president, Massachusetts Institute of Technology
Karen Holbrook, former president, Ohio State University
Shirley Ann Jackson, president, Rensselaer Polytechnic University
Maria Klawe, president, Harvey Mudd College
Ruth Simmons, president, Brown University
Shirley Tilghman, president, Princeton University

GT has yet to have a woman vice provost for research, provost, or president, although some of the other ADVANCE institutions do have women in such positions. Each of the 32 ADVANCE institutions is attempting an approach that fits its institutional history, culture, and needs and that it believes will advance STEM women to positions of leadership. Although many project elements overlap among institutions, each institutional project has unique elements. The Virginia Tech Web portal (http://research.cs.vt.edu/

advance/index.htm) permits access to the Web sites of all ADVANCE institutions. These might be viewed as more than 30 models for developing new leaders from women STEM faculty and transforming institutions of U.S higher education.

References

Adept.gatech.edu/ptac. Retrieved on June 23, 2005.

Advance.gatech.edu. Retrieved on June 23, 2005.

Babcock, L., & Laschever, S. (2003). *Women don't ask: Negotiation and the gender divide*. Princeton, NJ: Princeton University Press.

Braxton, J. M., Luckey, W., & Helland, P. (2002). Institutionalizing a broader view of scholarship through Boyer's Four Domains. *ASHE-ERIC Higher Education Report, 29*(2). San Francisco: Jossey-Bass.

Chodorow, N. (1978). *The reproduction of mothering: Psychoanalysis and the sociology of gender*. Berkeley: University of California Press.

Cockburn, C. (1983). *Brothers: Male dominance and technological change*. London: Pluto Press.

Commission on Professionals in Science and Technology (CPST). (2006). *Professional women and minorities. A total human resources data compendium*, 16th Edition. Washington, DC: CPST.

Dinnerstein, D. (1977). *The mermaid and the minotaur. Sexual arrangements and human malaise*. New York: Harper Colophon.

Eccles, J. (1994). Understanding women's educational and occupational choices. *Psychology of Women Quarterly, 11*, 3–29.

Eckel, P., & Kezar, A. (2003). *Taking the reins: Institutional transformation in higher education* (ACE/Praeger Series on Higher Education). Westport, CT: Praeger.

Friedman, T. (2006). *The world is flat: A brief history of the 21st century*. New York: Farrar, Straus, and Giroux.

Heifetz, R., & Laurie, D. (1997). The work of leadership. *Harvard Business Review, 75*(1), 124–134.

Keller, E. F. (1983). *A feeling for the organism*. San Francisco: Freeman.

Keller, E. F. (1985). *Reflections on gender and science*. New Haven, CT: Yale University Press.

Marasco, C. A. (2006). Women faculty gain little ground. *Chemical and Engineering News, 84*, 58–59.

Mason, M. A., & Goulden, M. (2004, November/December). Do babies matter (Part II)? Closing the baby gap. *Academe 90* (6): 10–15.

Merchant, C. (1979). *The death of nature: Women, ecology and the scientific revolution*. New York: Harper & Row.

Merton, P., Froyd, J., Clark, M. C., & Richardson, J. (2004). Challenging the norm in engineering education: Understanding organizational culture and curricular change. *Proceedings, ASEE Annual Conference.*

Meyerson, D. E. (2003). *Tempered radicals: How everyday leaders inspire change at work.* Boston, MA: Harvard Business School Press.

National Science Foundation. (2001a). *ADVANCE. Program solicitation.* Arlington, VA: National Science Foundation.

National Science Foundation. (2001b). *ADVANCE institutional transformation awards.* Retrieved October 1, 2001, from http://www.nsf.gov/advance

Noble, D. (1993). *A world without women: The Christian clerical culture of Western science.* New York: Oxford University Press.

Research.cs.vt.edu/advance/index.htm. Retrieved on August 26, 2008.

Rogers, E. (2003). *Diffusion of innovation* (5th ed.). New York: Free Press.

Rosser, S. V. (1990). *Female friendly science.* Elmsford, NY: Pergamon Press.

Rosser, S. V. (1997). *Re-engineering female friendly science.* New York: Teachers College Press.

Rosser, S. V. (2004). *The science glass ceiling: Academic women scientists and the struggle to succeed.* New York: Routledge.

Seel, R. (2000). Culture and complexity: New insights on organisational change. *Organisations & People, 7*(2), 2–9.

Seymour, E., & Hewitt, N. (1994). *Talking about leaving: Factors contributing to high attrition rates among science, mathematics, and engineering undergraduate majors.* Boulder, CO: Ethnography and Assessment Research, Bureau of Sociological Research.

Sonnert, G., & Holton, G. (1995). *Who succeeds in science? The gender dimension.* New Brunswick, NJ: Rutgers University Press.

Strang, D., & Soule, S. A. (1998). Diffusion in organizations and social movements: From hybrid corn to poison pills. *Annual Review of Sociology, 24,* 265–290.

Tierney, W. (1988). Organizational culture in higher education. *Journal of Higher Education 59*(1): 2-21.

Wajcman, J. (1991). *Feminism confronts technology.* University Park: Pennsylvania State University Press.

Woodbury, S., & Gess-Newsome, J. (2002). Overcoming the paradox of change without difference: A model of change in the arena of fundamental school reform. *Educational Policy, 16*(5), 763–782.

Xie, Y., & Shauman, K. (2003). *Women in science: Career processes and outcomes.* Cambridge, MA: Harvard University Press.

6

SPIRITUALITY, RELIGIOUS PLURALISM, AND HIGHER EDUCATION LEADERSHIP DEVELOPMENT

Robert J. Nash and Lara Scott

Since 2000, some programs in leadership development for higher education were paying increasing attention to spirituality and religious pluralism. Spirituality, in particular, is playing a pivotal role. Jon Dalton, director of the Center for the Study of Values in College Student Development, believes that attending to spiritual and religious factors in leadership training programs helps greatly in "communicating core values, integrating character education into curricula, shaping values, creating a diverse and inclusive community, guiding leaders' conduct, promoting holistic learning and robust cross-campus dialogue, and calling attention to praiseworthy moral behavior" (as cited in Chickering, Dalton, and Stamm, 2006, p. 255).

A few programs in higher education leadership and student affairs administration (Miami University of Ohio, Bowling Green, and the University of Vermont) are attempting to incorporate units on spirituality into their graduate training curricula via course offerings in cultural pluralism and diversity (see Chickering et al., 2006 for an update of such offerings). This chapter briefly examines some representative theories of spirituality and provides a few selective examples of how particular graduate leadership programs are attempting to teach this material. We focus primarily on our own efforts to infuse spiritual and religious aspects into leadership programs at the University of Vermont and at Champlain College.

Also in this chapter, in a move that is virtually unprecedented in the leadership literature, we present a brief rationale for fostering an informed religious literacy in higher education training programs (Nash, 2007). Learning about the actual content of a number of religions, we maintain, is the next logical step for enlarging the meaning of cultural pluralism and diversity to include religious difference. Religious identity is the core identity of billions of people on this planet and, closer to home, religious difference is becoming a potentially divisive issue on college campuses (see Cherry, De-Berg, & Porterfield, 2001; Riley, 2005). Finally, we examine four leadership qualities that we believe are necessary when talking with others about religious and spiritual differences, and we follow this up with a series of strategies for putting these qualities into action.

Leadership is a broad term that takes into account the assets each one of us brings to the world. As such, we are all leaders in our own way every day; we have the ability to touch lives, make meaning, and instill learning, both within ourselves and others, with our beliefs, words, and actions. The responsibility we hold while leading is powerful. For those of us working in higher education, we have the privilege of being surrounded by students (and faculty and staff) who are eager to learn and grow. They are at a place in their lives where they are intentionally striving to make meaning. They are in the process of creating themselves, and they are looking to us to help lead them down a variety of paths until they find the ones that fit.

We support the views of Warren Bennis (1989, 1993) who came to four conclusions about leadership after spending several decades studying the lives of effective leaders. Liesa Stamm (Chickering et al., 2006) summarizes these views as follows:

1. "Leaders are made, not born, and made more by themselves than by any external means."
2. "Leaders set out not to be leaders per se, but rather to express themselves freely and fully."
3. "Individuals who have become leaders continue to grow and develop throughout their lives."
4. "The primary distinguishing characteristic of a leader is a concern with a guiding purpose, an overarching vision." (pp. 249–253)

Leaders, according to Bennis, are created from educational experiences that invite them to examine themselves and the world around them and then share their learning with others. "Leadership effectiveness begins with self-awareness and self-understanding and grows to an understanding of others" (Komives, Lucas, & McMahon, 1998, p. 5). When looking inward, we begin a search for what we believe, a search for our passion, a search for our heart. Connecting the heart with the intellect, the spiritual with the material, makes the learner more whole and the leader more complete. As David Scott (2002) says, "Key to our future will be the concepts of the complete individual, with a greater sense of wholeness and connectedness" (p. 23).

As early as a decade and a half ago, the National Association of Student Personnel Administrators (NASPA) called upon leaders "to consider the student as a whole—his [her] intellectual capacity and achievement . . . emotional make up . . . physical condition . . . social relationships . . . vocational aptitudes and skills . . . moral and religious values . . . economic resources . . . and . . . aesthetic appreciations" (NASPA, 1987, p. 49). This idea of educating the *whole student* speaks to the importance of leaders in higher education who are not just managers or administrators but who themselves are whole human beings. In the words of Bennis (1993) such leaders are "continuing to grow and develop and who possess guiding purposes and overarching visions" (p. 90). Training others to be leaders requires leadership programs to be inclusive of *all* the facets of their defining identities. Thus, the major point that we make in this chapter is that religion and spirituality must be part of the mix in preparing students and faculty, and staff and administrators, to be holistic leaders.

For many people, religion and/or spirituality are foundational in their lives, because every action is intimately intertwined with their faith perspectives. Therefore, we need to welcome people into the college classroom, the office, and the administrative conversation with all the dimensions of themselves. Moreover, Love and Talbot believe "everyone searches for meaning in life" (as cited in Hamrick, Evans, & Schuh, 2002, p. 155). This suggests that even nonbelievers who may not connect with a particular religion or a more generalized spirituality must also be accepted as an integral part of the quest for wholeness, because they too are in the process of making meaning (Nash, 2003).

As educators, we strive for engagement, investment, and passion in our work with students and colleagues. Leaders who advocate for religion and spirituality to be part of the quest for wholeness model inclusivity and give all of us permission to bring the mind, the heart, and the soul into our conversation and learning (see Astin & Astin, 1999). Lewin and Regine write, "When the individual soul is connected to the organization, people become connected to something deeper—the desire to contribute to a larger purpose, to feel they are part of a greater whole, a web of connection" (as cited in Fullan, 2001, p. 52).

Some Basic Assumptions We Make About Spirituality and Religious Pluralism

The two of us coteach courses in a highly respected graduate program in the Higher Education and Student Affairs Administration (HESA) at the University of Vermont. The curriculum includes two courses for future higher education leaders that emphasize spiritual and religious difference: Higher Education in the United States and Religion, Spirituality, and Education. The first course, a core diversity requirement, contains a month-long unit on religious and spiritual awareness; the second one, an elective, is a semester-long comparative religions course that provides an overview of the five major wisdom traditions as well as several of the world's lesser-known religions.

The second course is the first of its kind ever offered in a professional school (Nash & Baskette, 2007), and in addition to providing essential information about the world's major religious traditions, we teach our leaders in training how to facilitate moral conversations throughout college campuses on controversial religious topics (Nash, Bradley, & Chickering, 2008). Also, in the early 1970s, Robert Nash created and offered the first applied ethics course ever offered in a higher education leadership program in the United States. It was in this course that one of us first heard graduate students (including administrators, faculty, and staff) talking about the religious and spiritual influences on their ethical behavior (see Nash, 2002).

Whenever we instruct these courses, we make the following assumptions about the need to foster an understanding of spiritual self-awareness and religious difference in our leadership development courses:

- First, we are convinced that most Americans know very little about the topics of religion and spirituality, even though they might have lots of uninformed opinions that they present as fact. This type of illiteracy is unacceptable in a 21st-century, multifaith, multireligious, global community (see Prothero, 2007).

- Second, educators in all settings need to reexamine their own latent biases both for and against organized religion and private spirituality, because often these invisible biases can come across in harmful ways to many believers, nonbelievers, and seekers. These three groups tend to take religion and spirituality very seriously. This self-examination process, although difficult and time consuming, is key to working with and understanding others. Its importance cannot be overestimated. At times, we will refer to this content more holistically as *religio-spiritual*, because we do not know how it is intellectually feasible to separate religion from spirituality and vice versa.

- Third, we believe it is crucial for higher education leaders to think about the role that the study of religion and spirituality plays in all areas of education in secular and sectarian venues. Educators must think seriously and systematically about the risks and benefits, the disadvantages and advantages, of dealing with such sensitive material in secular and private higher educational settings. To ignore issues of religion and spirituality in the 21st century is to miss what is vitally important to higher educators, given all their diverse clienteles. Historically, many American colleges and universities have very strong religious roots (Rudolph, 1990).

  The very popular dichotomy that administrators, educators, and students often posit between religion and spirituality, we believe, represents an unstated bias against organized religion and a bias in favor of private spirituality. We hear the following from our constituencies all the time: "I'm spiritual not religious," as if the former is intrinsically superior to the latter. Throughout most of human history, this type of assertion would simply be unintelligible, because, absent the formal beliefs and practices of a variety of organized religions, spirituality would have had no intrinsic (or extrinsic) meaning for billions of believers. Billions of believers would have considered spirituality alone to be ephemeral and groundless, because it would have been cut off at its roots.

- Fourth, it is important for all of us in higher education, and as leaders, to learn how to talk respectfully and compassionately with one another about a topic that, throughout history, has caused as much pain, suffering, and division as it has comfort, joy, and reconciliation (Nash, 2005).

- Fifth, if educators truly want to diversify their formal and informal curricula in academia, and if they want to develop offerings for staff and leaders that respect all kinds of difference, including religious and spiritual difference, then radically revisioning the nature and content of diversity education is necessary.

  Multiculturalism, diversity, and pluralism represent incomplete ideals unless they include religio-spiritual diversity (and nonbelief diversity as well), along with all the other worthwhile types of cultural differences. In the 21st century, religio-spiritual identity is the core identity of billions of people on this planet (Nash, 2001).

Closer to home, religious illiteracy is leading to an alarming growth of religious stereotyping on some college campuses. Fortunately, incidents of outright religious bigotry are not widespread, at least not at the present time. However, the sad lesson of history is that anti- and pro-religious bigotry (like all bigotry) starts small before it grows tall. Even now, on many campuses, members of minority religious groups are asserting their rights to autonomy, and in some cases, complete separation. Many Eastern religious groups demand their own faith centers instead of having to worship in formerly Christian chapels. Muslim groups are angry because they do not have a prayer space of their own. They are tired of sharing space with Christians or Jews. They want prayer rugs not pews. Also, Buddhists want a separate location for a meditation room. Jews want their own chapel sites complete with Torah scrolls. On some Catholic campuses, representatives of non-Christian religions are insisting on autonomous spaces for the full expression of their own devotions. In fact, several groups of evangelical Christians in secular universities are feeling ghettoized because their own worship areas are contracting in size, given the escalating demands for space by other religious groups.

Since the immigration boom of the 1960s, to mention only a few examples, there are presently 10 million Muslims, 3 to 5 million Buddhists, and 2 million Hindus in the United States. Their numbers are continuing to grow dramatically, and their children have now reached college age (Nash, 2007).

Deep Learning Opportunities at Champlain College

In summary, we want to prepare leaders to engage in what we think of as true leadership learning—what we call *deep learning*. This particular type of educational experience represents deep learning because it gets beneath the surface of taken-for-granted assumptions. It encourages vulnerability, mutual sharing, and honest self-examination. Students, staff, faculty, and administrators are able to participate in this kind of learning when their leaders are effective in providing a safe, inclusive space for deep conversations. At Champlain College, a small, private, secular institution in Burlington, Vermont, campus leaders experience a number of opportunities to talk about religion and spirituality. The following describe a few of these opportunities:

- Professional Development Days. Three times a year Champlain College staff attend full days of development where they are asked, in a variety of ways, to think about the interplay between who they are and the work they do. These days offer pause and reflection during the ongoing movement of an institution of higher learning to find ways to be more intentional and successful in what we do.

- Discussion Listserve. This Listserve offers the campus a space to discuss issues campus leaders are passionate about. From gas prices to the war in Iraq to questions about what cultural/religious holidays are observed on campus, people converse about topics and issues that are meaningful and oftentimes fundamental to their lives. This Listserve invites campus leaders to bring all aspects of themselves to work, including their cultures and religious and spiritual views. It offers the opportunity to the college community to publicly express passions and beliefs on campus, and it gives leaders a "practice" space before going into the student community.

- Spirituality Committee. Most recently this ad hoc leadership committee brought Arthur Chickering to campus to engage other campus leaders, including students, in a dialogue around religion and spirituality and identity development. The auditorium was full, clearly showing a desire to discuss this topic and make it visible on campus. In addition, with complete support of the president, discussion around ways for students to integrate their religious and spiritual development into their college experience at Champlain is moving forward.

- Multicultural Affairs Committee (MAC). This faculty senate–approved committee, chaired by a faculty member, brings another dimension of the religious and spiritual conversation to campus. While this committee has a wide-ranging focus around many multicultural issues, religion, spirituality, and meaning making are all part of what MAC does. MAC provides yet another arena for faculty, staff, and students to participate in dialogue, gain perspective, be true to who they are, and become whole people with complex identities on campus. One beneficial outcome of MAC cross-campus dialogues is that whenever students, faculty, and staff of color are asked to talk about various aspects of who they are, almost invariably, they talk about how their religious beliefs, as well as their racial identities, are instrumental in shaping their value systems.

- Mental Health Symposium. Offered for all Champlain students, faculty, staff, their families, and the community at large, the major goals for this symposium are to raise awareness about mental health issues, including the impact of religio-spiritual development, as well as to "create a compassionate climate for creative discussion, personal reflection, and education" (see http://www.champlain.edu/news/news_display.php?article = 08-27-07a.php). In the fall of 2007, Robert J. Nash and DeMethra L. Bradley were the keynoters for the symposium theme: What's Your State of Spiritual Mind?

Through opportunities such as these, it is clear that Champlain College values the religio-spiritual conversation and encourages all areas of campus leadership to continue the conversation outside the official Listserve, the MAC meeting table, and identity development days. With this value instilled in campus leaders, students, staff, and others begin to follow their role models and enter the religious and spiritual conversation, in small and large groups, by sharing different levels of knowledge, inquiry, and personal experience.

Whether one is a believer in religious faith, a believer in a more generalized spirituality, a believer in both, or a believer in neither, exploring those beliefs helps us give context to any taken-for-granted values we hold. Exploration invites us to put language to those ideals. "Being aware and trying to understand the different traditions, we can achieve a fuller and truer sense of who we are" (DrowningBear, 2002, p. 106). Knowing who we are as religio-spiritual beings allows us to interact with others in a genuine way, showing them some vulnerability at times and inviting them to witness us, their leaders, their staff, their faculty, and their administrators as real people struggling to create meaning in our own lives. As leaders, we humanize ourselves whenever we are vulnerable with people; we show them that it is OK *not* to know the answers to all the questions, and that learning is a lifelong process, full of questions *and* answers.

Developing a trusting relationship is essential in furthering personal growth and meaning making. "Leadership development is greatly enhanced when you understand how important relationships are in leadership. . . . You must know—yourself, how change occurs, and how others view things differently than you do" (Komives et al., 1998, p. 5). Leaders who, in the company of students, colleagues, and staff, are willing to explore and converse about all the dimensions of who they are, including their religio-spiritual identities, help others to look deeper into themselves. These openly vulnerable, mutually revealing conversations give new meaning to the term *multiple perspectives.*

It is obvious that campus leaders hold intellect in high regard, but when they are willing to explore the most profound elements of the self right along with students and all other constituents, it establishes the fact that *both* in-classroom and out-of-classroom knowledge, drive, and passion are significant. According to Chickering, campus leaders "can have a powerful impact on a college community by encouraging self-exploration, serving as role models, and making leadership opportunities available" (as cited in Hamrick et al., 2002, p. 146). Leaders who challenge others to know themselves and how they connect to the larger world are successful leaders. And successful leaders are far more likely to beget successful leaders.

Spirituality and Religion as a Quest for Personal Meaning

In this section, we talk about what the terms *spirituality* and *religion* represent for the two of us. Obviously there will be considerable overlap between the two terms, but there are also significant differences. For us, spirituality is more an affair of the heart than the head, although these two parts of the body are not irreconcilably opposed. Spirituality represents the quest for emotional, as well as cognitive, meaning that lies at the core of all cultures, people, and professions. We believe strongly that the quest for meaning in life is what a genuine professional education should be about. We think of leadership education not only as a social science or a practical science but as a series of interdisciplinary offerings that cut across several of the humanities—including psychology, philosophy, religious studies, history, literature, art, music, theater, and others. The humanities, in theory, cater more to heart learning than to head learning, although once again, heart and head are not mutually dichotomous in every case. We do not make an either-or distinction but rather a more-or-less distinction, one that neuroscience findings have affirmed (see Edelman, 2006).

"Knowledge fills the mind with information; spiritual growth creates the space for that information to become wisdom" (Sunim, 2002). Most of us enter institutions of higher learning to be changed; we search introspectively and look externally to put together the pieces of the puzzle called life. All of us must look inward to understand ourselves before we are able to look outward to understand what is going on around us and how it all fits. According to Love and Talbot, spiritual development is "an ongoing process and an important component of understanding oneself" (as cited in Hamrick et al., 2002, p. 155).

For us, any leadership training program needs to work with universal meaning as well as with particular meaning (what philosophers of religion call *transcendent* as opposed to *immanent* meaning), with the feelings as well as with the intellect, with the spiritual as well as with the material needs of human beings. Most important, leadership training programs that prepare educators and administrators for a variety of positions in higher education must put as much emphasis on the quest for personal meaning in life as they do on the shaping of particular management and leadership techniques and skill sets. Know thyself, the great Socratic dictum, is as important to us in a professional classroom as the training imperative, Know how to use the tools of thy trade. To know oneself spiritually is to experience a wondrous dimension of reality that is unmeasurable, often nonreplicable, and always deeply mysterious. We become aware that there is a deeper level of meaning to existence. We see, if only dimly, what one sociologist of religion, Peter Berger (1970), calls "fleeting signals of transcendence."

As leadership educators, we believe that an appreciation of religious pluralism begins with an understanding that the religious world is radically diverse and constantly changing. Moreover, for those of us who live and work on college campuses, to be ignorant of the expanding, diverse religious landscape throughout the world is to court international disaster in the decades ahead. For example, the number of evangelical Christians has increased almost exponentially, not just in the United States but throughout the world, constituting in some parts of the globe one-fourth of the adult population, and in this country, nearly one-third of all religious believers. The conclusion is inescapable: Campus leaders must know and understand the content of the various religions (Nash, 2007). We must become more religiously literate if we are going to encourage the growth of highly aware, inclusive, appreciative campus environments. Developing a culture of leaders who are knowledgeable about the actual beliefs of a variety of religions will begin a ripple effect from college campuses into the larger campus communities, throughout the city, state, and ideally the nation and world.

This work is not simple. It requires willingness to be challenged, interest in looking inward, and being able to hear new and/or different perspectives. "Religious pluralism requires active, positive engagement with the claims of religion and the facts of religious diversity. It involves not just a recognition of the different religious traditions and the insuring of their legitimate rights, but the active effort to understand difference and commonality through dialogue" (Rambachan, 2002, p. 173). When our campus leaders are ready to learn about the content of religio-spirituality, they will be better able to teach the next generation of leaders to be tolerant of a variety of faiths.

The Big Religio-Spiritual Questions

We have used the following "big" existential starter questions in our leadership seminars and consultancies, as well as in our leadership training institutes, in order to get our constituencies thinking deeply about spirituality and religion. We are convinced that leaders who take time to reflect on the meaning that religion and spirituality have in their own lives will then be able to inspire others to think seriously about the same. According to Hamrick et al. (2002), as students move away from home and have new experiences, "exposure to different belief systems, as well as complex challenges, often results in questioning of existing beliefs and a desire to explore the spiritual realm in depth" (p. 64). Leaders who are willing, and able, to support and encourage this exploration, not just with others but with themselves, give all the campus constituencies long overdue permission to think about a dimension of themselves that is often ignored on most secular campuses (Nash & Bradley, 2007a, 2007b).

Some of the questions below have been inspired by Sharon Daloz Parks (2000), but in all cases we have articulated them in our own way. We have also constructed a number of additional questions. Parks, who has worked with students, staff, faculty, and administrators for over three decades, has been able to evoke profoundly *spiritual* responses from a variety of campus constituencies. In her own words: "These are questions of meaning, purpose, and faith; they are rightly asked in age-appropriate ways in every generation, in youth, in young adulthood, and throughout adult life. Our students are being cheated in the schools and colleges because they are not being invited to entertain the greatest questions of their own lives or their times" (p. 7).

1. Do you make a distinction between religion and spirituality? If yes, what is the difference for you?

2. In a nutshell, what larger belief about the meaning of your life gets you up in the morning and off to work, and off to face your responsibilities, day after day, especially when you don't want to? In other words, what gives you the personal strength to carry on? What gives your life some kind of sustaining meaning? How do you deal with the brute fact of your mortality, your finitude, that someday—who knows when—you will die?

3. Is there a master plan to your life, do you think? Or is it all about blind chance? To what extent do you believe you have the freedom to create your own life?

4. Why is suffering so pervasive in the world, do you think? Why tsunamis? Why New Orleans flooding? Why political, religious, and nationalistic wars?

5. Why bother with spirituality and/or religion anyway? Is either really necessary?

6. Do you think your actions make any real difference to anyone or anything in the larger scheme of things? If yes, why? If no, why not?

7. When is the last time you had a conversation about religion or spirituality with a coworker, a family member, staff member, a student, a supervisor, or a faculty member (choose one)? How would you describe the conversation? If you haven't, why do you suppose you avoid it? Why doesn't it ever come up do you suppose?

8. Were you raised in a particular religion? If so, what was it? If not, why not, do you suppose? If you were, do you still practice that particular religion? If yes, why? If no, why not?

9. If you were ever asked, how long do you think you would be able to talk intelligently about the particulars of their faiths with students, staff, and others who might represent such backgrounds as Islam, Christianity, Buddhism, Hinduism, atheism, Judaism, or Taoism?

10. Do you remember ever getting any formal training about how to understand, and deal with, religious differences in your professional work with students, staff, and others? Why did this happen, or why not?

11. How would you characterize the general religious or spiritual leanings of the people in the place where you work or study?

12. Would you be comfortable talking about religion and/or spirituality with students, faculty, administrators, and staff who might come to you for professional or personal advice on these topics? Why or why not?

Teaching Leaders How to Talk About Religio-Spirituality on College Campuses

We have found in teaching our two HESA courses at the University of Vermont, and in our leadership workshops and consultancies throughout the country, that asking the big existential questions we list above in a nonthreatening way encourages all of our audiences to engage in powerful spiritual and religious self-examination (Nash et al., 2008). In what immediately follows, we identify, and discuss, four leadership qualities that we believe are invaluable in drawing out all the college constituencies that would otherwise be reluctant to talk about such controversial and personal material. Then in a next-to-final section, we present a brief series of strategies for helping leaders and their audiences talk about religio-spiritual issues.

We believe that the four qualities (inspired by Schwehn, 1993) we elucidate briefly in the paragraphs that follow are transferable to a number of settings and constituencies on college campuses. They are also useful for discussing all types of controversial topics, as we pointed out in Nash et al. (2008). In fact, we would go so far as to assert that, absent these personal qualities, most leaders' efforts in getting individuals and groups on college campuses to talk about what really matters to them are destined to fail.

The first quality is *humility*. This means that we must work hard to attribute the best motive to others, whenever they take the risk to express their thoughts in public (even, especially, when they honestly acknowledge their ignorance, based on stereotypes, about particular religio-spiritual beliefs and practices). In the name of humility, then, we need to listen carefully to these publicly expressed beliefs and inquiries. We do this because tolerance and compassion begin with an assumption that we are not the only ones who possess wisdom and insight into religio-spiritual truth. We too tend to stereotype and dismiss. We too hold fast to half truths. We too are liable to understate and overstate.

Humility is the awareness and recognition that learning is an ongoing, lifelong process and that no single person ever possesses all knowledge or all truth. Humility is the give and take, the teaching *and* learning, of true reciprocity. In this sense, we are all students; so too we are all teachers and leaders. On a college campus, humility takes the shape of faculty, staff, and students working hard to empower one another to share their authentic voices rather than proclaiming irrefutable truths. Without humility, leaders are more apt to rule than to lead, and others will tend to see them as arrogant rather than motivational.

The second quality is *faith*. This means trusting that what we hear from another person is worthwhile in some way, if only, and especially, to the speaker. In fact, we need to go one step further. We must have confidence that what others have to offer about their understanding of religio-spiritual beliefs might even be valuable to us in some way. In the words of Schwehn (1993), we need to "believe what we are questioning, and at the same time question what we are believing" (p. 49). In any campuswide conversation about religion, we maintain that success is measured by how well each of us is able to make the other person look good. To the extent that we try to make ourselves look good and the other person look bad, then *we* look bad.

Faith is being true to what we believe. According to Comte-Sponville (2002), faith is about "lying neither to others nor to the self" (p. 196). Questions that come to mind when thinking of faith in this manner are, What is it that you do when no one else is looking? Does your value base change, do decisions you would have made alone become different verdicts when others are around? Students and others may ask us, Do you practice what you preach? wondering if we, as role models and leaders, simply tell them what to do without doing it ourselves. Faith and integrity go hand in hand; living a life in full faith means that life is lived with integrity. Having faith is always challenging, but it is crucial for leaders to model being genuine and being at least open to the possibility that there might be a reality greater than the individual or the group. This may represent for some people a supernatural force such as a personal God (theism) or an impersonal first cause (deism). For others, it may suggest a transcendent spirit, an *élan vital*, or what the American philosopher William James once simply called the "More."

The third quality is *self-denial*. This suggests that at some advanced point in any dialogue about religio-spirituality each of us will need to reexamine at least a few of the assumptions (and misassumptions) about these topics we cherish. This includes, of course, our pet unchecked biases and uninformed stereotypes. Moreover, we will need to learn how to surrender ourselves to the possibility that what might be true to others could, at least in theory, be true to us as well. Self-denial is the inclination to acknowledge that we are willing, and able, to search for the truth in what we oppose and the error in what we espouse, at least initially. It means avoiding the opposites of self-denial—arrogance, unwavering certainty, and self-righteousness.

Self-denial speaks to the hard-won recognition that we do not have all the answers and that we are willing to embrace the idea of lifelong learning by seeking knowledge in many different ways from many different people. Each of us possesses a unique expertise of some kind, and it is empowering to share that knowledge with others in order to enrich their lives in some way. This, of course, entails the reciprocal expectation that we have something to learn from others as well. People who see their leaders as being confident but still willing to learn from others are more apt to behave likewise when they become leaders.

Finally, the fourth quality is *charity*. This is about attributing the best motive and looking for the good in others, including especially what others are willing to fight, maybe even die, for. Charity is about exercising generosity, graciousness, and even in some instances affection. This, of course, does not mean ignoring or excusing errors in judgment, faulty reasoning, or one-sided zealotry. Rather it means that any critique or correction must always come from a spirit of kindness and love, motivated always by a commitment to help and not to harm.

Charity is the willingness to build open, safe spaces on college campuses. Leaders can do this by showing all their constituencies that it is as important to *give* as it is to *take* from conversations about religion and spirituality. It is also important to listen respectfully to the views of others, even when they might be in conflict with our own. Open, safe spaces are all about mutual perspective sharing and listening to understand rather than merely to critique or to declare. With this goal in mind, the focus in campus conversations about religio-spirituality shifts from issuing edicts of right and wrong to asking genuinely open-ended, clarifying questions that reflect an honest interest in the meaning journeys of others.

Putting the Four Leadership Qualities Into Action: Strategies for Talking About the Deep Questions

When leading campus discussions on religion and spirituality, open-minded, agenda-free facilitators are worth their weight in gold. They need to be authentic inquirers who possess ample amounts of humility, faith, self-denial, and charity. They also must know how to translate these qualities into practical strategies for getting a variety of campus participants to open up when talking about the deep questions that we introduced in a previous section. Discussion leaders must understand that when talking in groups about religion and spirituality, the most important *product* is an unimpeded, unrushed *process*. Thus, patience is another key virtue in being an effective conversational facilitator. In this respect, one of our leadership workshop participants wisely said that the "opposite of talking isn't listening; it's waiting, and waiting takes time." What follows are several practical tips for leading successful conversations on the deep questions (Nash et al., 2008):

Humility

- Humility, openness, and a genuine spirit of free and open inquiry are the key virtues in promoting equality of participation in religio-spiritual conversations.
- Stress the importance of mutual vulnerability from all parties in the conversation by being vulnerable yourself. Vulnerability begets vulnerability; invulnerability begets defensiveness, intimidation, and ultimately sabotage or disengagement.
- Talk about those conversational qualities that best lend themselves to threat-free religio-spiritual interchange—for example, generosity, willingness to look for common ground, modesty, authenticity, and so on.
- Look for the truth in what you oppose and the error in what you espouse.

- Acknowledge openly that regardless of the official job title and associated power and influence, nobody has all the answers to the difficult, deep questions; in fact, very few of us even know how to ask these questions.
- Remember (early and often) that in conversations about religio-spirituality, a leader is less the privileged "sage on the stage" and more the equalized "guide on the side."

Faith

- Attribute the best motive and assume the best intentions of the one speaking.
- Ask evocative questions that are simple, clear, open ended, agenda free, direct, and directly relevant to the religio-spiritual questions being discussed.
- Draw out others often by asking clarifying questions or by rephrasing and summarizing what others have said.
- Explain, clarify, question, rephrase, respect, and affirm—always and often.
- Evoke, don't invoke or provoke.
- Respond, knowing full well that you (and I) made it all up—everything.
- Speak always for yourself and not for some group.
- All questions are up for grabs no matter who asks them. Good questions transcend formal rank.

Self-Denial

- Encourage all participants to organize, structure, and take full mutual responsibility for the process and product, the means and ends, of the religio-spiritual conversation.
- Sharing personal stories and perspectives is more humanizing and productive than making speeches and indulging in special pleading or guilt tripping.
- Affirmation leads to individual participation and celebration. Resist the urge to criticize, debunk, or critique.

Charity

- Charity begins with respect for the other. Here are a few examples of self- and other-respecting affirming responses: "Your words made me think about . . ." "I respect that you . . ." "I relate to what you just said in that . . ." "I'm sure you must have considered this . . . , so what do you think?" "Let me tell you where I'm coming from, and I'd love to hear your response . . ." "Please tell me why you feel so strongly about that point . . ." "I like very much what you are saying, but I'm just not there yet for me to own it. . . . Is this OK with you?" "Could you put what you just said into a story format? I react really well to stories about people's beliefs."

- Be openly grateful whenever appropriate. For example, "Thank you very much for what you've just said. I can see places where I resonate and places where I don't. I'd like to talk with you further about this." "Here's what you've added to my thinking, and I appreciate it greatly." "Do you know how important your voice has been in our conversation? Thank you for joining us in this space."

Conclusion

Envision a world where all people challenge themselves to find at least one piece of truth in an opposing point of view. What might that look like? When we picture a world like this, we see people less interested in themselves and more interested in others. We see curiosity and openness to what other perspectives might inform and enrich our own. We see a world where people embody the phrase *lifelong learning* about multiple perspectives. Translate that same idea into an institution of higher education and the outcome fulfills the very basic purpose of education: encouraging every single person on a college campus to gain self-insight, to know and articulate who they are and to reflect on what they know and believe—while at the same time being open to the truth in contrasting points of view in order to better understand others. For leaders to offer this type of experience to all their college constituencies, they must first experience it for themselves.

A capacious worldview on the leader's part can serve as an example to others for developing an empathy for differences in perspective—particularly religious and spiritual differences that might otherwise be threatening. This work is not easy. It requires deep examination of the self before reaching outward to others. The effort is worth it, however, because, in our experience, religio-spiritual dialogues among campus leaders and all their various audiences are often the most stimulating, as well as the most rewarding, of any activity that occurs in higher education.

References

Astin, A. W., & Astin, H. S. (1999). *Meaning and spirituality in the lives of college faculty: A study of values, authenticity, and stress.* Los Angeles: University of California Higher Education Research Institute.

Bennis, W. G. (1989). *On becoming a leader.* Reading, MA: Addison-Wesley.

Bennis, W. G. (1993). *An invented life: Reflections on leadership and change.* Reading, MA: Addison-Wesley.

Berger. P. L. (1970). *A rumor of angels: Modern society and the rediscovery of the supernatural.* New York: Doubleday Anchor.

Cherry, C., DeBerg, B. A., & Porterfield, A. (2001). *Religion on campus.* Chapel Hill: University of North Carolina Press.

Chickering, A. W., Dalton, J. C., & Stamm, L. (2006). *Encouraging authenticity & spirituality in higher education.* San Francisco: Jossey-Bass.

Comte-Sponville, A. (2002). *A small treatise on the great virtues.* New York: Henry Holt.

DrowningBear, B. (2002). The transformation of DrowningBear. In V. Kazanjian & P. Laurence (Eds.), *Education as transformation* (pp. 103–112). New York: Peter Lang.

Edelman, G. M. (2006). *Second nature: Brain sciences and human knowledge.* New Haven, CT: Yale University Press.

Fullan, M. (2001). *Leading in a culture of change.* San Francisco: Jossey-Bass.

Hamrick, F. A., Evans, N. J., & Schuh, J. H. (2002). *Foundations of student affairs practice: How philosophy, theory, and research strengthen educational outcomes.* San Francisco: Jossey-Bass.

Komives, S. R., Lucas, N., & McMahon, T. R. (1998). *Exploring leadership for college students who want to make a difference.* San Francisco: Jossey-Bass.

Nash, R. J. (1999). *Faith, hype, and clarity: Teaching about religion in American schools and colleges.* New York: Teachers College Press.

Nash, R. J. (2001). *Religious pluralism in the academy: Opening the dialogue.* New York: Peter Lang.

Nash, R. J. (2002). *'Real world' ethics: Frameworks for educators and human service professionals.* New York: Teachers College Press.

Nash, R. J. (2003). Inviting atheists to the table: A modest proposal for higher education. *Religion & Education, 30*(1), 1–23.

Nash, R. J. (2005). A letter to secondary teachers: Teaching about religious pluralism in the public schools. In N. Noddings (Ed.), *Educating citizens for global awareness* (pp. 93–106). New York: Teachers College Press.

Nash, R. J. (2007). Understanding and promoting religious pluralism on college campuses. *Spirituality in Higher Education Newsletter, 3*(4), 1–9.

Nash, R. J., & Baskette, S. M. (2007). Teaching about religious and spiritual pluralism in a professional education course. In M. R. Diamond (Ed.), *Encountering faith in the secular classroom: Turning difficult discussions into constructive engagement* (pp. 188–202). Sterling VA: Stylus.

Nash, R. J., & Bradley, D. L. (2007a). Moral conversation: A theoretical framework for talking about spirituality on college campuses. In S. L. Hoppe & B. W. Speck (Eds.), *Searching for spirituality in higher education*. New York: Peter Lang.

Nash, R. J., & Bradley, D. L. (2007b). The different spiritualities of the students we teach. In D. Jacobsen & R. H. Jacobsen (Eds.), *The American university in a postsecular age: Religion and the academy* (pp. 135–150). New York: Oxford University Press.

Nash, R. J., Bradley, D. L., & Chickering, A. W. (2008). *How to talk about hot topics on campus: From polarization to moral conversation*. San Francisco: Jossey-Bass.

National Association of Student Personnel Administrators. (1987). *Points of view*. Washington, DC: National Association of Student Personnel Administrators.

Parks, S. D. (2000). *Big questions, worthy dreams: Mentoring young adults in their search for meaning, purpose, and faith*. San Francisco: Jossey-Bass.

Prothero, S. (2007). *Religious literacy: What every American needs to know—and doesn't*. San Francisco: HarperCollins.

Rambachan, A. (2002). A Hindu perspective on moving from religious diversity to religious pluralism. In V. Kazanjian & P. Laurence (Eds.), *Education as transformation* (pp. 173–180). New York: Peter Lang.

Riley, N. S. (2005). *God on the quad: How religious colleges and the missionary generation are changing America*. New York: St. Martin's Press.

Rudolph, F. (1990). *The American college & university: A history*. Athens: University of Georgia Press.

Schwehn, M. R. (1993). *Exiles from Eden: Religion and the academic vocation in America*. New York: Oxford University Press.

Scott, D. K. (2002). Spirituality in an integrative age. In V. Kazanjian & P. Laurence (Eds.), *Education as transformation* (pp. 23–26). New York: Peter Lang.

Sunim, J. H. (2002). Buddhism as a pluralistic tradition. In V. Kazanjian & P. Laurence (Eds.), *Education as transformation* (pp. 135–142). New York: Peter Lang.

7

LEADERSHIP PROGRAMS FOR A FAMILY-FRIENDLY CAMPUS

Jaime Lester

A major concern in academic leadership over the last few decades has been faculty professional development. The impending retirement of large numbers of faculty has created an environment in which new faculty are needed to fulfill leadership roles. The emphasis has been on leadership development programs that train faculty and support them as they pursue academic leadership roles. An issue that has prevented faculty from considering academe and academic leadership is work/life balance, often-times referred to as *career flexibility*. Defined broadly as providing faculty with support over their life course, career flexibility specifically addresses multiple points of career entry, exit, and reentry from faculty work, cultural backlash, or undue professional compromise. The intended goal of career flexibility initiatives is to support tenure-track faculty career development while recognizing the diversity in faculty members' professional lives and ac-knowledging that not all faculty reach traditional milestones at similar times.

The need for career flexibility policies are very much linked to the leader-ship revolution, as career flexibility requires new approaches to faculty develop-ment that looks at leadership on multiple levels of the organization, examines the abuses of power, and considers culture and context. As suggested by Kezar and Carducci in chapter 1, revolutionary leadership scholars have introduced nonhierarchical, process-oriented, and democratic forms of leadership rather than relying on traditional principles of social control and hierarchy.

The purpose of this chapter is to discuss several of the approaches that leadership development programs have taken to address career flexibility.

Using nonpositional leadership, power, and organizational culture as outlined in the leadership revolution, it will become clear that organizers of leadership development programs have used new approaches to address career flexibility. In addition to the suggestions outlined by the two case sites, Northern University and Southern University,[1] this chapter concludes with additional suggestions for practice that address career flexibility in the context of leadership development programs.

There are several reasons why it is important to adopt career flexibility initiatives. First, the unfriendly culture of academia has remained one of the biggest obstacles to diversifying faculty ranks (Sullivan, Hollenshead, & Smith, 2004). Many work/life balance and career flexibility policies are rarely used because of lack of support, fear of retribution by tenure and promotion committee, and a lack of knowledge of the policies' existence (Drago & Colbeck, 2003; Finkel, Olswang, & She, 1994; Hochschild, 1997; Mason & Goulden, 2004; Raabe, 1997; Ward & Wolf-Wendel, 2004a). Second, the rigid career trajectories of faculty work have forced many women to leave academe or choose an alternative career path (Thornton, 2005). Although career flexibility initiatives do not exclusively apply to women, many women faculty in particular find it difficult to consider child rearing in rigid and linear academic career trajectories (Armenti, 2004). A lack of career flexibility results in many women leaving academe. In order to continue implementation of career flexibility initiatives, leaders from across institutions who have an understanding of the need for organizational change to accompany policies need to be developed (Ward & Wolf-Wendel, 2005). Career flexibility requires more than a policy; it requires organizational change fostered by leaders who have developed an understanding for the need for career flexibility policies (Hollenshead, Sullivan, Smith, August, & Hamilton, 2005; Ward & Wolf-Wendel, 2004a, 2005). Leadership development programs are an important venue to cultivate leaders from different institutional types to create organizational change.

Approaches to Leadership Development and Career Flexibility

Because of an increase in national attention to career flexibility issues and monies provided by external granting agencies, organizers of several leadership development programs across the country have incorporated discussions

---

1. Pseudonyms were used in order to protect the identification of the institutions.

of career flexibility in their current program curricula. These programs seek to create an awareness of career flexibility issues and the need for policies through integrated curricula that promote dialogue and learning among the program participants. The main goal of each program is to diffuse throughout the campus culture an understanding and acceptance of career flexibility policies and practices. The program participants become the change agents who seek to change the campus culture. In order to understand the experiences of the leadership development program organizers and to glean successful practices within the programs, interviews were held and resulted in several themes highlighted in this chapter. The themes—nonpositional leadership, use of power, and organizational culture—illustrate the current practices in career flexibility and leadership development and provide insight into the ways organizers of other programs may consider restructuring or creating new curricula. Each theme is presented with illustration from two campuses: Northern University and Southern University.

Nonpositional Leadership

The first approach used by the leadership development programs to infuse conversations of career flexibility concerns the definition of leadership. Several of the leadership development programs' definition of leadership relies on leadership as nonpositional—leadership as a collective process that does not rely on institutional hierarchy. A focus on nonpositional leadership engages individuals from all levels of the hierarchy who have the ability to create change. Conceptualizing leadership as nonpositional has been intuitively suggested in studies on career flexibility. Ward and Wolf-Wendel (2004a, 2005) argue that faculty colleagues need to be involved in policy development and creating an environment where the policies can be used. Colleagues serve as mentors to other more junior colleagues by providing support and advocacy for faculty who use career flexibility policies (Ward & Wolf-Wendel, 2004a). Senior faculty at many institutions also provide representation on faculty governance boards that have the power to advocate on behalf of the faculty for the development and implementation of career flexibility policies. Moreover, faculty colleagues provide the institutional memory of how policies will be interpreted by departments and colleges over time. Ward and Wolf-Wendel (2004a) and others also suggest that department chairs, deans, provosts, and presidents need to be engaged in order to address career flexibility (Hollenshead et al., 2005). Although department chairs, deans, provosts, and presidents are considered positional leaders, the suggestion is to engage leaders from across the institution (faculty, staff, and administrators) in a collective effort to create greater adoption, understanding, and eventually organizational change around issues of career flexibility. All groups of leaders need to come together in a dialogue to break down power barriers and discuss the importance of these policies for faculty.

A focus on nonpositional leadership at Northern University and Southern University has led to alternative definitions of leadership as well as multiple programs to target leaders from across the university. The underlying principle is that individuals at all levels of the university have an opportunity to effect change, increase the number of people who use career flexibility policies, create more exposure to these policies, and serve as change agents to cultivate an awareness of the need to accept new traditions of faculty work. In practice, a focus on nonpositional leadership requires a primary inclusion of faculty along with department chairs and upper administration in dialogue with faculty. Southern University has developed a series of workshops designed to bring together faculty from across the institution to discuss issues around faculty retention, equity, and career flexibility. Faculty meet in groups on a regularly scheduled basis to talk about the difficulties of balancing work and family and to discuss practices and policies that have assisted in their success. For example, faculty may share how a department chair allowed them to work primarily from home after the birth of a child, or how a department chair established a process to find teaching substitutes if family became ill. In addition, Southern invited other leaders from across the campus to engage in discussions to help them understand the needs and importance of career flexibility accommodations. Furthermore, the intent of the workshops at Northern and Southern has an underlying mission of creating change agents who graduate from the program with a greater understanding of the need for career flexibility. Empowering participants who are traditionally not considered leaders requires organizers of leadership development programs to cultivate a sense of empowerment and help participants develop strategies for affecting change. Often these strategies are shared during the dialogues within the context of the leadership development programs.

Use of Power

The second approach to leadership that serves as a foundation for curricula and development of leadership development programs that focus on career flexibility are the abuses of power that occur when individuals do not undergo a deconstructive process to examine hierarchical arrangements and other power dynamics. In the context of leadership, abuses of power marginalize groups or individuals, create unhealthy cultures, and establish an unequal distribution of resources (Kezar, Carducci, & Contreras-McGavin, 2006). For example, many faculty learn about policies and practices within their academic departments and they often rely heavily on department members to serve as institutional informants and advocates within the university administration (Quinn, Edwards Lange, & Olswang, 2004; Ward & Wolf-Wendel, 2004b). One study found that communication about policies is inconsistent, and decision making at the departmental level had a profound impact on how the policies were implemented (Quinn et al.). In this same study, some faculty members were not aware of the availability of the part-time tenure-track option because the department did not publicize or offer the part-time option. With so much emphasis placed on the role of the department in informing, advocating, and affecting the culture of the department, there are many ways in which individuals on the department level may abuse their power and either deter faculty from using career flexibility policies or unintentionally interpret the policies differently for diverse groups of faculty. Undergoing a process of deconstructing personal beliefs, biases, and the power inherent in a hierarchy is essential for those who have the power to have an impact on the development and implementation of career flexibility policies.

One of the approaches that Northern University applies to address abuses of power is to create a trusting environment and slowly integrate discussions of diversity into the curriculum. As one of the program organizers stated: "Do not hit people over the head with a diversity hammer." Northern has observed that individuals engaged in leadership development programs have deeply held beliefs related to policies that provide accommodation for groups or that seek to increase representation of groups (e.g., affirmative action and equal opportunity policies). Introducing career flexibility is often linked, in the minds of the participants, to affirmative action and other diversity-related policies, which creates tension, controversy, and resistance from the participants. These deeply held beliefs are also found by the Northern leadership program organizers to lead to the abuse of power. Leaders often make decisions based on deeply held beliefs, which may prevent the acceptance of career flexibility policies. Weaving issues of faculty and career flexibility into conversations about hiring, salary compression, and productivity assists in reducing the resistance that arises when deeply held beliefs and actions are questioned. For example, in a workshop on retention of faculty the organizers discuss career flexibility policies not as a mechanism to accommodate one group of faculty over another but rather as a way of creating equity among faculty. The program organizers ask the participants to share their own practices for promoting retention among faculty. Importantly, the participants are asked to recall the reasons why they sought to retain certain faculty over others. The reflection begins to create a dialogue on which faculty are accommodated and how those accommodations vary between faculty of different genders and ethnicities. These dialogues slowly address the leader's beliefs and the subsequent abuses of power that arise from basing decisions on those beliefs and offer an opportunity to change those beliefs without extreme resistance.

Furthermore, Northern University and Southern University use a cohort-based model to sustain an established and cohesive group of individuals in order to develop trust over time in order to have discussions of unconscious biases. Northern created cohorts of department chairs from the science disciplines who have similar issues and perspectives. By maintaining group cohesion and retaining cohorts of department chairs, Northern University cohorts reached a level that allowed for deconstructive dialogues regarding unconscious biases of faculty work, gender, and career flexibility. At Northern it took several years to establish trust and responsibility within the cohort in order to begin discussing these more controversial issues. At Southern University, the leadership development program includes a test of cognitive errors where individuals are given pictures of men and women in nontraditional gender roles and are asked to respond to a series of questions. The response time is recorded. The idea is that a longer response time indicates the unconscious bias that exists around gender. Simply, if it takes an individual longer to respond to a picture of a woman as a scientist then that person has an unconscious bias toward women and science. The test assists in uncovering unconscious biases that often lead to the misuse of power.

Organizational Culture

Finally, organizers of leadership development programs have approached career flexibility from a cultural perspective. Organizational culture and context stress that leaders need to be sensitive to institutional culture as well as external trends. Notions of faculty work have a long tradition in the academy and are rooted in traditional career trajectories. Establishing career flexibility initiatives question the long-held traditions of faculty work and require a cultural change in the minds of institutional constituents. Second, the existing culture can either help or hinder the implementation and adoption of career flexibility. When cultures are less apt to consider nontraditional notions of faculty work, establishing an understanding of the need for the policies as well as preventing backlash from using the policies is difficult.

The leadership development programs at Northern and Southern acknowledged the importance of organizational culture in addressing career flexibility and in educating program participants. In practice, the leadership development program organizers attempted to affect culture by creating change agents who diffuse the acceptance of career flexibility programs throughout the university and by capitalizing on cultural support and symbols to legitimize the program. The use of organizational culture has a two-prong purpose. On the one hand, individuals who are responsible for the introduction of career flexibility into leadership development programs actively sought to create institutional support for the programs by cultivating a culture of acceptance for career flexibility policies and the leadership development programs. For example, Northern and Southern asked college deans and the college administration to promote career flexibility policies and leadership programs in faculty orientation, college meetings, and speeches to college employees. On the other hand, leadership development program organizers sought to change the culture by cultivating change agents within the programs who would in turn go out into the college and promote career flexibility. The cultivation of change agents occurs during the dialogues that question deeply held beliefs and cognitive errors, which changes the values and views of the leadership program participants. As these participants work in the college, they have an opportunity to have an impact on the acceptance of career flexibility policies and change the organizational culture. This two-prong approach was designed to create a culture of acceptance and usage of career flexibility policies from the top (support from the administration) and the bottom (change agents among faculty).

Southern also capitalized on existing support from the provost's office, which established a position to support career flexibility including offering $1 million for dual faculty hiring. Southern takes a more holistic approach to changing the organizational culture by securing external and internal funds, collaborating with statewide training programs, creating formal roles to over-see career flexibility initiatives in the provost's office, and creating a variety of in-person and online programs to disseminate information widely. Collec-tively the variety of efforts in place to support career flexibility models sym-bolizes the institutional commitment to career flexibility as well as the new value placed on these policies and practices. For example, the funds provided by the provost's office and the new formal roles to support career flexibility models cultural change within the highest levels of the college and further emphasize the importance of career flexibility. Individuals within the college begin to understand that the rhetoric of career flexibility is supported by funds, new programs, and new positions to realize the career flexibility initia-tive. Each of these initiatives is viewed as a different mechanism to diffuse the importance of career flexibility and to change the organizational culture of the university. These initiatives also support the leadership development program by providing funds and, more importantly, by showing alignment between the organizational culture and the leadership programs. By existing in a culture that has shifted its focus to career flexibility, the leadership devel-opment programs appear to have institutional support and are aligned with the mission of the institution.

The approaches to leadership development and the practices of North-ern and Southern highlight effective strategies in fostering an understanding of career flexibility. At both universities there was an understanding of the importance of leadership beyond traditional leadership roles, such as presi-dents and provosts. These institutions' programs rely on leadership as a col-lective process by bringing together cohorts of department chairs and other individuals to learn collectively. Leadership teams can develop the trust re-quired to acknowledge the abuse of power and undergo a deconstructive process. Organizers of each of the leadership development programs found that questioning cognitive errors and other unconscious biases is essential in promoting the need of career flexibility policies. The dialogues and decon-structive process help to change the values and views of the program partici-pants who in turn have an opportunity to change the beliefs of others within the college. By gradually changing the beliefs of many, the organizational culture has an opportunity to shift to one that accepts career flexibility poli-cies. Finally, Northern and Southern are both undergoing a change in orga-nizational culture. Strategies such as creating positions in the provost's office, securing internal and external funds, and providing education and training in the context of leadership development are all strategies to help change the organizational culture to one that is more accepting of alternative faculty career trajectories.

Recommendation for Leadership Development Programs

The success of Northern and Southern illustrates the importance of leadership development programs in fostering career flexibility policies. In order to continue to make progress at these universities as well as at the many other postsecondary institutions across the country, organizers of leadership development programs can incorporate several strategies to create support for career flexibility policies, help unify the interpretation of these policies, and help deconstruct unconscious biases. The following are several recommendations for organizers of leadership development programs who have a desire to address career flexibility among faculty.

Leadership Teams and a Cohort Model

The leadership development programs that use the leadership team approach help to foster a trusting environment and help individuals get advice on issues that cross departmental boundaries. However, some intentionality behind the creation of these leadership teams is necessary. Bringing together people in logical pairing with comparative issues will allow networks and relationships to be built more easily, but there are many considerations when creating the teams. For example, department chairs in the humanities have a hard time understanding the issues in engineering when new faculty regularly have $1 million research starter packages. Disciplines also differ in terms of gender or recruitment of women faculty, and English, education, and social work traditionally have more women and less issues recruiting female faculty. These basic disciplinary differences may create misunderstanding and divides among the individuals in a leadership team.

Another issue that needs to be considered when creating the leadership teams is diversity. Having only one or two women and people of color on a team has the potential to "tokenize" those individuals. The few women and people of color may feel obligated or feel pressured to speak on behalf of their social identity groups. Consider the composition of the groups carefully with particular consideration to social identities. Create groups with several people from each identity group to prevent tokenizing a particular individual. Finally, a focus on nonpositional leadership may lead to the creation of groups across the institutional hierarchy. One group may have a few faculty, department chairs, a provost, and staff members. Embedded within these teams is a hierarchical power structure that reflects the institutional hierarchy, and individuals may fear being honest or critical of the institution. Leadership development program organizers need to create dialogues that address the power issues between group members. In addition the group needs to commit to confidentiality and job security in order to address the fear of those who are in lower levels of the institutional hierarchy.

Create Specific Curriculum for the Leadership Team

As leadership development programs continue to include leaders from multiple levels of the college, curricula will need to be developed to appeal to all the groups. Each constituent group will require a curriculum within the program that appeals to its perspectives as well as its experiences. For example, college deans are primarily concerned about the health of their college, which relies on productive faculty, appropriate use of resources, and fund-raising. To develop a curriculum for a leadership development program that includes discussions of career flexibility among deans, program organizers need to consider how career flexibility affects college resources, the productivity of faculty, and marketing that can be used for fund-raising. Organizers of leadership development programs may want to consider creating documents that outline the monetary value of having productive faculty as well as the productivity increase that is created when faculty use career flexibility policies. Also, organizers may consider bringing in newly recruited faculty to discuss the importance of career flexibility policies in their decision to accept a job offer within the college. Department chairs, however, are more focused on the management of their departments and are concerned with curriculum development, recruiting of students and faculty, course offerings, and other staff management issues. A leadership development program that focuses on department chairs may include an outline of the ways career flexibility policies can accommodate faculty without conflicting with course schedules and service responsibilities, such as recruitment and curriculum development.

Target Leadership Broadly

The majority of the interpretation and socialization around career flexibility occurs at the departmental level. Therefore, department chairs have been a natural group to target for discussions of career flexibility; however, leadership occurs on a variety of levels within postsecondary institutions. For example, senior faculty can be mentors who provide implicit knowledge and institutional memory around career flexibility and also vote on tenure and promotion. Organizers of leadership development programs need to consider targeting leaders from a variety of groups across the campus. Fostering cultural change requires a shift in the current culture and establishing an understanding of career flexibility among those individuals who will shape the culture in the future.

Targeting leadership broadly is a challenge for any leadership development program. Many faculty are overworked with too many responsibilities and receive few incentives for involvement in ongoing programs. Furthermore, student service and academic offices are often understaffed, relying on their few staff members to be physically present during normal business hours. Involvement in leadership development programs would close offices and decrease service to students and other individuals in the college. In order to address these issues that arise with a broader focus on leadership, program organizers need to devise incentives and support structures that allow faculty and staff to be involved in the program. For example, department heads can grant course releases to faculty for every semester they are involved in the program. Organizers of the leadership development program can also create ways to provide staff coverage during those hours that a staff member is attending program meetings or events. Organizers may also consider programming leadership development outside normal business hours, with monetary incentives for staff and faculty. Targeting leadership beyond positional leaders requires leadership development programs to contain creative incentives to remove barriers to participation.

Acknowledge the Need to Deconstruct Unconscious Bias

Career flexibility policies question deeply held beliefs and traditions about faculty work as a "life of the mind" that is boundaryless, that has undertones of gender inequities, and that contains internal biases related to gender and faculty work (Curtis, 2004). For example, Ward and Wolf-Wendel (2004b) found that administrators are concerned that family-flexibility policies that provide accommodations when faculty have children show favoritism to those women and men who have children. Organizers of leadership development programs need to acknowledge that participants enter into discussions and dialogues with these biases and fears. Slowly introducing conversations about career flexibility over time and when trust has developed is important to provide healthy and productive environments where biases can be questioned and deconstructed.

There are several suggestions on how to introduce conversations of career flexibility. First, leadership development program organizers need to carefully consider when to introduce these conversations. As noted by officials at Northern and Southern, cohorts of participants need to create a rapport and establish trust within the group before beginning to introduce conversations that lead to deconstructing biases. Although the issue of timing the discussions may slightly vary between each group, it is advisable to not introduce the conversations until participants have become actively engaged in discussions and converse with each other easily. For a multiyear leadership development program, questioning unconscious biases should not occur until after the first year. Second, conversations need to be aided by tools that help participants to understand that they have unconscious biases. Southern University uses an exercise that measures the response time of images of male and female scientists. This exercise is completed by all participants and illustrates the presence of unconscious biases.

Bring in Beneficiaries

Another suggestion for organizers of leadership development programs interested in career flexibility is to humanize the issues by bringing in individuals who would benefit or have benefited from these policies. Northern University brought women faculty into the discussions that used career flexibility programs. The participants had an opportunity to see that career flexibility accommodations do not lead to a lack of productivity. In fact, the beneficiaries brought into the leadership development program were often not publicly identified as individuals with children or increased home responsibilities; it was assumed that because they are productive faculty that they did not have large external demands. Beneficiaries serve as a way to humanize abstract policies and as a way to begin discussions of unconscious biases.

For those institutions that are still considering the adoption of career flexibility policies, using the experiences of individuals who did not benefit from these policies illustrates the need for them. Organizers of leadership development programs should consider gaining access to exit interviews of faculty who have left the institution or have follow-up discussions with faculty who explicitly left due to career flexibility issues. The exit interviews illustrate the impact on the individual and the potential impact on the university if policies do not change. There may also be faculty who are currently employed at the institution who did not seek other employment but who experienced hardship. Their stories of attempting to balance work and personal considerations serve to illustrate the benefits of adopting career flexibility policies.

External Support

One of the many reasons that leadership development program organizers have been able to incorporate discussions of career flexibility is because of internal and external support. External agencies provide contributions to the leadership development programs that have in turn legitimized the issues for the larger campus culture as well as the institutional administration. In addition, administrative support, in terms of both funding and championing the program, legitimize the program in the eyes of those audiences the leadership development program is attempting to target. Organizers of leadership development programs need to capitalize on the national attention being paid to career flexibility and external funds, and establish internal support in order to legitimize the issue and create interest in attending the programs. This suggestion does not relate exclusively to career flexibility issues but also to individuals who require active deconstruction and are sensitive in nature and may need the additional push and legitimacy provided by internal and external support.

Use Multiple Approaches

One element that can be effective for fostering an understanding of leadership development programs is data. Many institutions annually collect data on faculty and staff demographics, use of policies, salaries, and other measures pertinent to the institution. Accessing the data to provide evidence and to illustrate the need for career flexibility is a powerful tool to create dialogue, increase interest, and convince leadership development program participants of the need for career flexibility policies. For example, leadership development programs can present data on faculty demographics in order to project the number of faculty who will potentially have young children or aging parents, requiring new work arrangements outlined in career flexibility policies. Data on faculty productivity and retention can also illustrate the impact of career flexibility policies. Consider the impact of data that shows an increase in productivity among those faculty who use career flexibility policies. In addition, qualitative data provided in exit interviews may be available that address issues related to career flexibility. Faculty may note in their exit interview that they left because their institution did not accommodate them to care for children or aging parents or because of an illness. This information can be used to inform and educate the leadership development program participants.

Another form of data that leadership development programs should consider using is case studies from other institutions that have successfully created career flexibility policies. Case studies are powerful tools to illustrate the importance and effectiveness of these policies. Several types of case studies can be used, the first being case studies of specific policies. Northern University, for example, is one of the only institutions of higher education that has created a policy to allow tenure-track faculty to work on a part-time basis. This policy has proven effective and can serve as a best practice example for participants in the leadership development program. The second is case studies of institutions that have undergone significant changes to create organizational change around career flexibility. The process of creating institutional support, the development of policies, and implementation on a campuswide basis can serve as a holistic example of the challenges and opportunities in persuading an institution to be amenable to career flexibility. The final case study that is useful to illustrate the benefit of career flexibility is the individual case study. Similar to the recommendation of bringing in speakers, case studies of individuals can serve to personalize the issues and need for career flexibility policies. The details provided in a single story of the challenges faculty face in work/life balance and the importance of career flexibility to maintain their job responsibilities is a powerful tool.

In addition to using data and case studies, organizers of leadership development programs can bring in experts, question unconscious biases, and provide a forum for people to discuss adaptations of career flexibility policies in a multifaceted approach to foster an understanding of the need for alternative faculty work arrangements. Many of these curricular adaptations are included in this chapter and can serve as guides of creative methods to engage leadership development program participants. Addressing career flexibility in the context of leadership development programs requires that programs go beyond lecturing and one-time meetings to adopting a variety of methods to introduce difficult, yet important questions that arise around career flexibility.

Conclusion

The opportunities for leadership development programs to engage in career flexibility discussions are just beginning as many institutions across the country are just now realizing the need to create career flexibility policies to address the needs of a changing faculty workforce. There are many ways to incorporate career flexibility into leadership development programs, but one would be remiss to think that all colleges and universities are ready for these discussions. Organizers of leadership development programs are challenged to change existing curriculum and practices, such as the duration of the program, the inclusion of deconstructive dialogues, and the audience. Including career flexibility within the curriculum requires that leadership development programs move beyond short programming that lasts 1 day or a weekend and to more extensive efforts that last several months to several years. Organizers of these programs need to consider multiple audiences from across the institutional hierarchy and engage these individuals in groups to deconstruct unconscious biases and beliefs of faculty work. Each of these efforts takes time and resources as well as organizers who are willing to be creative to move beyond current practices.

In addition to the challenges faced in design, leadership development programs may also exist in a culture that is resistant to career flexibility discussions and policies. Northern University and Southern University were fortunate in that the institutions expressed a commitment and had a history of awareness of career flexibility issues. Not all colleges will be ready to consider alternative faculty work arrangements, and organizers of leadership development programs will be challenged to get institutional interest and support before programming can begin. One effective method for overcoming resistance is to seek external funding. Not only do funds provide the necessary monies for the development of programs, they also symbolize the importance of career flexibility to the external environment. Similarly, many institutions have competitor universities they often look to for cutting-edge practices and to benchmark success. When competitor institutions develop policies or improve programs, other institutions may be more likely to consider the importance of career flexibility policies. Resistance will come from individuals who hold unconscious biases related to career flexibility. As noted, these resistances can be addressed through a curriculum that supports a trusting environment and creates opportunities for dialogue. Using data, bringing in beneficiaries, and questioning biases through cognitive tests are just a few methods for instigating dialogue.

As more campuses begin to engage in career flexibility and as they look to leadership development programs as forums to hold discussions and educate leaders, more advice will emerge. The strategies outlined in this chapter are a beginning to a discussion of how to create organizational change and effective implementation of career flexibility policies that are being developed across postsecondary institutions nationwide. These suggestions and strategies are not meant to be the only possibilities for infusing or developing new leadership development programs, but they can serve as a guide and as conversation starters on ways to change leadership development curriculum. In order to change how postsecondary education views faculty work by providing alternative faculty work arrangements, leaders from all levels of the hierarchy need to be engaged in career flexibility issues. Organizers of leadership development programs have an opportunity to assist campuses to identify the issues and struggles in implementing these policies and to help individuals deconstruct unconscious biases that may affect career flexibility policies.

References

Armenti, C. (2004). May babies and posttenure babies: Maternal decisions of women professors. *The Review of Higher Education, 27*(2), 211–231.

Curtis, J. (2004). Balancing work and family for faculty: Why it's important. *Academe, 90*(6), 21–23.

Drago, R., & Colbeck, C. (2003). *The Mapping Project: Exploring the terrain of U.S. colleges and universities for faculty and families: Final report for the Alfred P. Sloan Foundation.* University Park: Pennsylvania State University. Retrieved May 1, 2007, from http://lser.la.psu.edu/workfam/mappingproject.htm

Finkel, S. K., Olswang, S., & She, N. (1994). Childbirth, tenure, and promotion for women faculty. *Review of Higher Education, 17*(3), 259–270.

Hochschild, A. R. (1997). *The time bind: When work becomes home and home becomes work.* New York: Holt.

Hollenshead, C. S., Sullivan, B., Smith, G. C., August, L., & Hamilton, S. (2005). Work/family policies in higher education: Survey data and case studies of policy implementation. *New Directions for Higher Education, 2005* (130), 41–65. San Francisco: Jossey-Bass.

Kezar, A., Carducci, R., & Contreras-McGavin, M. (2006). Rethinking the "L" word in higher education: The revolution of research on leadership. *ASHE-ERIC Higher Education Report, 31*(6). San Francisco: Jossey-Bass.

Mason, M. A., & Goulden, M. (2004). Do babies matter (Part II)?: Closing the baby gap. *Academe, 90*(6), 10–15.

Quinn, K., Edwards Lange, S., & Olswang, S. G. (2004). Family-friendly policies and the research university. *Academe, 90*(6), 32–34.

Raabe, P. H. (1997). Work-family policies for faculty: How "career and family-friendly" is academe? In M. A. Ferber & J. W. Loeb (Eds.), *Academic couples: Problems and promises* (pp. 208–225). Urbana: University of Illinois Press.

Sullivan, B., Hollenshead, C., & Smith, G. (2004). Developing and implementing work-family policies for faculty. *Academe, 90*(6), 24–27.

Thornton, S. (2005). Implementing flexible tenure clock policies. *New Directions for Higher Education, 2005* (130), 81–90. San Francisco: Jossey-Bass.

Ward, K., & Wolf-Wendel, L. (2004a). Academic motherhood: Managing complex roles in research universities. *The Review of Higher Education, 27*(2), 233–257.

Ward, K., & Wolf-Wendel, L. (2004b). Fear factor: How safe is it to make time for family? *Academe, 90*(6), 28–31.

Ward, K., & Wolf-Wendel, L. (2005). Work and family perspectives from research university faculty. *New Directions for Higher Education, 2005* (130), 67–80. San Francisco: Jossey-Bass.

8

CREATING FACULTY ACTIVISM AND GRASSROOTS LEADERSHIP

An Open Letter to Aspiring Activists

Jeni Hart

To whom it may inspire:
The purpose of my letter is to inspire current and aspiring faculty activists to believe that change in the academy can happen, and that their leadership can be a critical aspect of institutional change. Unfortunately, many faculty who are activists do not see themselves as such. Further complicating this is that many of these same faculty do not see themselves as leaders. Why, you ask?

Grassroots Activism

In terms of how activism is understood, such an idea is often narrowly conceived. When one hears the word activism, activities like sit-ins, boycotts, and protests come to mind. Those activities are part of how I understand activism as well. However, they do not sound like appropriate sorts of strategies faculty participate in on their own campuses. I beg to differ. I do think these strategies are very much a part of what some faculty consider as part of their campus activism; however, these activities do tend to come with more risk. Sit-ins, boycotts, and protests are very demonstrative and public forms of activism. Faculty who do participate in these sorts of activities may quickly be labeled troublemakers. Their collegiality may be called into question and contract renewal, tenure, and/or promotion may be jeopardized. Whether or

not this is fair, particularly given protection of academic freedom, or con-
scionable, is not the point of this discussion, rather the point is to recognize
that activism still comes with some degree of perceived or real risk in the
academy.

Having said that activism in the traditional sense can be risky, I would
argue that activism in a broader sense can be as well. Anyone who is committed to and actively pursues a cause is likely to draw some attention and is
likely to challenge the institutional status quo. For those who are afraid of or
disagree with change, activists are a threat, even if the activism looks less like
activism than one tends to think. For example, I have had the privilege of
researching two grassroots groups of feminist faculty activists on two campuses. These women faculty were passionate about improving the campus
climate for women. One group, the Faculty Women's Caucus (FWC) at the
University of Nebraska, did not have a public list of members. They also
rotated facilitation of the group, but only among tenured faculty. Both of
these efforts were intended to protect the activists, to avoid putting their jobs
at risk. The second group, the Association for Women Faculty (AWF) at the
University of Arizona, protected themselves by pursuing strategies that were
very much in line with their traditional roles as faculty. Rather than organizing a sit-in in the university president's office, they met with him on a regular
basis (much like university service and very much in line with the bureaucratic daily functions of administrative leadership). In these meetings, they
presented research findings, that is, hard data, to demonstrate their positions
(mirroring the research function of faculty) and then would host workshops
to educate the university community about the status of women on campus
(teaching). By acting like a faculty member should, even in pursuit of the
cause of gender equity, these faculty women stayed under the radar and ap-
peared to be less of a threat.

Although the women in both groups developed strategies to mitigate the
risk of being labeled troublemakers, instigators, or even not collegial, their
fight for gender equity was very much activism and still carried some element
of risk. They were not paranoid. In fact, their work was grounded in qualitative and quantitative measures of faculty climate, not only grounded in the
national research on faculty gender equity but in rigorous research about
faculty climate and equity at the University of Nebraska and the University
of Arizona. Ultimately, their work was activist, challenging the idea that activism can and does expand beyond sit-ins, boycotts, and protests to include

working as *activist professionals* and engaging in *professionalized activism* (Hart, 2005).

Strategies of the Activist Professionals

What I mean by working as activist professionals is demonstrated by the strategies of the women in the FWC. For activist professionals, activism is foregrounded in their organizational identity. Put another way, their activism is more transparent than their professional identities. These grassroots activists measure their success by agitating—by making headlines in the local press or even national headlines, as they did in raising awareness about the abusive behavior and apparent lack of institutional response involving a high-profile football player. However, their positions as professionals, that is, faculty members, also contribute to how they manifest their activism. The earlier description of how they mitigate risk for their members exemplifies that their role as academics is not forgotten. Further, like the women in the AWF, they also rely on activist efforts that look like teaching, research, and service to complement *leveraging the public* (Hart, in press) through the use of media, persistent calls to state legislators, and well-crafted petitions calling for institutional policy changes.

Strategies of the Professionalized Activists

The difference between an activist professional and someone who engages in professionalized activism is subtle. The women faculty activists in the AWF are more closely aligned with professionalized activism. First and foremost, their faculty identity guides their choice of strategies. The way they managed risk through the three tenets of faculty work—teaching, research, and service—models the primacy of professional identity. Moreover, they take great care in developing trusting relationships with administrative leaders such as the president, provost, and regents—that is, *prestige networking* (Hart, in press)—in order to foster allies who have authority to institutionalize their feminist agenda. But activism is still very much a part of their work. Those teaching, research, and service activities are above and beyond their expected faculty workload, and working toward gender equity drives each of those activities, which may or may not be the case for the teaching, research, and service they do for their department, contract renewal, promotion, tenure, and merit.

I hope I have been successful in showing how grassroots activism can and should be conceptualized more broadly. This sort of activism is happening on many campuses, not just at the two mentioned above, and activism is not a *dirty* word, but I reiterate that engaging in activism is not without risk. This risk exists for a number of reasons, including a perceived sense of inequity or discrimination for some in the academy—which is often the motivator for activism in the first place. In addition, faculty engaging in work that may be personally valued (i.e., activism) but may not be professionally rewarded may increase the risk of engaging in the activism. However, my purpose is to inspire activists, leaders, and change agents, and that being said, I argue that one's personal values, including any work toward social justice and equity, makes the work that is formally and externally rewarded more meaningful if one's value system is left intact. Sometimes, doing something because it is the right thing to do for oneself should not be pushed down the list of professional priorities.

Grassroots Leadership

Without abandoning my position on the value of activism in the academy, I would now like to suggest that those engaged in activism such as described above and in chapters 5 and 7 in this volume are grassroots leaders. This may sound peculiar to some. Leadership is often cast as a positional sort of endeavor. By this I mean that those who are at the top of a hierarchical structure and hold certain titles like president, provost, and dean are leaders in academe. With that understanding in mind, how could faculty involved in grassroots faculty activism be leaders, particularly if they purposely challenge in their activism the very hierarchical organization they are a part of? Yet, I argue that not only are these faculty change agents for social justice and diversity, they *are* leaders. Further, the academy would be a more accessible, equitable, and hospitable place by beginning to reconceptualize traditional notions of leadership in order to include activist faculty as leaders.

I am not alone in this argument. In *Rethinking the "L" Word in Higher Education: The Revolution of Research on Leadership*, Kezar, Carducci, and Contreras-McGavin (2006) highlight the work of Astin and Leland (1991) who use empirical evidence to show how faculty can be more than leaders in an academic senate or as instructional leaders. Astin and Leland explore the leadership roles that faculty take in the context of collective action. Ultimately, their perspectives challenge us to look at faculty as leaders for social change. Since then, others, including Allan (2003), Nelson and Watt (2004), and myself (Hart, 2005, 2007, in press), have looked at activism among academics and have explored successes and failures of faculty leaders who have collectively sought social change.

Grassroots leadership is often about motivating and inspiring change within a collective or a nonhierarchical organization. In many respects, this should come naturally to faculty who traditionally organize in collegiums (Birnbaum, 1988). Of course, it is not that simple—for if it were, all faculty would be engaged in this sort of leadership on campus. However, it does happen.

Examples of Operationalizing Grassroots Leadership

For faculty who are committed to social justice and social change, grassroots leadership is about operationalizing that commitment. The organizations at Nebraska and Arizona described above are collectives and they came together because of a common cause, equity issues for faculty women. The collectives started rather informally, over a lunch in a café, and from lunches of two faculty on each campus grew two groups that have been active on each campus for over 20 years. The need for the organizations came from the faculty themselves, and each year the faculty involved continue to redefine their strategies and agenda items. The organizations are organic; they do not rely on an administrative leader to convene the group or to provide topics for discussion. Ultimately, each group ebbs and flows based upon emergent issues, and participation ebbs and flows based upon individual faculty time and interest in particular agenda items. Their power comes from being self-defined and redefined and by not being beholden to administrative mandates. Their power comes even more so from each person's commitment to the purpose of the organization. The work does not fall on one individual, rather it is a group that has a common purpose, that can raise consciousness, propose policy change, and chip away at inequities and injustices.

This is not to suggest that a collective is mandatory for grassroots leadership and activism. Collectives, or social movements, do have a unique power and influence; however, grassroots leadership can also come from an individual. Again, it is about the organic nature of motivating and inspiring change. Some do this through their own scholarship. Others do this by engaging in service learning with their students. Still others do this by speaking up in meetings and critically challenging the status quo. These are all models of activism and of leadership. These activities are "radical enough." In fact, Debra Meyerson (2003) refers to these everyday leaders as *tempered radicals*. The lessons learned from her research parallel much of what I learned by studying the women faculty at Nebraska and Arizona and can serve to further inspire potential leaders, both radical and tempered. Ultimately, the purpose of grassroots leadership and activism is about contributing to social change—no matter how small or how great. For example, it may take 50 articles about the chilly climate for faculty women to convince an institution that it does exist. If the scholar who was going to write article number 50 decided that his or her commitment wasn't radical enough and thus opted to write about something else, people within the chilly climate institution may never believe there is a problem. Each grain of sand adds to the mountain. Put another way, an individual can and does make a difference solely or as part of a collective.

Examples of Facilitating Change

I want to return to the work of the FWC and AWF. There were missteps and recalcitrance that made change difficult. However, the leadership from these grassroots groups did result in real change for the Nebraska and Arizona universities. The first change that members from each group discussed is unique to collectives—eliminating isolation. The women faculty involved in the FWC and the AWF felt that their organization was successful because it provided a mechanism to bring together like-minded women from across campus who may otherwise work in isolation. The women involved were not just the faculty whose academic work focused on gender—but they were all interested in their experiences and in the experiences of other women faculty. Had it not been for the grassroots collectives, these women may never have come together for moral and professional support, which was an unintentional collateral benefit.

At the University of Nebraska, the efforts of the FWC resulted in other changes as well. For example, the FWC raised the "pill bill" with the Nebraska regents. Now, the university health insurance program covers the cost of contraception devices for all female beneficiaries. Another change fostered by the FWC is the student judicial process. All the students participate in one judicial process—there is no longer a separate process for athletes, Greek-affiliated students, and other student groups. This procedural change grew out of a highly publicized case of alleged domestic violence by a well-known football player. The FWC discovered that the football player had a separate, and perceptively unequal (i.e., outcomes were often less severe for athletes than for nonathletes who were involved in similar violations), judicial process. By talking directly to the football coach, contacting *Sports Illustrated*, and appearing on the nationally televised news program *48 Hours*, faculty in the FWC made the campus aware of the multiple disciplinary processes, and the university changed the system.

Similarly, the work of the women in the AWF resulted in positive climate changes on campus. The AWF conducted a salary study that resulted in a new procedure that eliminated gender-based salary inequities for faculty. While the money dried up for equity, it did make a difference for many faculty at that time. A subcommittee within the AWF proposed a policy to stop the tenure clock for childbirth and adoption. Through continued pressure from the committee, the university adopted the policy not once, but twice—faculty can stop the clock two times within one's tenure clock. The AWF also drafted an alternative duties policy for faculty who have a child, to be used in conjunction with or instead of a tenure clock stoppage that the university adopted.

The message here is that grassroots leadership resulted in change, change for social justice and gender equity. The methods used by each group varied, as described in the first section of this wo-manifesto, but it is not the method that is the focus. Rather the focus is to emphasize that grassroots leadership is both activism and leadership, and that change can be "radical" or "not radical enough." In the end, what is important is a common purpose and inspiration and motivation to make a difference.

Why So Few?

How many grassroots leaders and activists are there on our campuses? I believe there are some—as is evidenced by the women in the FWC and the AWF—who do identify as such. But I think if we took a census, the numbers who self-identify would be relatively small. Why is that? Why so few?

I believe that the numbers are small because of the following reasons:

- Activism and leadership are defined too narrowly by too many.
  Earlier, I discussed that there may be a concern that one is not radical enough. As a result, it is easy to dismiss one's very important contributions toward organizational and social change. Further complicating this idea of "radical enough" is the assumption that you must be radical to do this work. Certainly, there are radical activists engaged in this sort of leadership, but I believe the numbers are small, in part because the work is seen as radical. Radical activism has a stigma attached to it; this sort of activist is stereotyped as marginal and, thus, academics (particularly those who must rely on the reviews of others for their academic success) are reluctant to embrace this work.

  In addition, if one is not identified as a positional leader (e.g., president, dean, chair), one sometimes fails to see one's self (or others) as a leader. This is problematic. Leadership for social change is very much leadership and should be embraced as such. In fact, failing to broaden the definition of leadership to include the kinds of leadership described in this text only serves to devalue critical contributions to academe. In fact, I would argue that a traditional, top-down, hierarchical definition of leadership fortifies the perceived lack of leadership experiences of many women faculty and faculty of color. It is true that the numbers of women and people of color in academic leadership positions are scant, but that is only if we look at the traditional view of leadership. We need to reexamine who is a leader with a broader vision to see that while we may still have problems in terms of structural diversity in traditional leadership (and this concern should not be dismissed), we actually have a very diverse group of leaders in higher education who are making a difference.
- Grassroots activism and leadership seemingly lack tangible rewards.
  Faculty, particularly faculty at research institutions, know that the currency for promotion and tenure is scholarship. This message is not ambiguous. Further, grassroots activism and leadership tend to fit neatly into the service category of faculty work. Of research, teaching, and service, campus service is the least valued in terms of tenure and promotion (and external reputation). Even at institutions that are not as heavily focused on scholarly productivity, research still matters and

so does teaching—certainly more than service. This lack of rewards makes it difficult in a system with finite time to willingly engage in grassroots activism and service. I do think this is a problem (and one that activists and leaders should keep on their agendas). If anyone is going to change the faculty reward structure, it is faculty themselves. I'm not suggesting that we make research or teaching less valuable. What I am saying is that if we tell faculty they are being evaluated according to a 40-40-20 configuration (or whatever configuration faculty may have), then they should actually be evaluated according to that configuration.

In addition, the work that comprises activism and leadership is often scholarly service (Hart, Grogan, Litt, & Worthington, in press). The work generates new knowledge (e.g., campus climate studies, policy briefs) and shares knowledge (e.g., through professional development opportunities, workshops, conferences). Service is all too often lumped into a devalued category, further marginalizing the significant contributions faculty activists and leaders are making to the campus community and often to academe more broadly. Moreover, grassroots activism and leadership includes individual scholarship intended to result in social change. That scholarship fits much more easily into the work that "counts," namely, research, but like service, it is often considered less legitimate by reviewers (Stanley, 2007) and promotion and tenure committees than work that follows the scientific method or is not about social justice. This too is a problem that warrants the support of grassroots faculty activists and leaders. Just as leadership needs redefinition, I argue that scholarship needs to be redefined to include scholarly service and nonpositivist inquiry. This idea is not new. Ernest Boyer (1990) challenged us to think about scholarship in different ways. He urges the professoriate to include the scholarship of engagement, or scholarly service, as knowledge production and worthy of reward. More recently, Katie Hogan (2005) and Kelly Ward (2003) supported Boyer's call and reinforced the redefinition of scholarship. Without these changes, the rewards for grassroots activism and leadership seem to be minimal.

That said, let me return to a point I made at the beginning of my letter. Part of the reward of grassroots activism and leadership for social change is the intrinsic value of doing work that is personally important and interesting. Those engaged in social change efforts know that part of the benefit is in doing the right thing, the thing that one believes in and espouses. For those interested in social change and equity work, grassroots activism and leadership is a natural part of life. That part of life is an end to itself. Don't get me wrong, tenure, promotion, and publication all have advantages. But should they come completely at the expense of doing what someone believes in, as a complement to one's institutionally and professionally defined job?

- Grassroots activism and leadership can be risky.
  I have said more than once in this letter that grassroots activism and leadership can be risky. It is because of the risk involved, the potential risk to one's academic career, that some activists and leaders may opt out completely or defer their involvement until they receive tenure. The women in the AWF were professionalized activists who chose purposeful strategies to appear less radical and more in line with traditional faculty roles. The women in the FWC used slightly different strategies, but the idea of risk was never completely off their radar. It is critical for each potential grassroots leader to recognize the range of risk within activism and remember that "not radical enough" is activism too.

- Faculty work has become more national and international in scope.
  Gone are the days when most faculty retire at the institution of their first academic position. Instead, faculty are nomads. Part of that movement is because of the globalization of higher education and the push for faculty to have an impact on the national and international arenas. The focus of faculty work has become predominantly focused on scholarship, and the value of service to one's local academic community continues to diminish, particularly in terms of the faculty reward structure. External professional forces (and internal institutional forces in terms of the currency of grant-person-ship and other forms of scholarship) have contributed to a nationally and internationally concerned professoriate. Further, those faculty not on the tenure track who desire a tenure-stream position are often hard pressed to find a position at the home of their nontenure-track line, again adding to the mobility and outward focus of so many faculty.

    However, grassroots leaders and activists who may have a thriving national and international network often also have a deep commitment to their home campuses. For example, the women faculty in the

FWC and the AWF were engaged in deliberate ways to improve the quality of life at the University of Nebraska and the University of Arizona. These academics were not only interested in their own scholarly agendas, but they were also very much interested in social change and equity locally. In fact, it seems to make sense that grassroots leaders and activists would be less likely to leave their institutions for other colleges and universities because of their levels of stewardship and involvement. These faculty will likely remain at their institutions over time, particularly if their activist work is recognized. Too often we see faculty paying a "loyalty tax" to their institutions. Those most invested and involved in their institutional communities are paid less (most often because of salary compression) and get little reward, formally or informally, for trying to improve the climate. While economics may make it difficult to eliminate the inequities of compression (this is not to suggest that compression should be ignored, however), less economically driven rewards can and should be considered for those faculty who are grassroots activists and leaders.

Advice for Grassroots Leaders and Activists

Grassroots leaders and activists most often want to "rock the boat, and . . . stay in it" (Meyerson, 2003, p. xi). That is exactly what the women faculty in the FWC and the AWF have done. What follows are some words of wisdom that I hope will encourage aspiring and current leaders and activists to work for social justice and change.

- Little efforts can mean a lot.
  Never take for granted the random acts of kindness that can make a difference. It is not always necessary to threaten the status quo explicitly—this is how these leaders manage to stay in the boat. For example, in meetings you can reinforce the points of view of others who are being silenced or marginalized. You can correct assumptions and stereotypes. You can confront discriminatory or exclusive language of colleagues and students.
- Within a collective, you have allies.
  Grassroots leaders and activists can act in isolation. However, finding like-minded individuals to create alternative networks can mitigate

isolation and the burden of blazing the trail alone. The women in the
FWC and the AWF relied on the collective for support. At the core
of their networks was their passion for gender equity. The women
came from different disciplines and fields, and in the case of the AWF,
many of the women did not consider themselves feminist. Yet despite
their differences, a common good brought them together to work
toward social change. These activist networks created a social movement, minimizing the risk of being singled out for making waves.

- Consider the relationship you want to have with the college or university administration.
Sometimes, this decision is easily made—if the administration is re-
calcitrant about the issues germane to you, a less formally sanctioned
collective is likely the best way to organize. However, if the administration seems willing to work with you on the issues, an organization
that is recognized or sanctioned by the university may be the most
effective way to start your organization. Often, the extent to which
the administration embraces certain social change efforts is difficult
to ascertain. When this is the case, grassroots leaders and activists
should weigh the benefits of an institutionally unsanctioned versus
sanctioned collective.

The FWC was a more fluid and less formal organization. The
FWC membership was predominantly off the radar screen of university administration. While annually one or two faculty managed the
organization, they acted only to call meetings when issues were
brought to their attention. Further, they were not the only members
who could call meetings. Any woman faculty member at the University of Nebraska could e-mail the list of women faculty to call for a
meeting or an online discussion. Members moved in and out of the
collective, depending upon whether the issue of the moment was of
particular concern. There were no monetary resources for the FWC,
and by and large, the group was not sanctioned by the university.
This lack of sanctioning meant that the FWC could more easily work
behind the scenes, establishing relationships with the press, organizing petitions, and calling legislators to raise critical issues. As a collective, these leaders had the freedom to define the organization's agenda
and to modify it quickly and easily. However, because they were unsanctioned, sometimes it was difficult to find allies in the formal university structure. As leaders and activists, they could be more easily

dismissed as on the fringe and as troublemakers. Moreover, the lack of financial resources made it difficult to do everything the leaders envisioned.

The AWF was a much more formal organization, with a mission statement, charter, dues for membership, and chain of command. This structure was the source of a certain degree of legitimacy in the eyes of others at the University of Arizona. This degree of legitimacy also provided easier access to resources. The organization was grassroots, though, and emerged through the work of faculty and was not externally mandated by university administrators; nor did the organization receive institutional funding, allowing for a certain degree of flexibility in how monetary resources (i.e., organizational dues) were allocated. Yet, the AWF, because of its sanctioned status, did run the risk of co-optation by the university administration. The lure of complacency and conformity to the will of the administration, including never-met promises to consider policy change, can be compelling. But, as Meyerson (2003) suggested, mindfulness about the potential pitfalls that may compromise change in any sort of organization, whether unsanctioned or sanctioned, can go a long way to avoid them.

- Leverage small wins (Meyerson, 2003).
  Mole hills eventually do become mountains. Remember, change takes time, but it can and does happen. While many of us want to see revolutionary change, it rarely happens overnight. But each little success moves us one step closer to realizing the ultimate goal. By leveraging the small wins, each subsequent victory seems much more attainable, not only to the leaders and activists but even to the naysayers.
- Never underestimate your ability to create change and inspire others. Talking with a colleague over coffee or lunch can lead to great things. Such was the case for the FWC and the AWF. Two women, one at the University of Nebraska, and the other at the University of Arizona, called upon two other colleagues to talk about the status of women faculty on their campuses. These informal meetings became the start of two grassroots activist leadership organizations. Soon these pairs of women became collectives, creating agendas and strategizing to improve the campus climate for other faculty women. What began

as conversations among colleagues over cups of coffee grew into two successful networks of leaders.

The emergence of the FWC and the AWF led to changes in the institutions; new policies were established and new networks were created. While these changes were not revolutionary, they mattered to the faculty involved and to each institution. However, it is important to mention that changes on a smaller scale matter too. Two other points made above highlight the power of what may seem small and less significant. I reiterate the consequence of the seemingly inconsequential.

When I was a doctoral student, I volunteered as part of a class project with the AWF. The president of the organization was an English professor who was passionate about improving the climate for women at the University of Arizona. I was moved by her indefatigable energy as an activist, leader, and scholar. She motivated me to learn more about grassroots leadership and activism and to become an activist and leader myself. Her inspiration sparked a new generation of faculty activists. What seemed like an insignificant meeting and an insignificant class assignment has become central to my research agenda and to who I am personally and politically as a scholar.

A Final Thought

Grassroots activism and leadership is not for everyone. However, I do believe there are many activists and leaders in the academy engaged in this work for social justice, and there are many more who aspire to see social change within the academy. These leaders have so much to offer students, the colleges, and universities they work for, and themselves. Currently, the risks seem high and the rewards seem low. I challenge all activists within the academy, including activist administrators, to consider how the risks and rewards might be redefined, and do it—just as I hope that I have done in trying to redefine leadership and activism. Administrators can do a great deal to support grassroots activists and leaders, but the grassroots nature of this leadership means that it is organic and must come from the faculty (or whoever is the core of the collective or individual effort). This is to say that administrators should not form groups to be grassroots collectives, as that is the very antithesis of grassroots. Rather, administrators should foster an environment that allows for these groups to emerge, which may include more formal advocacy groups that can complement the activities of grassroots leaders and activists (e.g., campus committees on the status of women or diversity planning groups).

I embrace Jennifer Baumgardner and Amy Richards's (2005) definition of activism, which is that activism is a process where one (as an individual) or many (as an organized collective) expresses "values with the goal of making the world more just" (p. xix). And like Baumgardner and Richards, the faculty involved in the FWC and the AWF used feminism as the guiding value system their strategies emerged from. Feminism is not the only guiding value system, but it is one of many. Whatever value system guides social justice for you, I hope that this letter helps you to see that grassroots activism and leadership are invaluable processes in trying to eliminate inequity. In most cases, such activism and leadership are messy, and as such, they allow for myriad forms in myriad locations, including the academy.

In activist solidarity,

Jeni

References

Allan, E. J. (2003). Constructing women's status: Policy discourses of university women's commission reports. *Harvard Educational Review, 73*(1), 44–72.

Astin, H. S., & Leland, C. (1991). *Women of vision, women of influence: A cross-generational study of leaders and social change.* San Francisco: Jossey-Bass.

Baumgardner, J., & Richards, A. (2005). *Grassroots: A field guide for feminist activism.* New York: Farrar, Straus, and Giroux.

Birnbaum, R. (1988). *How colleges work: The cybernetics of academic organization and leadership.* San Francisco: Jossey-Bass.

Boyer, E. L. (1990). *Scholarship reconsidered: Priorities of the professoriate.* Princeton, NJ: Carnegie Foundation for the Advancement of Teaching.

Hart, J. (2005, Summer). Activism among feminist academics: Professionalized activism and activist professionals. *Advancing Women in Leadership Online Journal.* Retrieved June 7, 2005, from http://www.advancingwomen.com/awl/social_justice1/Hart.html

Hart, J. (2007). Creating networks as an activist strategy: Differing approaches among academic feminist organizations. *Journal of the Professoriate, 2*(1), 33–52.

Hart, J. (in press). Mobilization among women academics: The interplay between feminism and professionalization. *National Women's Studies Association (NWSA) Journal.*

Hart, J., Grogan, M., Litt, J., & Worthington, R. (in press). Institutional diversity work as intellectual work. In W. Brown-Glaude (Ed.), *Reconstructing the academy: Faculty take the lead.* New Brunswick, NJ: Rutgers University Press.

Hogan, K. (2005). Superservicable feminism. *Minnesota Review, 63/64,* 112–128.

Kezar, A. J., Carducci, R., & Contreras-McGavin, M. (2006). Rethinking the "L" word in higher education: The revolution of research on leadership. *ASHE-ERIC Higher Education Report, 31*(6). San Francisco: Jossey-Bass

Meyerson, D. E. (2003). *Tempered radicals: How everyday leaders inspire change at work.* Boston: Harvard Business School Press.

Nelson, C., & Watt, S. (2004). *Office hours: Activism and change in the academy.* New York: Routledge.

Stanley, C. A. (2007). When counter narratives meet master narratives in the journal editorial-review process. *Educational Researcher, 36*(1), 14–24.

Ward, K. (2003). Faculty service roles and the scholarship of engagement. *ASHE-ERIC Higher Education Report, 29*(5). San Francisco: Wiley.

9

CHANGING OF THE GUARD IN COMMUNITY COLLEGES
The Role of Leadership Development

Pamela Eddy

C hange is underfoot in community colleges. Community colleges are relative newcomers to the mix of higher education institutions, yet currently represent 45% of all colleges and universities and educate almost half of American college students (National Center for Education Statistics [NCES], 2005). A portrait of current community college presidents shows that 45% are over 61 years old (American Council on Education [ACE], 2007) and a 2001 report indicated that 80% of sitting presidents are expected to retire in the next 10 years (Shults, 2001). The need exists to train replacements for these retiring leaders. The potential need for filling hundreds of presidential openings raises concern regarding succession planning but also provides a context for viewing the possibilities available with the shifting of community college leadership. Undeniably, community colleges are seen as more women friendly and have the largest number of women at their helm, with women presidents filling 29% of the positions. Likewise, community colleges provide more opportunities for minorities to reach the presidential office, with 14% representing presidents of color. Presidential and other leadership openings may provide even more opportunities for women and leaders of color to advance.

In addition, community colleges are at the nexus of change. Pressing issues include changing student demographics, heightening needs for remedial education, technology demands on budgeting and programming decisions, faculty turnover, and shifts in programming emphasis, including the introduction of the community college baccalaureate. Paralleling these trends on community college campuses are advances in leadership theory that demand different thinking about development of current and potential community college leaders. Traditional development practices no longer meet the demands required of new leaders and must be revised.

In this chapter, potential leaders will obtain an overview of current leadership development opportunities in the community college sector. In addition, I offer advice for rethinking current programs and creating new ones to better align leadership research with training opportunities. This chapter begins with a portrait of community college leadership development historically. Next, the chapter provides a review of current leadership development options. These options include not only university-based programming but also professional organization leadership development institutes. Readers in charge of creating and delivering training and those seeking training can gain information regarding the various learning options available. Those in charge of training can learn new ideas, addressing some of the critiques of current program offerings. Finally, I outline important issues to consider in planning the future of community college leadership development. Viewing the chapter information from the vantage point of a user of development services and a provider of training allows for a more complete analysis, ultimately providing a blueprint for better programming.

Shifting Portrait of Community College Leaders

In 1960 there were 590 2-year colleges; the number of these institutions grew to 1,683 in 2004—an increase of 185% (NCES, 2005). Comparatively, 4-year institutions grew by less than half this rate (NCES, 2005). Coupled with this expansive growth in the community college sector was a need to lead these institutions. Early leaders often came from the public school sector since many of the early 2-year colleges were extensions of the public school system. The explosive growth of community colleges in the 1960s showcased a time of development of formal programs to educate those in higher education administration (Goodchild, 1991). University-based programs specifically targeting community college leadership development emerged. In 1968 the W. K. Kellogg Foundation funded the American Association of Junior Colleges Clearinghouse on Community Services (Shaw, 1969); one of the functions of the forum was to provide short-term institutes on community service leadership, conferences, and workshops. The foundation also supported graduate-level community college leadership programs in the 1960s and 1970s, some of these programs still exist today albeit with several iterations since their inception (Amey, 2006). A few years ago the Kellogg Foundation provided support for the American Association of Community Colleges (AACC) Leading Forward initiative (Ottenritter, 2004). The purpose of this initiative was to conduct research, including summits, to address the leadership issues facing community colleges. Development opportunities and training for community college leaders, however, have changed little over the past 40 years.

Almost half of all community colleges are publicly controlled with an overall student enrollment average of 10,957, whereas privately controlled 2-year colleges almost equal in number have an average of only 705 students (Hardy & Katsinas, 2007). Sixty-four percent of these public institutions are located in rural areas (average number of students 5,812), whereas 23% are in suburban locations (average number of students 15,528), and 14% are in urban centers (average number of students 28,401; Hardy & Katsinas). These contextual differences underscore that one form of development does not fit all community college needs.

The range of public community colleges includes some 553 presidents leading rural institutions, 195 at the helm of suburban institutions, and 112 leading in urban settings for a total of 860 public 2-year college presidents. These leaders have primarily ascended to their positions via previous presidencies (26%), from chief academic affairs officer posts (34%) or from senior executive positions (28%; ACE, 2007). With almost 90% of community college presidents coming from the senior ranks of leadership, it is important to understand the impact of the career pathway on the creation of learning opportunities for future leader development.

Recent changes in the Carnegie Classification System (Carnegie Foundation for the Advancement of Teaching, 2007) resulted in a more detailed format of differentiation among community colleges. Community colleges now have distinct categories based on location (rural, suburban, urban) and size (small, medium, large), as well as control (public or private; Carnegie Foundation for the Advancement of Teaching). The ability to disaggregate information on 2-year colleges underscores the impact of institutional contexts on leading and hence what is required to develop leaders for various types of institutions. The needs and demands of a large urban-based 2-year college are markedly different from those of a small rural campus, resulting in a differing array of strengths and experiences required in leaders for working in each location. Thus, the development of leaders for the various institutional types may need to focus on different approaches and targeted recruitment efforts (Leist, 2007). These basic facts and trends are presented to help the reader understand the leadership development needs within this unique sector.

To best appreciate the current state of development training and its influence on careers, it is important to consider the roots of research regarding community college leadership and the influences of shifts in leadership theory over time. Twombly (1995) reviewed four eras of community college leadership that complement the historical organizational development of generations of community colleges outlined by Tillery and Deegan (1985). She charted the following: 1900–1930s when the "great man" theory dominated; the 1940s–1950s in which leaders sought to become independent from secondary schools and forge an identity of their own; 1960s–1970s in which the present-day version of the community college was born with strong, dominant leadership that was necessary during those pioneering days; and the 1980s–1990s where attention to resource issues was more necessary (Twombly), and models from business began to be used that emphasized efficiency and strategic planning (Rowley & Sherman, 2001). The most recent decade of community college leadership may be categorized by adaptive leadership, with a focus on leaders as learners (Amey, 2005; Heifetz, 1998; Kezar, Carducci, & Contreras-McGavin, 2006).

The context for the leaders of community colleges throughout the eras was influenced by popular leadership theories of the day. Bensimon, Neumann, and Birnbaum (1989) completed a comprehensive exploration of the theories and models of leadership within higher education. These authors classified the theories into the following six categories: trait theories, power and influence theories, behavioral theories, contingency theories, cultural and symbolic theories, and cognitive theories. Even though these classifications parallel the eras of community college leadership, it does not imply that the leadership theories pertain solely to each of the five eras noted above. Rather, many of the leadership approaches are still in place today in leadership development practices.

Preparation of the leaders of the future requires consideration of advances in leadership research. Kezar et al. (2006) expanded Bensimon et al.'s

(1989) topography to include the latest theories on leadership. Some of their examples of revolutionary concepts extend previous leadership theories and apply new paradigms. The authors included in their emerging list of new leadership concepts "ethics and spirituality, collaboration and partnering, empowerment, social change, emotions, globalization, entrepreneurialism, and accountability" (Kezar et al., p. 71). Underlying several of these concepts is the ability to deal with change (Linsky & Heifetz, 2002) and the capacity to operate from a multiple frame perspective that emphasizes the relationships inherent in the politics of leading and the managing of meaning to aid in sense making for the organization (Bolman & Deal, 2006; Eckel & Kezar, 2003; Eddy, 2003; Fairhurst & Sarr, 1996; Weick, 1995). Better understanding how community college leaders learn can help in the development of future leaders and provide individuals with an enhanced understanding of their own leadership.

Leadership Development Programming

In recognition of the anticipated turnover in community college leaders, the AACC established its Leading Forward initiative to help plan for the expected leadership demands (Ottenritter, 2004). The AACC established a set of competencies to allow for conversation about desirable traits and requirements necessary to lead the modern-day 2-year college (AACC, 2005). While this cataloging harkens to Vaughan's (1986) earlier work on traits required for the successful president, the current listing moves beyond a mere checklist of required attributes and provides a more holistic approach to leadership. In fact, a key assumption underlying the created competencies listing is that leadership can be learned and that a variety of means can be used during the development process, which is assumed to be a lifelong endeavor. The six leadership competencies developed by AACC include organizational strategies, resource management, communication, collaboration, community college advocacy, and professionalism (AACC, 2005). Each factor contains a listing of potential illustrations of acquisition of these competencies—in effect offering potential leaders with a template to judge how they could acquire these attributes and noting areas of skill and experiential deficiency. The efforts of the AACC, however, represent a passive approach to changing practice in the development of future leaders. Those responsible for community college leadership development can become more proactive and use the AACC competencies as a road map to design programs.

Since community college leaders emerge via a variety of routes (Amey, VanDerLinden, & Brown, 2002), it is important to view leadership development holistically. Indeed, 38% of current community college presidents have never been a faculty member and 67% have been employed outside of higher education for some portion of their careers (ACE, 2007). Thus, to fully understand the development process, it is critical to consider the community college context as one that provides leadership development through on-the-job training via experiential learning and is influenced by more than an academic culture.

Beyond this experience-based time, formal leadership development programs exist. These programs, however, are primarily geared toward identified presidential aspirants versus the development of leaders throughout the institution. Hull and Keim (2007) reported on the type of development opportunities sitting community college presidents engaged in or had plans for participation. Three specific programs are reviewed here: the AACC Presidents Academy and Future Leaders Academy, the Chair Academy, and the League for Innovation in the Community College's development training. The Chair Academy, while targeting incoming department chairs, may be the only training leaders at smaller or resource-pressed institutions ever receive. Finally, doctoral programs with a focus on community college administration provide another formalized way to educate future leaders. Hull and Keim found that the Chair Academy had the highest levels of participation by current presidents at 23.8%, with the AACC training following at 19.9%, and the training offered by the League at 14%. Individuals may have participated in more than one form of training, thus potentially overstating the total level of training by leaders. A full 69% of the study's respondents, however, felt that more development was needed but cited budgetary constraints as a limiting factor for increased involvement in these institutes by their campus members.

In general, the current major development programs in place for aspiring and new community college leaders come up short. The majority of the agendas of these developmental opportunities focus on skill acquisition, which although an important consideration for leaders, does not prepare individuals for the larger demands of becoming visionary leaders of these complex organizations. The demand for community colleges to be responsive institutions and all things for community members is no longer tenable

(Vaughan, 2005). Thus, leaders need to make tough, ethical choices regarding access, programming, faculty assignments, and resource decisions while still supporting the mission of their cultural-bound institutions.

In considering the training of community colleges leaders, it is important to keep in mind that a key platform for community colleges is diversity—of students, faculty, and leaders. As noted, community colleges have more diverse presidential leadership, in part because of the unique training opportunities that focus on aspiring women leaders and leaders of color. However, even these gains have slowed in recent times. A comparison of women leading community colleges between 2006 and 2001 shows only a 2% gain, whereas for the same time period leaders of color acquired a mere 1% more presidential positions. Thus, developing a diverse cadre to lead community colleges still requires attention given the stagnant growth in recent years of the number of women and leaders of color obtaining presidencies.

AACC

The AACC formed its Leading Forward initiative as a result of a 2001 mission review and its concern regarding the pending shortage of leaders. Leadership development was specifically added as a strategic action area and goal. One manifestation of this shift resulted in a series of summits to determine ways to improve the leadership pipeline and to develop consensus over critical leadership attributes (Ottenritter, 2004). These sessions provided the basis for the development of the leadership competencies listed on page 189. AACC offers several opportunities for skills acquisition for those interested in seeking a presidency, those in the early days of being the chief executive officer, and those seeking continuing professional development. Several of these initiatives are outlined in the following paragraphs. (See the AACC Web site under events for upcoming workshop offerings, http://www.aacc.nche.edu).

A preconference workshop at the annual AACC conference provides particular focus on new presidents. The one-and-a-half-day seminar, The New CEO Institute: Hit the Ground Leading, includes seasoned and new leaders' reviewing issues pertinent during those first years on the job. Common topics include working with the board of trustees, figuring out the culture of the institution, technology issues, and recounting lessons learned by more seasoned presidents. Hearing about working with people within the existing culture of an institution is a critical step in providing the type of leadership training required for the future. However, since this topic is covered in only a portion of the short time individuals have during the workshop, just a brief exposure to cultural theories and their application are offered.

A number of networking opportunities are built into the group's time. Other shorter preconference workshops target those aspiring to a presidency. Topics of recent sessions covered interviewing simulations for the potential applications, and panel discussions covering insights for those contemplating an upward move. The focus on the skills required to navigate the job interview may allow individuals to be successful in obtaining a position, but time is not devoted to the larger issues of how to function within the position. Individuals new to the job often must wait until they are in a position to attend training, leaving them to fend for themselves through their early days in a presidency.

The AACC Presidents Academy is open to CEOs from member institutions. The membership-only requirement for attending may limit participation of newly minted presidents whose institutions do not belong to AACC or are from resource-poor colleges. Sessions are held in the summer over a 5-day period. Typically these sessions include sharing of best practices on issues critical to presidents. Topics may include navigation with the board of trustees, the role of the spouse, communication tips, managing conflict, politics, and mechanisms to maintain balance. Key to these learning opportunities is the chance to put theory and lessons to practice through the use of case studies and exercises. This is particularly important for more recent presidents as they do not always have direct experience with the situation being reviewed, and the case examples allow them to contextualize the information.

Similar in format to the Presidents Academy is the Future Leaders Institute. This 5-day leadership seminar spotlights midlevel community college leaders contemplating a move up the career ladder. Generally, participants are those currently in deans' positions or higher. While topics similar to those found in the Presidents Academy are covered, the institute also includes assessment of leadership styles and reflection on guiding ethics and approaches to change. Many of the sessions focus on issues central to relationship building and working with a variety of people. These topics represent moves in the right direction for leadership development with their focus on ethics, people, and change. In general, however, these sessions are still taught using a classical paradigm with a focus on a positivist perspective, which assumes that knowledge is based on scientific tests and that a truth may be discovered, versus using an interpretative symbolic lens, which assumes social construction of reality, or a postmodern perspective, that rejects a single representation of issues and critiques assumed structures (Hatch & Cunliffe, 2006). The latter approaches call for the creation of multiple interpretations that value a variety of institutional voices. A reliance on a classical paradigm limits the ability of leaders to understand the broader cultures in operation at the college and, as a result, detaches leaders from the diverse populations they serve and lead.

The Chair Academy

The Chair Academy started at the Maricopa Community Colleges in Phoenix, Arizona, in 1992. The impetus for this professional development program evolved from the lack of training available for first-line leaders at a community college, namely department chairs. Faculty members promoted to lead the department generally do so without the benefit of any formal training or exposure to leadership theory or practice. The creation of the Chair Academy sought to remedy this situation by focusing on those mid-level leaders new to the position. Often, these first-time leaders may not have intentions of seeking any further promotions (Wolverton & Gonzales, 2000), thus, this training may be the only formal development they receive. Almost two-thirds of current presidents got their start as faculty members, generally following a traditional pathway to their presidency including the requisite stop at department chair. A key element in the formation of the program was to focus on tying in experiential learning and application of learned leadership concepts to practice. For some, this training is their first exposure to a systemic study of leadership. Additionally, the potential for participants to gain credits from attendance at the academy meets the needs of midlevel administrators also seeking advanced credentials through doctoral programs.

The structure of the program begins with a 5-day initial session and is capped a year later with another 5-day session. The first week of training involves the creation of an individual professional development plan, allowing each person an opportunity to tailor his or her practicum experience and mentoring relationship to best suit the person's needs. Seminar topics include the complex role of the organizational leader, leading and managing effective work teams, strategic planning and scenario thinking, managing conflict productively and engaging in crucial conversations, and leading and learning. Incorporated into the week are a series of leadership assessments in which surveys are administered and tallied that place individuals in particular leadership quadrants. The use of instruments to access leadership styles may be limiting because of an inherent assumption that there is a "correct" style one should aspire to. The shortcomings of these assessment instruments, however, may be partially overcome with the focus on understanding the complexity of leadership and the links between leading and learning. Given that this training is often the first opportunity for individuals to study leadership and obtain exposure to critical thinking on current theories, it can provide a critical linchpin in addressing changes in leadership development in community colleges.

The first 5-day session of the academy focuses on assessing skills and developing individual plans to address any deficits apparent from participant results of these leadership surveys. In the interim between the first 5-day seminar and the second, a year-long practicum allows participants an opportunity to put to practice the lessons learned. Participants work on their individualized learning plan with the oversight of an assigned mentor. The use of leadership survey instruments allows participants to assess their initial profile and then to evaluate their growth at the conclusion of the year-long program. The assumption inherent in this training approach is that deficits are evident and can be "fixed" through work by the participants. This philosophical approach may result in dissuading some potential leaders as they do not conform to expected patterns of the type of leadership supported by the assessment instruments, which in some cases continue to support dated concepts of what it means to lead.

Mentors are available for support and guidance, and an electronic system connects participants not only to mentors but to one another as well. Reflective journaling allows participants an opportunity to document their growth over the year but also instills the practice of reflection as a leadership skill (Amey, 2005). This aspect of the program supports important qualities needed in leaders of the future, in particular since it allows a focus for the participants on developing their own ethical lens of leading and provides a means to better understand the organizational cultures in which they will lead. The Chair Academy provides students with a way to obtain up to nine graduate credits to apply to a degree program. This feature allows participants to augment graduate work with a concentration in leadership studies and provides an incentive for others to begin a graduate program.

The leadership academies are hosted at various locations across the United States and to a limited extent internationally. The availability of multiple hosting locales increases the access to development opportunities for individuals from smaller colleges or from institutions with more limited resources. Since the position of department chair is often the first step in a career path toward a presidency, training at this midcareer level allows for a wider participation of aspiring and potential leaders for the future. The feature of increased access, in terms of training offerings and in members' doing frontline leadership, underscores the importance of the Chair Academy in addressing training demands. Rethinking how best to leverage these positive aspects of training to include expanded definitions of leadership, work on self-assessment for ethical development, and opportunities for increasing cultural competency would aid participants as they prepare for leading the community colleges of the future.

League for Innovation in the Community College

The League for Innovation in the Community College—hereafter referred to as the League—was founded in 1968 to provide guidance to the fast-growing community college sector. In particular, at its inception the League developed templates for curriculum and instruction for emerging graduate programs focused on community college leadership development. It also created a 400-page manual to help guide founding colleges with operational procedures (League, 2007). One of the purposes of the League is to develop leaders for community colleges; several programs support this goal.

The Executive Leadership Institute focuses on preparing senior-level administrators for advancement to a presidency. Key elements in this program include review of the application process and tips for interviewing. An assessment is provided to help participants determine which type of institution and presidential role is the best fit for them. Important aspects of the job are reviewed, including working with the board, fund-raising, and determining leadership preferences—both as the internal leader and the representative for the college—dealing and planning for strategic change, and review of national trends. A mock interview is also provided. Legal and ethical concerns are also covered. As with the AACC training, much of the focus of the

League training is on skills to obtain a presidency and tools to determine a match between the aspiring president and an institution. The League boasts that since 1988, 43% of its participants have been successful in obtaining a presidential position.

As evidenced in other leadership development trainings, the focus on learning about yourself as a leader and a learner are important foundational steps for an individual but may not provide enough background regarding the larger issues of leadership theory required in working within complex 2-year college systems. For instance, even though it is important to know how you might fit in an institution, more central is knowing how to work within the cultures of the institution. The ability to align with the existing campus culture (Kezar et al., 2006) and to aid in meaning making for others (Eddy, 2003; Weick, 1995) can enhance success.

The League's specialized program, Expanding Leadership Diversity in the Community College, helps prepare midlevel administrators from urban institutions for promotion to upper-level positions. It is important to focus on increasing diversity in the leadership ranks because community colleges provide the most diverse student body of all institutional types (37% of community college students are students of color compared to only 27% at 4-year public universities; NCES, 2005). The intentions of this program focus on increasing the number of leaders of color at community colleges, which is critical given that the number of leaders of color at 2-year colleges increased by only 5% in 20 years. Although the program ended in 1999, the training format it offered to up-and-coming minority administrators and urban educators followed an outline similar to that of the Executive Leadership Institute. Participants were paired with a mentor, underwent leadership assessments, developed an individualized development plan, and attended skills-based seminars. Additionally, participants worked on a community issues project using a problem-based learning strategy. Participants wrote a report on how they would address one of the critical issues identified and how they would do so in a collaborative fashion. Finally, an internship experience allowed participants an opportunity to experience a different institutional context and to practice some of the skills they were acquiring in the program. In the absence of this program, current minority leaders are encouraged to apply to the Executive Leadership Institute. The demise of this specialized program, however, does not negate the problem of the lack of minority leaders in community colleges.

The League, in partnership with the American Association of Women in Community Colleges and the Maricopa Community Colleges, also sponsors the National Institute for Leadership Development for women leaders. This program has prepared over 4,000 women for leadership positions in community colleges (League, 2007). What is not known, however, is why fewer women have acquired larger percentages of community college presidencies in the last decade. Is the lack of larger representation by women at the helm of 2-year colleges because of the glass ceiling or because of women's opting out in the pipeline? Either reason requires further investigation to better understand how to work on equity in leadership.

This program focuses on giving participants a better understanding of their identity, their leadership skills acquisition, identification of leadership and community college issues, and the development of personal confidence. The vehicle for application of the training opportunities is the creation of a pragmatic project pertinent to the participant's home institution. The problem-based focus of the long-term project allows for an opportunity to practice skills introduced during the training session. A mentor is assigned to help oversee the project and to offer advice. Taking an active role in a campus-based project gives the women participating an opportunity to experience the influence of the campus culture on planning and change; however, even though the institute provides great networking exposure, it offers little to create a foundation to think more broadly about current leadership theory. In particular, knowing more about multiframed leadership, using expanded paradigms to better understand multiple voices inherent in organizations, and managing relationships and campus understanding are key to leaders' success.

University-Based Programs

Some of the first university-based programs were supported by the W. K. Kellogg Foundation in the 1960s. Today 70% of current community college presidents have doctorates in education or higher education (ACE, 2007), making university programs an important site for training leaders. Several programs are specifically designed for community college leadership. A study funded by the American Association of Community Colleges sought to investigate how "community college leadership programs are meeting current challenges and how their approaches differ from those of the Kellogg junior college leadership programs of the 1960s" (Amey, 2006, p. 1). Modern-day program characteristics include the following: "accessible, low cost, high quality, tailored for working professionals, provide mentoring opportunities, and allow for personal reflection and assessment" (p. 1). In general, the impetus for the development of university-based programs takes one of three formats. One model relies on a champion, generally a university faculty member, who sees a need and aids in the development of a program. Another model builds on a nondegree program that evolves into a degree program. Finally, another model showcases a partnership involving university faculty, community college presidents, and state community college association commitment.

The *Breaking Tradition* (Amey, 2006) report investigated six university-based leadership development programs. The site programs often originated as pilots, typically with a champion, either an individual or small group, lobbying for their development. The degree-based programs target mid- to upper-level administrations and use a cohort model for course delivery. A small cadre of faculty were the linchpins in the program operations and thus were the gatekeepers of the curriculum offered. These university-based faculty designed the program curriculum either in consultation with community college leaders or from the program director's personal experience or interaction with community college leaders in the state (Amey). Three of the programs offer a particular academic focus on diversity that complements the diverse demographics of their location. The other three sites focus attention to increase diversity within their programs and include curricular foci on diversity topics. A clear community college leadership focus was evident.

Because these programs are relatively new, long-term success and placement rates are unknown. A critical issue is the sustainability of the programs, considering the labor-intensive nature of their operations. Larger cohorts, the dependence on interpersonal relationships among key faculty and community college members, and the role of resources are all critical factors in long-term sustainability. Challenges facing program viability are turnovers in university personnel, shifts in community college personnel, and loss of program champions. While the analysis only reported on a small number of university programs, the elements of concern revealed in the study can apply to other programs that offer flexibility for community college administrators seeking an advanced degree.

Not all university programs are as focused on preparing community college leaders as the ones reviewed in Amey's (2006) research. A review of higher education doctoral programs in general, however, indicated that most program curricula have changed little over time. Programs that offer a doctorate of education, often those most available at regional institutions and in reach of more community college administrators, have more core required courses and a skills-based focus with topics including organizational theory, history of higher education, higher education law and finance, and policy (Eddy & Rao, 2008).

Despite increased theorizing about leadership and the press of issues on community colleges, little has changed in the ways leaders have been trained over time. Leadership development in community colleges is primarily focused on skills acquisition, interviewing strategies to obtain a presidency, and networking in the profession. Innovative and flexible programming, such as the university-based options highlighted in Amey (2006), may provide a model for program options. The risk inherent in the focus on a champion for the program initiation and design, however, is that training may become too narrowly focused and faculty may burn out.

Planning for the Future

Leadership development for community college leaders needs to address several key issues concurrently. First, traditional training forums with a primary focus on skills acquisition are no longer sufficient to prepare leaders. In addition to the requisite ability to understand college finance, curriculum development, and legal issues, leaders need to appreciate the organizational cultures of their institutions and their role in constructing meaning for campus members. A need exists to develop the cultural competency of community college leaders to allow for intentionality by leaders in putting cultural knowledge into play in leading the institution. How leaders talk about changes facing their campuses provides a key in getting buy in from the various constituencies of the college to requested strategic initiatives (Fairhurst & Sarr, 1996). When leaders understand the culture of the college, they can more readily frame the vision for the future and outline the steps to reach institutional goals.

Second, training and development programming needs to recognize the diversity of settings present in the community college sector. Community colleges are not a homogenous group. The colleges themselves range in size from less than 1,000 students to well over 25,000 students, from rural to suburban to urban locales, from student bodies primarily interested in trans-fer or vocational training, and from poor to rich districts.

Next, college administrators need to consider how succession planning can aid in preparing campuses for the anticipated changeover in leaders. Planning ahead and providing training along the career pathway creates smoother transitions. Furthermore, advanced planning allows campus mem-bers a chance to contemplate advancement opportunities. Oftentimes, indi-viduals do not consider themselves as potential candidates for upper-level positions until someone taps them or suggests the option to them (Eddy, 2007).

Finally, future development training needs to value different means of learning about leading. Preparation as lifelong learners confronts the need of leaders to constantly address the changing pressures facing higher education. Additionally, leadership development needs for the up-and-coming future leaders may differ based on gender, race and ethnicity, or previous commu-nity college experience. Specially focused development opportunities exist for some of these subgroups, including women and rural leaders. As pre-viously noted, the League supports a program in conjunction with Maricopa for women leaders—the National Institute for Leadership Development. Other general development programs for women include the Bryn Mawr College Summer Institute for Women in Higher Education Administration, hosted in conjunction with Higher Education Resource Services (HERS), and a management institute at Wellesley College for women administrators and professional faculty, both described in chapter 2 of this volume.

Cultural Competency

Cultural competency for leaders signifies the ability to understand the orga-nization's culture—what is valued, what the college history is, what the com-mon traditions are (Rhoads & Tierney, 1992). New leaders must spend time understanding the essence of their college and fitting the needs of the college with their own underlying individual leadership preferences. Leaders come to their positions with underlying schemas that dictate how they make sense of new information and how they approach change (Eddy, 2004, 2005). Thus, development training should focus on providing up-and-coming lead-ers with the ability to recognize how to match the needs of different organi-zational cultures with appropriately matched actions. The current practice of having participants in leadership training take a series of assessment instruments that highlight individual leadership orientations addresses part of the need for leaders to identify their personal approach to leadership. The next critical step, however, is understanding how an individual's leadership preference fits in a variety of different organizational cultures. Case study analysis can provide a first step in acquiring insight into the intersection of individual schemas and different cultural scenarios. Actual visits and exchanges at a variety of campuses provide real examples of this as well.

Berquist and Pawlak (2008) provided a guideline for leaders on six cultures of the academy, including the collegial culture, the managerial culture, the developmental culture, the advocacy culture, the virtual culture, and the tangible culture. New leaders may find they have a preference for operating in a managerial culture based on a hierarchy, but their new institution's culture is a virtual culture with an emphasis on open and shared systems. The ability to operate using a multiframe perspective (Bolman & Deal, 2006) is critical for leaders in this situation. The ability to understand that the culture of the new institution requires a particular set of actions that differ from the leader's previous institution is an example of cultural competency. New leaders must first make sense of the situation for themselves, which may involve altering their own schema, before they can help shape meaning for campus members (Eddy, 2005; Weick, 1995).

Community college leaders need to acquire the ability to lead in culturally bound systems while facing pressures that often originate outside their immediate region. The very origins of community colleges are founded on providing for local community needs, which shift over time. Leaders must acquire an appreciation of area needs and an understanding of how the culture of the region and the college affect actions and changes within the college. Thus, while all community colleges may have a similar cultural underpinning for their mission and foci, each is unique and ultimately requires different responses.

Knowledge of the campus culture assumes that the leader can articulate the values and traditions of campus importance. Bolman and Deal (2006) discussed how organizational culture is like a theater. The ability to direct the various actors allows a leader to tell the campus story and to help others see the same meaning in the plot lines. Understanding the culture can help leaders consider how best to address change initiatives and how to make decisions. Cultural competency provides leaders the capacity to assess a situation and determine the best course of action based on institutional needs.

Complementing this ability is the development of communication skills that allow for framing of situations for campus members and the community, which can lead to increased understanding and, ultimately, buy in (Eddy, 2003; Fairhurst & Sarr, 1996; Weick, 1995). The capability to influence the understanding of situations by others allows leaders a means to move forth change initiatives.

Preparing to Lead in Rural and Urban Settings

The new Carnegie classification schema now includes seven different categories, underscoring the need for attention regarding the influence of context on leading. The ends of the continuum of classification are rural and urban community colleges. Suburban 2-year colleges, located squarely in the middle, ultimately provide the normative model and, as such, represent the prototype for what the public envisions when discussing community colleges. Given this orientation, the ends of the continuum are reviewed as they represent a marked duality in the 2-year college system. Rural community colleges make up 60% of all community colleges (Carnegie Foundation for the Advancement of Teaching, 2007), accounting for the majority of all community college presidents. Leaders in rural areas face the challenge of leading a smaller institution with fewer resources and greater economic constraints. The Rural Community College Initiative (RCCI, 2007) works to support rural community college leaders in three areas: civic engagement, educational access, and economic development. Through funding from the Ford Foundation and support from MDC, Inc.; North Central Regional Center for Rural Development; and the Southern Rural Development Center, the RCCI conducted two phases of community college involvement. Two-year colleges located in 10 different states have participated since the program's inception in the mid-1990s. Several land-grant universities in the participating states partner with the community colleges.

One example of a partnership to develop community college leadership is the MidSouth Partnership for Rural Community Colleges (MSP), a regionally specific grow-your-own leadership development program that helps community college leaders build sustainable rural communities (Clark & Davis, 2007). The MSP was initiated in 1998 and is an ongoing collaboration of Alcorn State University, Mississippi's John C. Stennis Institute of Government, and community colleges across the mid-South. This partnership grew from the RCCI program outlined above, with the distinct goal of building sustainable rural communities while renewing and expanding a diverse cadre of effective community college leaders. Key elements of the MSP leader development process include a week-long retreat with follow-up programming, cross-disciplinary academic degree programs with a rural development emphasis, public policy analysis and doctoral dissertation research by practitioners, and systemic linkage to national rural and educational issues (Clark & Davis).

Similarly, the Expanding Leadership Diversity program offered by the League focused on particular issues facing urban leaders. Particular issues pressing urban areas are the focal point of the in-field experience for participants of this training, which then allows for an opportunity to practice what participants are learning in a real-time manner. Training for diverse leaders to guide urban institutions often focuses on training for leaders of color. The Lakin Institute for Mentored Leadership (sponsored by the National Council on Black American Affairs, an affiliate of the AACC) and the Hispanic Leadership Fellows Program (of the National Community College Hispanic Council) provide training for leaders of color. The Lakin Institute provides training for 25 potential African American community college presidents each year (see http://www.league.org/league/conferences/lakin.htm). "The Hispanic leadership program targets Hispanic vice chancellors, vice presidents, provosts and deans who aspire to a community college presidency" (Hull & Keim, 2007, p. 700). (For more on Lakin, see http://www.ccc.edu/ roundtable/index.shtml; for the Hispanic Leadership program, see http:// ced.ncsu.edu/ahe/ncchc/)

Additionally, the Institute for Community College Development, housed at Cornell University, provides a rotation of training topics, several of which focus on labor relations issues. Even though union issues cross institutional location borders, the impact of union concerns on urban and suburban community colleges is greater given their number of employees. Access to this form of specialized development aids leader preparation for these larger-sized institutions located in more metropolitan areas.

Succession Planning

With almost half of all sitting community college presidents over the age of 60, it is critical to address succession planning. Indeed, the focus of the

AACC Leading Forward Initiative calls attention to the need to prepare leaders for the pending retirements anticipated in community colleges. Since many colleges are regionally bound, grow-your-own programs may be helpful in developing the leaders of the future. In particular for women, VanDer-Linden (2003) found that despite the rhetoric of women being willing to move for promotion, those in her study indicated they were place bound and did not have many opportunities to move up within the organization. Arguments for the preparation of rural leaders also emphasize the need to hire leaders familiar with working in a rural culture, making grow-your-own programs popular in these institutions (Leist, 2007). Similarly, arguments for urban areas follow the same logic. The League's Expanding Leadership Diversity initiative focused on developing a pool of minority community college leaders and urban leaders. The focus on community problem-solving experiences to address critical issues facing the region was particularly useful in giving aspiring leaders an enhanced understanding of what it meant to lead in an urban environment.

Often, taking a position as a department chair is the first step in advancing within the college hierarchy. Thus, it is important to include development opportunities for these emerging leaders. This critical first step into leadership makes the Chair Academy increasingly important; however, the lower participation rates in this training program highlights that many front-line leaders are missing this development opportunity (Hull & Keim, 2007). Creating institutionally or regionally based training for department chairs may provide a viable alternative to the expense of sending new chairs to a nationally situated training site. University-based higher education programs may act as a convener site to provide regionally based training.

If provided with appropriate training, this first administrative position may serve to encourage individuals for future promotional positions because they will feel prepared; contrarily, lack of support may discourage them from seeking further advancement. Another key aspect of this first-line administrative position is encouraging interest and ultimate selection from a wide array of faculty members. As noted, gender parity is lacking in presidential positions, as is diversity in more presidents of color. Active recruitment at the grassroots level of the administrative hierarchy, namely at the chair level, of a diverse pool of applicants begins to address issues farther up the pipeline.

In addition to tapping future leaders for front-line leadership positions, the flattening of the hierarchy places more emphasis on leadership throughout the college. The increased demands of the top leadership position require an increased reliance on others in the institution to take on leadership roles (Bensimon & Neumann, 1993). Pushing down leadership functions within the hierarchy requires preparation of leaders along the pathway to take on more leadership functions and in turn to begin honing their leadership skills all along the pipeline. Linked to the demand of responsibility of leading throughout the organization are the larger issues facing community colleges. No longer are the challenges facing the college limited to the attention of top-level administrators. Dealing with issues pressing community colleges regarding diversity, economic development, technology, and changing faculty work roles require versatile and facile leaders throughout the college. Developing leaders along the career pathway allows for increased diversity and exposure for individuals not representing the administrative hegemonic majority—namely white men.

Developing Leaders as Learners

The increased complexity of educational leadership requires leaders to have a learning orientation and a philosophy of continuous improvement regarding their own development (Amey, 2005). Leadership development programmers need to recognize that one-size-fits-all training no longer works. As noted above, leaders require different skills based on the location of their college and the culture of the institution and the area. Thus, an individual may attend a national or state training forum and learn about budgeting or working with community partners, but then this basic knowledge needs to be situated contextually through training and practice on his or her home campus. As adult learners, leaders need to situate what they are learning within their past experiences (Knowles, 1980), which in this case are tied to their home campus.

Leaders need to understand not only their preferred way of leading but that of others within the organization. Adult learning theory operates for leaders and their staff. Knowles (1980) identified several key characteristics within andragogy—how adults learn. First, adults want to be self-directed in their learning. They also want to tie what they are learning into their bank of experiences. Adults are also motivated internally to learn and are ready to learn required and necessary skills. Finally, adults want to put their newly acquired learning to practice and application. In considering leaders as learners, it is obvious that newly appointed leaders are highly motivated to learn how to do the job of leading. Thus, development opportunities should be formatted based on the concepts of adult learning to allow for links to what participants know and opportunities to practice applying the new knowledge.

Davis (2003) identified seven distinct ways of learning for administrators: (a) learning new skills—behavioral learning, (b) learning from presentations—cognitive learning, (c) learning to think—inquiry learning, (d) learning to solve problems and make decisions—using mental models for learning, (e) learning in groups—collaborative learning, (f) improving performance—learning through virtual realities, and (g) learning from experience—holistic learning. The skills focus of current development practices begins to address the issue of acquiring the basic tools to do the job. The mentoring programs and practicum experiences associated with some of the trainings underscores the need for these adult learners to put to practice the new knowledge they are acquiring. What is missing from the current training opportunities is instilling the ideal of continuous learning and use of reflection to provide feedback for leaders to change their practice. Since the majority of community college leaders do not participate in formal national training programs (Hull & Keim, 2007), it is important for campus administrators to consider how they will create learning opportunities for development that address the needs of their participants using a learning orientation. Individuals must also reflect on their preferred modes of learning and in particular identify their basic underlying values and assumptions about leadership since these mental maps may ultimately create limitations for them.

Reflective practice (Amey, 2005; Brookfield, 1994; Cooper, 1994) allows leaders to realize their own orientations to leading and may provide them with heightened awareness of ways to use their skills to their best advantage and how to improve in their weaker areas. Learning to become reflective practitioners requires practice and is an ongoing process. The critical assessment of one's expertise and limitations requires the ability to question underlying assumptions and beliefs currently in practice (Amey, 2005). Argyris (1976) outlined the process of double-loop learning in which the knowledge gained from questioning these beliefs and assumptions is used to change behaviors. Incorporating reflective practice into development training provides the foundation to making this a lifelong practice and one that will aid leaders in their own learning. Just as in other learning, reflection requires practice before individuals embrace the concept. A difficulty for leaders today, however, is creating the space required for reflection.

In the shift to thinking of leaders as learners, an outcome should be an expansion of our conception of what defines leaders. As noted, the numbers of women and leaders of color does not have parity in the community college sector. The specialized trainings reviewed in this chapter provide an enhanced focus on preparing a diverse set of leaders for the future. Of more importance, however, is how reflection on leadership begins to expand the notion of what it means to be a leader. Thus, an anticipated outcome of this process is the creation of a wider acceptability of alternative ways of leading. The ability to appreciate a cornucopia of institutional voices enhances the ways problems facing the college are viewed.

Conclusion

The current period of transformation of higher education and the public demand for accountability and the ability to support economic development and growth demands much of future leaders. Central to the success of current and future leaders is leadership development. Previous research on leadership development strategies (Watts & Hammons, 2002) similarly called for a need to address the shortcomings of how community colleges develop leaders. Missing from these calls for change, however, were a focus on the need to develop cultural competency and acknowledgment of the continuum of needs for leaders in different contexts. The plans for the future outlined above contribute to filling this gap in developing leaders for the future by providing tools required to develop these competencies. Acknowledging the range of leaders required to lead today's community colleges underscores the need for differentiated training opportunities based on regional needs that recognize the role understanding culture adds to the ability of leaders to be successful. Changes in leadership ranks provide a unique opportunity for community college presidents to recraft what it means to be a leader of these transforming institutions. We do not have to settle for what has traditionally comprised the leadership ranks—predominately top-down administration by a group of white men (Amey & Twombly, 1992). Opening up the ranks of leadership to a wider band of leaders can provide different views and perspectives of how we should be leading these organizations. The consideration of individuals for leadership development should not rely on a cookie-cutter approach in which we attempt to replicate the last set of leaders. Indeed, the times demand a different type of leader, one who has multiple competencies and is invested in reflective, lifelong learning of the job. Development of these current and future leaders is imperative for meeting the demands on community colleges in the new millennium.

The foundation of the community college philosophy is its nimbleness to adapt to change. The current leadership transition is an opportunity for this nimbleness to stand out. During this period of transition, we risk losing some of our institutional history as less-experienced leaders take over. However, the fresh ideas new leaders present are required to meet the building pressures facing colleges. Honoring past practices and preparing for the future presents a tall order in leadership development during this changing of the guard. Preparing aspiring leaders to reach their potential quickly is important in a smooth transition as retiring leaders are replaced.

References

American Association of Community Colleges. (2005). *Competencies for community college leaders*. Washington, DC: American Association of Community Colleges.

American Council on Education. (2007). *The American college president: 2007 edition*. Washington, DC: American Council on Education.

Amey, M. J. (2005). Conceptualizing leading as learning. *Community College Journal of Research and Practice, 29*(9/10), 689–704.

Amey, M. J. (2006). *Breaking tradition: New community college leadership programs meet 21st-century needs*. Washington, DC: American Association of Community Colleges.

Amey, M. J., & Twombly, S. B. (1992). Revisioning leadership in community colleges. *The Review of Higher Education, 15*(2), 125–150.

Amey, M. J., VanDerLinden, K., & Brown, D. (2002). Perspectives on community college leadership: Twenty years in the making. *Community College Journal of Research and Practice, 26*(7), 573–589.

Argyris, C. (1976). Single-loop and double-loop models in research on decision making. *Administrative Science Quarterly, 21*(3), 363–375.

Bensimon, E. M., & Neumann, A. (1993). *Redesigning collegiate leadership: Teams and teamwork in higher education*. Baltimore, MD: Johns Hopkins University Press.

Bensimon, E. M., Neumann, A., & Birnbaum, R. (1989). Making sense of administrative leadership: The "L" word in higher education. *ASHE-ERIC Higher Education Report, 31*(6). Washington DC: George Washington University.

Berquist, W. H., & Pawlak, K. (2008). *Engaging the six cultures of the academy.* San Francisco: Jossey-Bass.

Bolman, L. G., & Deal, T. E. (2006). *The wizard and the warrior: Leading with passion and power.* San Francisco: Jossey-Bass.

Brookfield, S. D. (1994). *Becoming a critically reflective teacher.* San Francisco: Jossey-Bass.

Carnegie Foundation for the Advancement of Teaching. (2007). *The Carnegie classification of institutions of higher education.* New York: Carnegie Foundation for the Advancement of Teaching. Retrieved June 15, 2007, from http://www.carnegie foundation.org/classifications

Clark, M. M., & Davis, E. (2007). Engaging leaders as builders of sustainable rural communities: A case study. *New Directions for Community Colleges, 2007*(137), 47–56. San Francisco: Jossey-Bass.

Cooper, J. E. (1994). Metaphorical "I": Journal keeping and self-image in administrative women. *Initiatives, 56*(1), 11–22.

Davis, J. R. (2003). *Learning to lead: A handbook for postsecondary administrators.* Westport, CT: Praeger.

Eckel, P. D., & Kezar, A. (2003). *Taking the reins: Institutional transformation in higher education.* Westport, CT: Praeger.

Eddy, P. L. (2003). Sensemaking on campus: How community college presidents frame change. *Community College Journal of Research and Practice, 27*(6), 453–471.

Eddy, P. L. (2004). The impact of presidential cognition on institutional change. *Community College Enterprise, 10*(1), 63–77.

Eddy, P. L. (2005). Framing the role of leader: How community college presidents construct their leadership. In M. J. Amey & B. Laden (Eds.), Conceptualizing leadership as learning [Special issue]. *Community College Journal of Research and Practice, 29*(9/10), 705–727.

Eddy, P. L. (2007, April). *Climbing the ladder and looking back: Reflections of women leading community colleges.* Paper presented at the annual meeting of the American Education Research Association, Chicago, IL.

Eddy, P. L., & Rao, M. (2008). *Higher education leadership preparation: Emerging trends and program implications.* Manuscript submitted for publication.

Fairhurst, G. T., & Sarr, R. A. (1996). *The art of framing: Managing the language of leadership.* San Francisco: Jossey-Bass.

Goodchild, L. F. (1991). Higher education as a field of study: Its origins, programs, and purposes, 1893–1960. *New Directions for Higher Education, 1991* (76), 15–32. San Francisco: Jossey-Bass.

Hardy, D. E., & Katsinas, S. G. (2007). Classifying community colleges: How rural community colleges fit. *New Directions for Community Colleges, 2007*(137), 1–17. San Francisco: Jossey-Bass.

Hatch, M. J., & Cunliffe, A. L. (2006). *Organization theory: Modern, symbolic, and postmodern perspectives.* New York: Oxford University Press.

Heifetz, R. (1998). *Leadership without easy answers.* Cambridge, MA: Belknap Press.

Hull, J. R., & Keim, M. C. (2007). Nature and status of community college leadership development programs. *Community College Journal of Research and Practice, 31*(9), 689–702.

Kezar, A. J., Carducci, R., & Contreras-McGavin, M. (2006). Rethinking the "L" word in higher education: The revolution of research on leadership. *ASHE-ERIC Higher Education Report, 31*(6). San Francisco: Jossey-Bass.

Knowles, M. S. (1980). *The modern practice of adult education: From pedagogy to andragogy.* New York: Cambridge Books.

League for Innovation in the Community College. (2007). *About the League.* Retrieved June 19, 2007, from http://www.league.org/league/about/about_main.htm

Leist, J. (2007). "Ruralizing" presidential job advertisements. *New Directions for Community Colleges, 2007*(137), 35–46). San Francisco: Jossey-Bass.

Linsky, M., & Heifetz, R. (2002). *Leadership on the line: Staying alive through the dangers of leading.* Cambridge, MA: Harvard Business School Press.

National Center for Education Statistics. (2005). *Digest of education statistics: 2005* (NCES Publication No. 2006-030). Washington, DC: U.S. Department of Education. Retrieved July 24, 2008, from http://nces.ed.gov/programs/digest/2005menu_tables.asp

Ottenritter, N. (2004, April). *Leading forward: AACC and leadership.* Paper presented at the 46th annual conference of the Council for the Study of Community Colleges, Minneapolis, MN.

Rhoads, R. A., & Tierney, W. G. (1992). *Cultural leadership in higher education.* Washington, DC: Office of Educational Research and Improvement.

Rowley, D. J., & Sherman, H. (2001). *From strategy to change: Implementing the plan in higher education.* San Francisco: Jossey-Bass.

Rural Community College Initiative. *About the RCCI.* (2007). Retrieved June 19, 2007, from http://www.mdcinc.org/rcci/aboutrcci.htm.

Shaw, N. (Ed.). (1969). *Community service forum.* Washington, DC: American Association of Junior Colleges.

Shults, C. (2001). *The critical impact of impending retirements on community college leadership* (Leadership Series Research Brief No. 1). Washington, DC: American Association of Community Colleges.

Tillery, D., & Deegan, W. L. (1985). The evolution of two-year colleges through four generations. In D. Tillery & W. L. Deegan (Eds.), *Renewing the American community college* (pp. 3–33). San Francisco: Jossey-Bass.

Twombly, S. B. (1995). Gendered images of community college leadership: What messages they send. *New Directions for Community Colleges, 1995*(89), 67–77.

VanDerLinden, K. (2003, April). *Career advancement and leadership development of community college administrators.* Paper presented at the American Educational Research Association, Chicago, IL.

Vaughan, G. B. (1986). *The community college presidency.* Washington, DC: American Council on Education.

Vaughan, G. B. (1997). The community college's mission and milieu: Institutionalizing community-based programming. In E. J. Boone & Associates (Eds.), *Community leadership through community-based programming* (pp. 21–58). Washington, DC: Community College Press.

Vaughan, G. B. (2005). (Over)selling the community college: Access at what price? *The Chronicle of Higher Education, 52*(10), B12.

Watts, G. E., & Hammons, J. O. (2002). Leadership development for the next generation. *New Directions for Community Colleges, 2002*(120), 59–66. San Francisco: Jossey-Bass.

Weick, K. E. (1955). *Sensemaking in organizations.* Thousand Oaks, CA: Sage.

Wolverton, M., & Gonzales, M. J. (2000, April). *Career paths of academic deans.* Paper presented at the annual meeting of the American Educational Research Association, New Orleans, LA.

HIGHER EDUCATION LEADERSHIP DEVELOPMENT PROGRAMS IN THE MARKETPLACE

Sharon A. McDade

K ezar and the contributing authors in this volume argue that leadership development programs must change, or revolutionize, if they are to play a significant role in the future production of college and university leaders. In particular, Kezar argues on p. xiii in the preface that traditional leadership development "programs bring together hierarchical, positional leaders; focus on skill and trait development; and reinforce the importance of social control and persuasion, teaching competencies that transcend context." The calls made by Kezar and the other contributors suggest innovation in leadership development, although many of the threads in this volume have been raised before (which they acknowledge), at least in discussion among leadership development program developers. Why have not the format, audience, and focus of leadership development programs changed? And what could compel these programs to change as called for by the authors of the chapters in this book? This chapter focuses on the marketplace of higher education leadership development programs—what changes and what remains the same—and speculates why.

In this chapter I share observations and experiences relative to the revolution in leadership development Kezar and colleagues make claim to in this book. After setting the context for the chapter by defining the marketplace and describing my background in leadership development, I consider several aspects of the academic marketplace: the audiences, individual versus collective development, the costs, curriculum and instruction, research (or lack thereof) on leadership development and programs, and the marketplace of leadership development programs. Consider this to be a dialogue with the other chapters in this book in an attempt to raise questions for the higher education community on how the ideas and calls for revolutionizing leadership development might be considered and implemented.

Context: Marketplace and Personal Background

One could conceptualize leadership development within a marketplace—customers for it, an expected demand, and providers trying to understand consumers and needs. As a result of this market environment, formats and curricula are changed to be responsive to market demands. Although leadership development programs may have existed informally prior to 1960, several national, formal leadership development programs were created in the 1960s and following decades (McDade, 1988): the American Council on Education (ACE) Fellows Program was founded in 1965 (ACE, n.d.-a), Harvard's Institute for Educational Management (IEM) in 1970 (Harvard Graduate School of Education Programs in Professional Education, n.d.), and Higher Education Resource Services (HERS) in 1972 at Brown University with institutes started in 1976 at Wellesley College and Bryn Mawr College (HERS, n.d.; HERS Wellesley, n.d.). Each of these started with a unique format, audience, and curriculum delivery method. The Fellows Program, a year-long experiential learning opportunity, was aimed at faculty and those in early academic leadership roles, although recently midlevel managers have participated. IEM was originally a 6-week residential program; although now shortened, it retains its case-study format. The audience has always been senior-level administrators (presidents, vice presidents, deans, etc.). HERS is "an intensive residential professional development experience for women in mid- and senior level positions in higher education administration. [It is] offered in both a month-long summer program and in multiple weekend series during the academic year" (HERS, n.d., p. 1). Thus, there has been a long history of programs at the national level serving higher education leadership development needs.

My commentary on leadership development programs comes from a career of working with them and researching them. I served as director of the IEM at Harvard University from 1984 to 1990, and during that time created the Management Development Program and contributed to the launch of the Harvard Seminar for New Presidents. After 17 years as an academic researching leadership development programs and leadership development in higher education, I am now merging the threads of my career as director of the ACE Fellows Program. In between my roles with these two premier leadership programs of U.S. higher education, I have been involved with dozens of other leadership development programs, either as an instructor, director, or creator. I have served since 1993 as the external evaluator for the Hedwig van Ameringen Executive Leadership in Academic Medicine (ELAM) Program (Drexel University, n.d.). I have written several books (Green & McDade, 1994; McDade & Lewis, 1994) and many articles about leadership development, including the book referenced by Kezar in the preface (McDade, 1988) that she claims is essentially the only book about leadership development programs to date.

The Audiences of Audiences for Leadership Development

Who goes to leadership development programs? In chapter 1, p. 12, Kezar claims that "leadership development programs need to expand their definitions of leaders and leadership and recruit participants who occupy different rungs of the administrator ladder as well as represent a cross-section of the university's organizational subunits." While I agree, I also note some issues to consider that can problematize this direction. I also provide ideas for creating new audiences for leadership development.

First, the national marketplace has clearly defined programs by leadership levels focused on certain hierarchical positions, as Kezar notes, and this may be difficult to change. Programs are most typically categorized in the marketplace by the audiences they serve. For example, many of the major institutionally focused associations sponsor leadership programs for presidents as part of their service function to member institutions. The Council of Independent Colleges (CIC) provides an annual Presidents Institute that "is CIC's premier event, bringing presidents of independent colleges and universities together for networking, problem-solving, and sharing of ideas" (CIC, n.d., p. 1). The National Association of Independent Colleges and

Universities (NAICU) sponsors an annual leadership conference for member institution presidents (NAICU, n.d.). ACE sponsors an array of presidential programs (for example, ACE, n.d.-h). The American Association of Community Colleges (AACC) hosts annual programs for heads of community colleges "dedicated to the professional renewal and recognition of community college CEOs" (AACC, n.d., p. 1). (See chapter 9 in this book for a specific focus on the leadership programs of AACC.) As many of these programs attract presidents who return multiple times for renewal and networking, the programs vary tremendously from year to year with curricula that strike a balance between exploration of issues regarding the execution of the presidential office (for example, work/life balance) and hot topics of the day. The AACC may be the most holistic of this group, because of work by this association to articulate six competencies of leadership (Amey, 2006; Ottenritter, 2004), which are now being infused in all of its leadership programs. Thus, these programs serve a specific audience—the presidents—and there is a clearly defined market of programs designed to serve the leadership development needs of this audience.

Given recent discoveries about the age of presidents and the anticipated retirement of an entire generation of institutional leadership (ACE, 2007), many associations have initiated, or have provided, more focus on programs for developing the next generation of college and university CEOs. Since presidents typically emerge from the vice presidential level, particularly provosts (ACE), the primary focus of these new programs tends to be on leaders in senior positions. Such programs include the American Association of State Colleges and Universities' (AASCU) Millennium Leadership Initiative (AASCU, n.d.) and ACE's Advancing to the Presidency: A Workshop for Vice Presidents (ACE, n.d.-b). While it is important for programs to help groom senior officers for presidencies, there is also a need for the development of another range of programs that look farther down in the hierarchy for candidates for leadership.

This book calls for attention to faculty and administrators in the lower rungs of the administrative hierarchy and faculty. Some associations that serve functional areas and disciplinary groups within the academy provide leadership programs for such audiences. For example, the Association of American Medical Colleges (AAMC) provides a suite of leadership programs across functional management areas as well as for faculty who are interested in leadership, with 25 groups and areas listed on its Web site (AAMC, n.d.).

This is perhaps the most robust range of leadership and professional development programs provided by a single association, serving functional and cross-functional areas at all stages of the administrative hierarchy, including focused programs for the advancement of women and minorities. In particular, the faculty leadership programs, dedicated to the proposition that "faculty vitality is essential for the sustained health of our medical colleges and teaching hospitals" (p. 1) already exemplify many of the characteristics that Gallant and Getz call for in chapter 4 in this book on facing organizational complexity and change. This may be a model for other disciplinary associations and higher education administrators to follow and to help them lead the revolution.

Other programs serve administrators across functional areas. The nationally known programs attract audiences from senior (IEM) or middle management (such as the Management Development Program and Institute for Management and Leadership in Education; Harvard, n.d.) or by gender (see ACE's Office of Women in Higher Education [ACE, n.d.-g] and ACE's Center for Advancement of Racial and Ethnic Equity [ACE, n.d.-d]). Chapters 2 and 3 in this book describe HERS and programs that serve administrators and faculty of color and provide important critiques of how these programs (and this category of programs) can revolutionize. As useful and important as these programs are, there is always a need for more programs that bring together participants from across functional areas.

The bulk of faculty leadership development programs tend to be sponsored by disciplinary associations, yet these are few in number compared to need or demand. For example, the American Psychological Association sponsors an Education Leadership Conference (American Psychological Association, n.d.). Other associations sponsor leadership academies for faculty serving as department chairs. For example, the Modern Language Association provides leadership support for faculty in department chair roles through its Association of Departments of English (ADE, n.d.) and Association of Departments of Foreign Languages (ADFL, n.d.). ACE "offers a series of general national workshops for division and department chairs and deans specifically designed to focus on departmental leadership" (ACE, n.d.-e). Multiplied across the hundreds of disciplinary associations serving higher education faculty, there are many leadership development workshops and seminars. Although no inventory of the complete range and number of these programs has been conducted, they are known to exist and serve a vital function in development of the grass roots of faculty leadership capacities. These programs need to be studied and organizers may benefit from the ideas in this book, but without documentation the curriculum and impact are unknown.

As this very short introduction to types of leadership programs shows, the marketplace provides a range of programs by levels of the administrative and faculty hierarchy as well as a range of programs aimed at bringing together people from across functional groups by hierarchical levels. Thus, the spirit of Kezar's call in chapter 1 for expanding the definitions of leaders and leadership may be met in the future by broadening the emerging avenues. Yet, no matter how many programs exist to serve any particular audience within higher education, they serve only a small percentage of that audience in any particular year and time.

The call by Kezar and the other authors of chapters in this book is correct (and the volume of their call needs to be amplified) in that more programs are needed to serve greater numbers of participants from the higher education community. Perhaps the only audience levels that are well served by the number and variety of programs are presidents and senior officers. Most presidents and senior officers will attend at least one if not many of these programs at various times in their term of office as their needs, interests, jobs, and institutional affiliation change. In the lower levels of the hierarchy and among faculty, the ratio of programs to population diminishes. Many professors will never attend a national leadership development program. Even at the first rung of academic leadership—the department chair— few, in proportion to the numbers, will attend a national departmental leadership program. Thus, the call in this book for more leadership programs, with a particular focus on faculty and those in first-tier and middle management positions, is on target with the needs of audience members in the academy.

Individual Versus Collective Leadership Development

A key criticism of the current selection of national leadership development programs embedded in this volume is that almost all serve individuals and not teams. This does not acknowledge that the leadership of colleges and universities is conducted by teams—from the president's senior cabinet to the department chairs of a college. There are two sides to this criticism.

The Individual Side of Leadership Development

A first side in this discussion is that almost all the national leadership programs do serve individuals—and this does foster, and grows from, the concept of the individual as leader. This makes sense from the viewpoint of the move up the leadership hierarchy. There are fewer "like" administrators, and it is necessary to leave one's institution and go to a conference or meeting to find others in similar jobs and with whom education about the leadership challenges of these jobs would make sense. Thus, chief academic officers (there is only one per institution) may find particular benefit in a leadership program specifically for them, where they can share problems and issues with others in similar situations (see ACE, n.d.-f). This is also the premise of many of the leadership programs for women and people of color. There may be so few such individuals in leadership within a single institution that they need to attend a conference with a focus on their affinity group to find people in similar situations and needs (see Drexel University, n.d.). Thus, while serving individuals, these programs are also serving the collective of higher education.

Many leadership programs provide not only support for individual leaders at a particular management level but also tend to the interests and needs of these individuals for growth toward higher levels in the administrative hierarchy. Career growth, from this perspective, is an individual activity. People progress at individual rates, develop their interests and aspirations individually. Therefore, attending leadership programs is appropriate for the way individuals identify themselves as leaders and seek their own individual leadership growth. Looking at the national leadership programs through this lens, the programs provide an opportunity for individuals to network, to test themselves against others, to seek individualized feedback, and to try on new leadership personas away from their own institutions as they stretch, through program curricula, into new and different leadership conceptualizations (Green & McDade, 1994; McDade, 1988). Many of the national leadership programs provide extensive individual feedback on leadership styles and capacities through instruments such as 360, Myers-Briggs, and similar typologies. But, as the chapter authors note, there should be more emphasis on teams and an extension in the marketplace of programming for teams and their development. I will address this question as I continue this section.

The Team Side of Leadership Development

The second side of the criticism raised in this book is that current leadership development programs do not foster and emphasize teams and collaboration. This was noted as an important area in which leadership development programs need to be revolutionized since the work of colleges and universities ultimately takes place in teams and work groups. Team-building leadership programming is expensive for a campus in that it involves the cost of sending multiple campus members to a program. Nonetheless, important team-building and team-focused leadership development programs exist in at least five ways that can be used as a direction for integrating the revolutionary principles.

First, a few national leadership programs do serve campus teams, despite the barriers to team development at a program away from campus. Some of the best examples of this focus on teams and team building from a national platform may be offered by ACE's Campus Internationalization (ACE, n.d.-d). These programs, forums, and laboratories stress team participation and team building among members within an individual institution, through supported networking and collaboration, across institutions that share internationalization agendas. These can serve as models to build on in the future.

Second, although the designs of many national leadership programs may not serve teams as participants, some incorporate collaboration and team education into their curriculum. For example, Rosser's chapter 5 in this book puts the spotlight on the National Science Foundation ADVANCE program, which, as Rosser states, includes the characteristics of "context specific, globalized, process oriented, collaborative, and dealing with cognitive complexity" (p. 118). In a similar vein, the ELAM program also emphasizes a curriculum of collaboration and cooperation, and models these concepts in program activities and alumni follow-up (Drexel University, n.d.). Thus, some models exist in which we can consider the incorporation of teams and collaboration in leadership programming.

Third, programs and activities that serve teams more typically exist at the institutional level and are most prevalent in informal and ad hoc activities. While faculty and administrators go away from campus for individualized learning, institutions bring leadership training to their own campuses for team leadership training. If the team is at one place, it is more efficient in resources and time to bring the training to the team. This encompasses an entire range of programs—retreats for presidential cabinets, boards of trustees, department chair groups within a college, senior officers serving a vice president—that never get documented in the national literature on leadership development yet serve the needs of teams throughout higher education. The major activity of many of the senior officers of institutional associations is to provide this kind of team leadership development for member institutions. Cadres of consultants specialize in this type of training. The wealth of these leadership development opportunities is immense. Because of the match of these opportunities to the specific needs of an institutional team, the possibilities of these training activities employing many of the revolutionary perspectives advanced in this book are high. However, we do not know much about these institutional team-building and team leadership development activities because there has been virtually no research or even commentary in the scholarship of practice about them.

Fourth, institutional-based leadership academies constitute a formal version of team-building leadership programs. Many institutions provide an internal leadership development program or academy that has specific intentions of bringing together managers in a particular category or rising leaders from across the institution (McDade & Lewis, 1994). While some of these academies have been in place for many years, others come and go depending upon institutional needs, funding, and the interests of new presidents.

It is, perhaps, in these institutional leadership academies that the revolutionary leadership training advocated by authors within this volume may best be found. These academies are typically developed from an institutional needs assessment, thus ensuring that the interests of participants are closely and specifically attended to. Often these programs are created in conjunction with institutional centers that focus on leadership, ensuring that cutting-edge leadership practices and theory are applied (see Buffalo State University's Investment in the Future Institute, Durlak [2007]). It is in these programs that campus teamwork may have its best focus, as the mission of most of these programs is to bring people together from across the campus so they can learn to work together to facilitate networks and teams throughout the institution.

Fifth, many presidents or deans of colleges may create team building in their cabinets or among key leaders within their institutions through sequential training. Although I have never seen any empirical research on this topic, I know that this actively existed during my tenure as IEM director, and I have seen this as an external evaluator for ELAM. During my IEM tenure, many presidents sent all members of their cabinets through IEM, one vice president a year, until all had the IEM training. These presidents thought that the investment of time and resources was appropriate as the cabinet members then shared a language and analytical orientation to leadership developed through their participation in IEM, even though they attended one member at a time. Many medical schools use ELAM in the same way, by annually nominating a woman academic to ELAM so that since its inception in 1995, a number of institutions now have eight or more similarly trained women leaders in service to the college or university. This allows ELAM graduates at a medical college to share language, leadership knowledge, networks, and problem-solving techniques that enable them to function as teams and to infuse their collaboration and cooperation throughout the college.

Thus, the contributors to this book are correct in many ways about individual versus collective leadership learning. Yes, the bulk of the major national leadership programs do serve individuals and emphasize individual leadership, perhaps driven by the market for people who want to advance their careers and use these programs for important development toward advancement and leadership capacity building for the challenges of the next level of responsibility. Yes, these programs can and should provide more focus on collective and collaboration leadership and team functioning. In contrast, a vast array of leadership development programs may serve teams and foster collaborative leadership, but these programs are not inventoried or their efforts documented in any comprehensive way for the academy to know of their existence or their benefits. Perhaps the call for revolutionizing leadership in this book will cause a greater documentation of these efforts so that their contributions can be better known and program models shared for the mutual benefit of all institutions.

The Costs of Leadership Development—Who Pays and Why?

The revolution in leadership development called for in this book raises an important question about the cost of such efforts. Revolutions are expensive.

Someone or something has to pay. If the goal is to revolutionize the mission, format, structure, curricula, and participants in leadership development programs, who or what pays for the revolution? Although some programs are funded through foundation or endowment monies, the vast majority of the national leadership programs have only two streams of funding—institutions and individuals. Some national leadership programs provide scholarship funding under special circumstances, but this is not common. Campus-based leadership development is almost exclusively funded through institutional funds, with occasional support from grants specific to the purpose or task.

Why do institutions pay for leadership development and what is expected for the investment? Institutions want and need to develop existing leaders and emerging leaders for the betterment of the organization. There is clearly a better return on investment for institutions to sponsor internal leadership academies, pay for consultants for special leadership development programming, or create internal centers to support development (for example, centers for faculty development). The investment in leadership academies multiplies in reward as more institution members go through the experience. Bringing a consultant or instructors for modules in a special focus leadership program ensures maximum exposure of the concepts for affected campus members. These investments ebb and flow, depending upon institutional finances and the emphasis chosen by senior campus leaders (and, in particular, the president) on leadership development. Thus, investment in campus-based leadership development reaps institutional rewards beyond individual participation. However, there is little research on these activities, or even on the formal campus-based leadership academies. This is often because there is little empirical research to measure impact, and such academies are so often at the whim of presidential attention and financial support. If there is no documentation of impact, it is hard to sustain what can often be deemed an "extra" when times are tough and basic student and faculty needs must first be serviced. Thus, whether any of these programs could serve as revolutionary models may never be known to the larger higher education system because funding is mercurial and documentation is sparse. However, this volume is exceptional in pointing to and capturing some of these campus-based efforts.

Why do institutions invest money for individuals to go to off-campus leadership development programs when the explicit purpose of these programs is, for the most part, individual leadership development? Travel and tuition costs are typically high. While the association-based programs try to keep tuition costs low for most programs to encourage member institution participation, the national leadership programs, separate from associations, must advance a tuition that covers the costs of the program. If only a few individuals can go to a program, is that investment worthwhile for an institution? The benefit may be measured not in monetary amounts, but in revitalization, new ideas, expanded networks, and leadership augmentation that the individual brings back to his or her job and to the institution. The time away from a high-pressure and demanding job may provide an opportunity for reflection, and the change of pace may be worth more than the cost of the tuition and thus make the individual investment highly worthwhile for an institution. Tension is always involved when officials at an institution consider investing in individual leadership development (knowing there will be career advancement benefits for the individual while anticipating benefits that the individual will bring back to the job and campus) versus the payoff from sending teams that are working on major initiatives for campuses. While it would make sense that an institution might best benefit from the investment in team development, the reality of the marketplace is that few team-oriented programs exist. Perhaps an audience for team-oriented programs exists but is not being accommodated in the marketplace.

Why do individuals pay and what do they want from the experience? It can be speculated that individuals tend to invest in leadership development programs for career advancement and job fulfillment. When it is your checkbook applied to the cost of a leadership program, the bottom line is clear—what can this experience add to your own career? That a number of leadership development programs have survived over multiple decades (for example, IEM, ACE Fellows Program, HERS) is a testimony to how well these programs have addressed individual career advancement and leadership development needs. That several of these programs have active alumni organizations and alumni fund-raising (for example, ACE Fellows Program, IEM, ELAM) are also testimonies to the individual value that participants have placed on these programs and on the impact in their leadership and careers.

While each of the major national programs have certainly evolved and improved throughout its history, each has a core programmatic element it has remained true to—its brand in the marketplace. People pay for the brand experience because of its uniqueness in the marketplace and for the brand name of the sponsoring organization. While certainly people would not have paid the high costs of the major national programs over the decades if the programs were not delivering results, the fact that sufficient numbers of people did choose to pay to participate in these programs each year attests to the fact that their core curricula must be delivering acceptable results. Considered in this light, organizers of these programs may not want to revolutionize too much so that they do not stray too far from their national brand in the marketplace. While it would be safe to assume that none of the national organizations are offering exactly the same program as it existed in the inaugural year, and that these programs have changed over their lifetimes, there is no publicly available documentation or research that captures such evolutions. Other national programs have come and gone over the same decades. That key national programs have evolved and stayed viable in the marketplace is shown by their longevity and existence today. Of course, all programs need to continue to evolve—and perhaps even revolutionize—to remain fresh and useful in the assessment of audiences in the marketplace.

The costs—whether borne by institutions, individuals, or a combination of both—is a major factor in the potential for revolution in leadership development programs. Revolution costs money: money for innovation, new materials, new instructors. It is not that the major national leadership development programs are not innovating and changing (they had to innovate and change to stay competitive in the marketplace), it is that they have done so in an incremental manner, thus folding innovation costs over the long haul. New programs build the costs of innovation into their early years, when a program is finding its feet and figuring out how best to address its market. The costs for innovation in campus-based programs may be lowest of all because virtually everyone associated with the program may be volunteering as part of institutional service. The cost for innovation in such programs may be more about time as a resource instead of dollars. Again, there is no research within higher education that investigates these factors, and no efforts to look at literature regarding marketplace, costs, and innovation borrowed from other fields to contextualize these dilemmas. But, I suspect campus-based programs can more easily incorporate these ideas. That national and regional programs can act on these ideas is evident in HERS, which recently overhauled its program at minimal cost and did not fear branding concerns. However, HERS does have a long-standing reputation as a maverick and perhaps changing the curriculum is part of its branding. Perhaps other leadership programs can also see that as part of their branding.

Curriculum and Instruction

What gets taught, how it is taught, and who teaches it are also important, interwoven threads when considering the revolutionizing of leadership development. The calls for revolutionizing leadership development in this book particularly request curriculum that promotes learning, empowerment, and change. Quite possibly, every leadership development program, regardless of type, would argue that its does these three things. Why might the authors of this volume argue otherwise? Perhaps because, at a basic level, leadership programs tend to have a common curricula and use similar instructional methodologies.

As this book often reminds us, leadership is best studied in a contextualized way. Thus, all the leadership development programs include references to higher education—its structure, issues, problems, and challenges. At the national leadership programs, this contextualization is more generalized across higher education, but then there is the benefit in seeing how leadership plays out in various types and segments of higher education as leaders may find themselves in another sector or campus type in coming years. The campus-based leadership programs are obviously deeply contextualized within the culture of the host institution. If these programs are considered on a continuum, then faculty and administrators early in their careers may be exposed through campus-based leadership programs to institution-specific leadership contextualization. As people advance up the hierarchy, they are exposed to a cross-institutional context. It may be that neither type of contextualization is better than the other, but that both need to exist to serve learning needs at different points in the career development continuum. As the chapter authors pointed out, a specific institutional culture would seem to be overlooked in programs that try to generalize leadership lessons, but I wanted to point out that context is addressed at some level in the current programs.

Current programs incorporate some of the teaching modalities argued for in the chapters, and the push to continue to reevaluate reflection practices or the type of experiential learning provided, for example, could be powerful.

There are varieties of learning modalities across the programs. The ACE Fellows and ELAM programs include residential seminars that intersperse experiential learning of Fellows working with and mentored by senior officers. The Harvard suite of programs is based on case-study learning. Case studies are widely used across all the programs and perhaps constitute the core of the learner-centered experiences within these programs. Self-analysis and reflection may be the other most common learning method in these programs, as most use some varieties of assessment instruments and build analysis and reflection related to these instruments into the program schedule. This is another important opportunity for building in revolutionary principles.

A reality of leadership development programs is that to ensure variety and expertise according to subject, all rely on an array of instructors who come into the program and teach units. This typically may mean a finance expert who teaches financial issues, a legal expert for legal issues, a panel of presidents to talk about leadership as the topic, and so on. I am unaware of any higher education leadership program that has a stable of dedicated faculty who do nothing but teach in and develop that program. Instead, all the programs tap as faculty members people who do their full-time work elsewhere and come into the program for a specific task. While some programs pay for the services of these faculty, many do not. In particular, the campus-based programs tend to rely on volunteers from the institution. Association-based programs often rely on volunteers from that institutional or functional area. These volunteers teach in these programs as part of their service commitment to higher education.

Volunteer or paid, it is impressive how much time and energy faculty put into their modules. But the reality is that these people are hired as experts on a particular topic. How that topic fits into the overall mission and purpose of the program, into the overarching curriculum design may only reside with the program director and that director's ability to articulate the mission and purpose in a hiring phone call. Because instructors have other jobs and fit teaching in these programs into small pockets of their time, there is little incentive or time for entire faculty to gather and discuss curriculum design, teaching methodology, and program learning objectives. The result is often close to what happens in a conference or annual meeting—here is one session of this topic and here is another on another topic, and let us make certain we have diversity of topics and presentation modes so that the day is lively, engaging, and motivating.

Such instructional selection and design may not lend itself to the revolutionary calls for leadership development expressed in this book. It may also be difficult to fold the revolutionary curricula and learning modalities noted in this book into established programs that evolve incrementally. Perhaps the reason HERS was able to successfully revolutionize was because it has a stable group of faculty who have taught in the program for years and have worked closely with each other in developing program modules. Perhaps it is only possible to infuse a program with the full range of revolutionary expressions as called for in this book if created new, in a holistic way, with a group of planners who then also facilitate the program to operationalize the common understanding of the design.

Perhaps the reality is that no one program can encapsulate all the elements of revolutionary leadership as articulated in this book. Perhaps a program is successful if even one or some of the elements discussed in this book are included, so there is a balance between traditional and revolutionary. A market is healthy when an array of programs with a variety of curricula, learning modalities, and instructional options speak to all audience groups at every stage of their careers, and to all institutional development needs.

Research (or Lack Thereof) on Leadership Development and Programs

The preface and several chapters in this book allude to the fact that we know little about leadership development in higher education. The circle of people who research and write on this topic is small, with some of them contributing to this volume and the rest cited in the reference lists. That Kezar can point to such an important topic on which the seminal book was written almost 20 years ago suggests that we need updated investigation into how, where, and in what manner higher education develops the leadership of its membership. With the anticipated turnover in leadership at all levels of the academy—from senior faculty to presidents (ACE, 2007)—leadership development is a timely topic. Yet, little research exists.

A key limitation of discussion about leadership development is the lack of empirical research on what happens in leadership programs and the impact of these programs. Very little on campus-based programs exists, which makes sense given the grassroots nature of these programs. Administrators of these programs are busy executing the programs and have little time for or training in evaluation. Association-based programs are directed by skilled and knowledgeable people with many demands on their time, usually hired for their knowledge and expertise. Association research activities are more typically focused on bigger national issues, and researches do not invest resources in evaluating membership activities such as leadership development programs.

Only a few programs, most notably ACE Fellows and ELAM, have consistently produced evaluative research over the lives of the programs. In particular, the ELAM program is stellar in this regard with a string of publications emanating from a Robert Wood Johnson grant, with more such publications in the pipeline. In summary, this research is documenting the contributions of the program to the leadership and careers of its participants over the long term and finding significant impacts pre- and postparticipation, and compared to women who did not go through the program (Dannels et al., in press; McDade et al., 2008; McDade, Richman, Jackson, & Morahan, 2004; Morahan et al., 1998; Morahan et al., 2006; Richman, Morahan, Cohen, & McDade, 2001).

With more research on leadership development and leadership development programs within higher education, we would be able to answer questions raised by the contributors to this book about how best to situate and advance leadership advancement within the academy. We would know if leadership development requires revolutionizing, what types of revolutionizing have the best impact, and how best to proceed with the revolution called for in this book.

The Marketplace of Leadership Development Programs in U.S. Higher Education

Leadership development programs and experiences constitute a market of educational opportunities. Institutions and individuals select programs and experiences related to a mix of reasons—match to needs and interests, availability, costs, function, program structure, curriculum, learning and teaching modalities, networking opportunities, and contextualization. As in any marketplace, the broader the array of options, the better the selection for players in that market to find best matches. In that marketplace conceptualization, there is room for the traditional, tried-and-true, as well as for the revolutionary or some combination of both. Hopefully this book will spur the development of revolutionary programs or revolutionary elements within programs that will expand the marketplace and encourage the development of an even greater range of choice.

References

American Association of Community Colleges. (n.d.). Events: Presidents Academy. Retrieved December 6, 2007, from http://www.aacc.nche.edu/Content/NavigationMenu/NewsandEvents/Presidents eAca demy1/Presidents_Academy.htm

American Association of State Colleges and Universities. (n.d.). The Millennium Leadership Institute. Retrieved December 6, 2007, from http://www.aascu.org/mli/index.htm

American Council on Education. (2007). *The American college president: 2007 edition.* Washington, DC: American Council on Education, Center for Policy Analysis.

American Council on Education. (n.d.-a). ACE Fellows Program. Retrieved December 6, 2007, from http://www.acenet.edu/AM/Template.cfm?Section = Fellows _Program1&CFID = 2117 9059&CFTOKEN = 46650703&jsessionid = 163037 c46781gCo5C$

American Council on Education. (n.d.-b). Advancing to the presidency: A workshop on successful presidential search and transition. Retrieved December 6, 2007, from http://www.acenet.edu/AM/Template.cfm?Section = Advancing1

American Council on Education. (n.d.-c). Center for Advancement of Racial and Ethnic Equity (CAREE). Retrieved December 6, 2007, from http://www.acenet.edu/AM/Template.cfm?Section = CAREE&Template = /TaggedPage/TaggedPageDisplay.cfm&TPLID = 58&ContentID = 20366

American Council on Education. (n.d.-d). Campus internationalization: Institutional networks. Retrieved December 6, 2007, from http://www.acenet.edu/AM/Template.cfm?Section = inst_networks

American Council on Education. (n.d.-e). Department leadership programs. Retrieved December 6, 2007, from http://www.acenet.edu/AM/Template.cfm?Section = chairs_workshop

American Council on Education. (n.d.-f). Institute for New Chief Academic Officers. Retrieved December 6, 2007, from http://www.acenet.edu/AM/Template.cfm?Section = CAOS1

American Council on Education. (n.d.-g). Office of Women in Higher Education (OWHE). Retrieved December 6, 2007, from http://www.acenet.edu/Content/NavigationMenu/ProgramsServices/OWHE/OWH E_main 1.htm

American Council on Education. (n.d.-h). Presidential roundtables. Retrieved December 6, 2007, from http://www.acenet.edu/AM/Template.cfm?Section = Pres _Round

American Psychological Association. (n.d.). APA education directorate. Retrieved December 6, 2007, from http://www.apa.org/ed/elc/home.html

Amey, M. J. (2006). *Breaking tradition: New community college leadership programs meet 21st-century needs*. Washington, DC: American Association of Community Colleges.

Association of American Medical Colleges. (n.d.). Councils, organizations, and professional development groups. Retrieved December 6, 2007, from http://www.aamc.org/members/facultydev/start.htm

Association of Departments of English. (n.d.). ADE summer seminars. Retrieved July 26, 2008, from http://www.ade.org/seminars/index.htm

Association of Departments of Foreign Languages. (n.d.). ADFL summer seminars. Retrieved July 26, 2008, from http://www.adfl.org/seminars/index.htm

Council of Independent Colleges. (n.d.). Conferences and events: Presidents Institute. Retrieved December 6, 2007, from http://www.cic.edu/conferences_events/presidents/index.asp

Dannels, S. A., Gleanson, K., Jackson, G. B., McDade, S. A, Chuang, Y. , McLaughlin, J. A., et al. (in press). Impact of executive leadership in academic medicine (ELAM) program: Comparison of ELAM participants and two comparison groups. *Academic Medicine.*

Drexel University. (n.d.). The Hedwig van Ameringen Executive Leadership in Academic Medicine (ELAM) Program for Women. Retrieved December 6, 2007, from http://www.drexelmed.edu/ELAM/index.html

Durlak, M. A. (2007). Investments in the future: Ensuring that resources are in place to promote continued progress. Retrieved December 6, 2007, from http://www.buffalostate.edu/insider/index.asp?article = 2987&vol = 19

Green, M. F., & McDade, S. A. (1994). *Investing in higher education: A handbook of leadership development*. Washington, DC: American Council on Education/Oryx Press.

Harvard Graduate School of Education Programs in Professional Education. (n.d.). Higher education programs. Retrieved December 6, 2007, from http://www.gse.harvard.edu/~ppe/highered/

Higher Education Resource Services. (n.d.). HERS institutes. Retrieved December 6, 2007, from http://www.hersnet.org/Institutes.asp

Higher Education Resource Services, Wellesley College. (n.d.). Higher Education Resource Services. Retrieved December 6, 2007, from http://www.hersnet.org/HERSWellesley.asp

McDade, S. A. (1988). Higher education leadership: Enhancing skills through professional development programs. *ERIC/ASHE Higher Education Research Report, (24)*(1). Washington, DC: ERIC Clearinghouse on Higher Education.

McDade, S. A., & Lewis, P. H. (Eds.). (1994). Developing administrative excellence: Creating a culture of leadership. *New Directions for Higher Education*, 89. San Francisco: Jossey-Bass.

McDade, S. A., Nooks, K. A., King, P. J., Sloma-Williams, L., Chuang, Y., Richman, R. C., et al. (2008). A window into the culture of leadership within higher education through the leadership definitions of women faculty: A case study of ELAM women faculty alumnae. *Journal About Women in Higher Education*, *1*(1), 74–103.

McDade, S. A., Richman, R. C., Jackson, G. B., & Morahan, P. S. (2004, April). Effects of participation in the Executive Leadership in Academic Medicine (ELAM) Program on women faculty's perceived leadership capabilities. *Academic Medicine* 79(4): 302–309.

Morahan, P. S., Kasperbauer, D., McDade, S. A., Aschenbrener, C. A., Triolo, P. K., Monteleone, P. L., et al. (1998, November). Training future leaders of academic medicine: Internal programs at three academic health centers. *Academic Medicine*, *73*(11), 1159–1168.

Morahan, P. S., Yamagata, H., McDade, S. A., Richman, R., Francis, R., & Odhner, V. (2006, June). Case study: Experiences from ELAM Program regarding new challenges facing inter-institutional social science and educational program evaluation research in academic health centers. *Academic Medicine*, *81*(6), 527–534.

National Association of Independent Colleges and Universities. (n.d.). Fall Leadership Conference. Retrieved December 6, 2007, from http://www.naicu.edu/events/fall-2008-leadership-conference

Ottenritter, N. (2004, April). *Leading forward: AACC and leadership*. Paper presented at the 46th annual conference of the Council for the Study of Community Colleges, Minneapolis, MN.

Richman, R. C., Morahan, P., Cohen, D. W., & McDade, S. A. (2001, April). Advancing women and closing the leadership gap: The Executive Leadership in Academic Medicine (ELAM) program experience. *Journal of Women's Health and Gender-based Medicine 10*(3), 271–277.

II

REFLECTIONS ON THE LEADERSHIP MARKETPLACE

Adrianna Kezar and Laurel Beesemyer

S haron McDade's reflection chapter on the revolutionary principles of leadership within the framework of the marketplace is helpful for placing the ideas described in this book in a meaningful context—one that is growing more powerful. While McDade is focused on the general concept of the market where consumer demand shapes product development (i.e., leadership development) and providers attempt to sell their product through classic business techniques such as branding and creating a niche, the concept of the marketplace for leadership development programs is very apropos these days. Many commentators have noted that market forces are becoming more prominent in the globalized world in which neoliberal philosophy encourages institutions to use the rules of the marketplace to shape institutional behaviors even within educational settings (Bok, 2002; Slaughter & Rhoades, 2004). Some neoliberal commentators believe that education, health care, government, and leadership development will be enhanced in performance if they follow the lead of consumers, focus on efficiency and cost savings, and downplay professional expertise. One of the main examples of this trend is the health management organizations (HMOs) that have been heavily critiqued for the downfall of health care in this country. Therefore, ending the book by examining these revolutionary principles in relation to the marketplace is an important way to help readers place the ideas we are arguing for in a broader context. The contributors to this book challenge these very trends of marketization and allowing a small group of consumers to establish definitions of leadership development for the entire population of leaders and potential leaders. We do not believe that the rules of the marketplace will help develop the best leadership development programs in higher education that can serve the public good.

As McDade suggests, it is the market that has created the current leadership development programs that we critique in this book. The top-down, authority-based, command and control, individualistic, values-neutral leadership development programs that are predominant in the current marketplace are the result of the needs and demands of those with authority and power who are the current market for such programs. Current customers are typically the presidents and provosts at elite institutions who create opportunities that reinforce their own power. It is these individuals who can pay for programs and who craft development programs to maintain and sanction their power and right to lead in certain ways. Such practices typically go unquestioned under the assumption that the market is unbiased and will therefore provide the best products and services as opposed to those programs that have established themselves as an elite brand with a consistent offering that enhances the consumer's self-image rather than necessarily being a program that enhances an entire institution.

Other leadership development opportunities developed in the 1980s and 1990s for middle-level administrators or faculty, as McDade notes, but these often copied existing programs, creating the notion of what leadership development should be in higher education. While these early elite and traditional programs certainly did not create a monopoly, their positioning as the first and most well-known programs served to shape other programs that developed and to spread their imprint on new leadership development. A typical practice when creating new leadership development programs is to search for existing programs and to model new programs after existing ones to enhance their standing and legitimacy among consumers.

How exactly has the marketplace influenced the leadership development programs that exist in higher education? As McDade notes, the marketplace of programs was shaped by a few elite programs developed at institutions such as Harvard or Brown. These programs attempted to attract individuals in positions of authority who typically have a great deal of money to spend on leadership development. These individuals come to the programs to focus on their personal leadership development rather than on a vision for change and the development and success of others on their campuses. They learn about strategic planning, budgeting, legal issues, and other elements that help those in positions of authority manage the institutions.

We define leadership in this book as the process of working collectively in an empowered and values-defined fashion to create change. Most of what calls itself leadership development in the marketplace would not be leadership development by our definition, which is informed by the revolutionary leadership principles. But the current marketplace, created in the 1960s and 1970s, conceptualizes leadership as management by those in positions of authority to maintain the status quo of the institution. It is this very definition of leadership that we argue against in this book. We believe that leadership has been and should be reconceptualized according to the revolutionary principles that emerged from the 1960s civil rights and women's movements. These principles have also been demonstrated to be important in a more globalized and interdependent world and represent fundamentally new ways to think about how to best lead social institutions.

In this final reflection, we wanted to challenge the elite, traditional, and what McDade refers to as programs with brand power. It is these programs, she speculates, that may not change because of their large market share and because they seem to serve an audience that demands their services. However, the problem with such a conceptualization is the assumption, inherent to the argument, that consumers are well informed of all the possible options and are choosing the best one, which disregards the power of branding. Branding is a powerful tool in that it is capable of building trust among consumers for an intangible product, which is the case of leadership development programs. More traditional leadership programs rely in large part on their elite status, which appeals to leaders' self-perceptions and the perceptions of others rather than the comprehensiveness of the program or its ability to actually develop visionary leaders. The danger is also that the brand may evolve but the product might not, which leads to the question of whether the product is really the best or merely that it is recognized and from that recognition comes trust, whether founded or not. McDade sees potential for the revolutionary programs in campus-based, smaller, and while not specifically noted, potentially less-elite or lesser-known programs. However, given the state of the marketplace how are such programs to compete in the short run and build up the cachet of a branded program to survive long enough to have a real impact on the ways leadership development is conceived and implemented? Thus, we challenge the notion of the market being the arbiter of what is best for leaders and higher education institutions, and the role the market plays in enabling the development of new programs that reproduce the traditional leadership paradigms.

Certainly a few well-respected programs exist that have been able to break away from reproducing the same traditional paradigm, but there has not been an ensuing reproduction of more revolutionary practices as yet or at least that has been documented in any way. HERS is one of the more highly regarded programs and it has always been shaped by the revolutionary leadership principles. Many of the programs highlighted in this book, such as ADVANCE or the institutions using principles of case-in-point pedagogy or spirituality, are located at well-regarded institutions. We believe the revolutionary principles have potential within all programs. This highlights not only the fact that the market may be imperfectly suited to the actual needs of institutions and their leaders but that there are ethical implications as well. Should some elite programs hide behind branding and niche or should they explore changes conducive to the good of higher education? Isn't leadership itself about taking risks? What better way to model leadership than for the elite leadership programs to examine their underlying assumptions about leadership and exhibit a willingness to change? As McDade points out, the elite programs created and reproduce the marketplace for leadership development, so we wonder what their responsibility is in changing this environment to embrace more democratic principles evidenced in the revolutionary leadership ideas. Such elite, highly successful, and, most important, visible programs are in a position to influence leaders and leadership development to take new directions. If their organizers enact change, other programs may be more likely to follow suit. Many of the elite programs and the programs that are modeled after them are not reflecting the contexts of institutions whose leaders they serve, which does a disservice to the entire higher education community and which, given higher education's standing within society as the agent of democracy, calls into question higher education's ability to serve the public good. In other words, the possible and actual pools of leaders and leadership teams are more varied, as are the constituencies higher education institutions serve, and it does institutions and society as a whole a great disservice if organizers of leadership development programs in general and the most powerful ones in particular do not reexamine their practices. While we have no definitive evidence about whether the organizers of such programs have considered these principles, the chapter authors' collective review of programs and our own knowledge of programs suggests that few principles have been enacted. This is certainly not to say that leadership programs do not engage in some ongoing changes, but whether program organizers actually examine their underlying assumptions is quite another task, one we are calling for in this book.

While we do not want to overextend the amount of power elite programs have, we do not want to let them off the hook in considering change because of their historic standing or elite status. As McDade and others consider why leadership development in higher education has not evolved as quickly as would be desired to embrace the revolutionary principles, we hope that this reflection piece will spur organizers of leadership development to be self-critical and to examine the decisions they make in choosing curriculum and program goals as ethical decisions, not merely market-based decisions about meeting immediate customer needs and protecting market branding. Also, we need for the organizers of these elite programs to consider their reach to leaders of color, leaders at less-elite institutions, teams of leaders, and leaders at different levels within the institution. We are excited about the potential that McDade points out among disciplinary and campus-based programs or within the professional programs that support specific functional areas such as student affairs, but we believe that the revolution will be incomplete if organizers of the traditional programs do not examine their assumptions.

McDade suggests there is room for traditional and revolutionary programs. While this may be true, we believe this may not be the most ethical choice. What leadership do we need to serve the public good in higher education? That is the question we pose. By serving the public good, we define the public good for higher education as reinforcing democratic principles of stakeholder involvement, access and equity, traditional commitments of citizenship development, and the promotion of community and public interests, and other similar commitments as documented in Kezar, Chambers, and Burkhardt (2005). For us, it is not a choice between traditional programs and revolutionary programs but a choice for leadership to serve the public good or to not serve the public good.

Many current programs promote an image of leadership and leaders that we believe do not serve the public good. Leaders focus on personal advancement, learn management skills, and focus on maintaining power and reinforcing bureaucratic norms, which limits their potential or desire to organize the institution for change. Leaders are also not learning ethical frameworks and are not attuned to the ethical components of leadership and are not sensitive to important cultural differences among people or contexts. Without leaders who are values-oriented, ethically and spiritually guided, capable of working as part of a collective, change-oriented, empowerment-focused, relational and emotionally intelligent, there are fewer people to safeguard some of the most important values of higher education institutions, values that are essential for the public. Higher education institutions are meant to foster a community that speaks and critiques for the public good and in which people differ in deep and influential ways. "The public good needs to be seen as dynamic, as a project in which varied actors participate, speaking through different cultural understandings" (Calhoun, 1998, p. 24). Leadership development programs need to reflect this dynamism if higher education is to effectively serve the public good.

We want to end this book by encouraging leadership developers to be bold, to play a leadership role themselves in reshaping the direction of leadership development so that it serves the public good.

References

Bok, D. (2002). *Universities in the marketplace: The commercialization of higher education.* Princeton, NJ: Princeton University Press.

Calhoun, C. (1998). The public good as a social and cultural project. In W. W. Powell and E. S. Clemens (Eds.), *Private action and the public good* (pp. 20–32). New Haven, CT: Yale University Press.

Kezar, A., Chambers, T. C., & Burkhardt, J. D.(2005). *Higher education for the public good: Emerging voices from a national movement.* San Francisco: Jossey-Bass.

Slaughter, S., & Rhoades, G. (2004). *Academic capitalism and the new economy: Markets, state, and higher education.* Baltimore, MD: Johns Hopkins University Press.

ABOUT THE CONTRIBUTORS

Laurel Beesemyer is a graduate student and provost's fellow at the University of Southern California. Her research interests include governance and organizational theory.

Tricia Bertram Gallant is the academic integrity coordinator at the University of California, San Diego. Her work is primarily in the areas of higher education administration, leadership, and academic ethics, and she occasionally serves as a consultant in the University of San Diego case-in-point conferences.

Rozana Carducci is a doctoral candidate in the University of California, Los Angeles, Division of Higher Education and Organizational Change. Her research focuses on leadership in student affairs organizations, organizational studies of higher education, and critical methodology.

Pamela Eddy is an associate professor of higher education in the Department of Educational Policy, Planning, and Leadership at The College of William and Mary. Her research focuses on leadership and community colleges.

Lynn M. Gangone is dean of the Women's College of the University of Denver. Her research focuses on the history of women's organizations and their influence on women's advancement in higher education. She serves on the HERS Board as treasurer and has served as faculty at the HERS Bryn Mawr Summer Institute for Women in Higher Education Administration since 1996. She has worked in higher education for over 25 years as a senior campus administrator, national and state association executive, lobbyist and policy analyst, and faculty member.

Cheryl Getz is the department chair and assistant professor of leadership studies in the School of Leadership and Education Sciences at the University of San Diego. Her work is primarily in the areas of higher education administration, group relations, and leadership training. She regularly acts as a case-in-point conference director and serves as consultant and facilitator to a variety of groups and organizations in higher education.

Jeni Hart is an assistant professor in the higher education and continuing education emphasis in the Department of Educational Leadership and Policy Analysis at the University of Missouri, Columbia. Hart has conducted research on activism among feminist faculty and the status and work lives of faculty women and faculty of color. Broadly, her agenda centers on gender issues, the faculty, and organizational transformation within academe.

Jerlando F. L. Jackson is an associate professor of higher and postsecondary education and coordinator for the higher, postsecondary, and continuing education program at the University of Wisconsin, Madison. Jackson's central research interest has been to explore workforce diversity and workplace discrimination in higher education. He is the lead editor of *Toward Administrative Reawakening: Creating and Maintaining Safe College Campuses* (Stylus Publishing, 2007).

Adrianna Kezar is an associate professor at the University of Southern California, and focuses on research related to leadership, change, diversity/equity, and organizational behavior. She has published 10 books and over 75 refereed journal articles. She has developed several leadership development academies, including the Institute for Emerging Women Leaders, and has participated in leadership development institutes as a faculty member, including HERS.

Jaime Lester is an assistant professor in the Department of Leadership and Counseling at Old Dominion University. Lester's research agenda includes gender equity in higher education, retention and transfer of community college students, socialization of women and minority faculty, and leadership.

Bridget R. McCurtis is a doctoral student and research fellow in the Department of Educational Leadership and Policy Analysis at the University of Wisconsin, Madison. Her primary research interests include leadership development for leaders of color and college student experiences with leadership programs. McCurtis serves as vice president and chief program officer at the Jackie Robinson Foundation, a nonprofit focused on scholarship, mentoring, and leadership development for talented students of color.

Sharon A. McDade is currently director of the fellows program at the American Council on Education. She served as a faculty member at George Washington University and Teachers College at Columbia University. She has studied and worked with leadership development for two decades.

Robert J. Nash is professor of higher education, interdisciplinary studies, and educational studies at the University of Vermont. He is an official university scholar in the social sciences and humanities. He is the author of nine books and over one hundred articles and book chapters.

Elizabeth M. O'Callaghan is a doctoral student and research associate in the Department of Educational Leadership and Policy Analysis at the University of Wisconsin, Madison. Her research interests include women's leadership and persistence in historically male-dominated disciplines and domains of higher education.

Sue V. Rosser has served as dean of the Ivan Allen College of Liberal Arts at Georgia Institute of Technology in Atlanta since 1999, where she also is professor of public policy and of history, technology, and society. She has authored 10 books and over 120 refereed journal articles on theoretical and applied issues surrounding women and science, technology, and medicine.

Lara Scott is assistant director of residential life at Champlain College. She received her graduate degree from the Higher Education and Student Affairs Program at the University of Vermont. She has cotaught graduate courses in the higher education program with Robert J. Nash.

AACC Leading Forward Initiative, 187, 204
AACC Presidents Academy, 190, 192
academic leadership
  and career flexibility, 151–154
  employment trends in, 66–70
  women in, 119, 121–122, 176
ACE Fellows Program, 74–75, 76, 77, 214
activism, grassroots, 169–183
adaptive leadership, 112
adaptive learning, 103–105
Adler, Nancy, 27–29, 53–54
ADVANCE initiative, 119, 122–129, 220, 236
affirmative action, 41
Allan, E. J., 173
American Association of Community Colleges (AACC), 10, 187
American Association of Junior Colleges Clearinghouse on Community Services, 186
American Council on Education (ACE) Fellows, 10, 214
American Indian Higher Education Consortium (AIHEC), 76
Amey, M. J., 198–199
analysis-in-action, 113
Applications of the Tavistock Group Relations Approach, 111
Association for Women Faculty (AWF), 170–171, 174–175, 181
assumptions, revolutionary, 5–8
Astin, H. S., 172–173
authority vs. leadership, 97–98
awards, leadership, 122
Awareness of Decision in Evaluation of Promotion and Tenure (ADEPT), 126–127

Balukas, J. V., 42
Bennis, Warren, 132, 133
Bensimon, E. M., 14, 21, 188

Berger, Peter, 140
Bernstein, A., 42
Berquist, W. H., 16–17, 201
bias
  deconstructing, 165–166
  in faculty promotions, 126–127
  religious, 135
  unconscious, 156, 161–162
Birnbaum, R., 11–12, 17, 188
Body and Soul, 28
Bolman, L. G., 3, 17, 201
boundaries, 105–106, 112
Bourassa, Donna M. Mid-Level Management Institute, 75
Boyer, Ernest, 177
Bradley, DeMethra L., 138
branding, 235–236
Breaking Tradition, 198
Burkhardt, J. D., 237

campus culture, 16–18
campus service, valuing, 176–178
Carducci, R., 51, 172
career
  development, impediments to, 79–81
  flexibility, 151–154, 156–159
  mapping, 54–58
Carnegie Classification System, 187
case-in-point pedagogy, *xvii*, 95, 98–106
Center for the Study of Values in College Student Development, 131
Chaffee, E. E., 17
Chair Academy, 190, 193–195, 204
Chamberlain, M. K., 41, 42
Chambers, T. C., 237
change agents, faculty, 172–174
chaos
  learning from, 99, 109
  navigating through, 10–13, 33

character education, 131
Chickering, Arthur, 137, 139
Chodorow, 120–121
citizenship, global, 29
classroom, as organizational system, 100–105
codes of conduct, 20
cognitive complexity, 12
collaboration
  among scientists, 118–119
  global, 29–30
collaborative leadership, 13–16, 22
Committee for the Concerns of Women in
    New England College and Universities,
    41
communication skills, cross-cultural, 26, 29
community colleges
  characteristics and history of, 185–189
  contextual leadership in, 202–203
  succession strategies for, 203–205
competency, cultural, 200–202
Comprehensive Approach to Leadership De-
    velopment for People of Color (CALD-
    PC), 81–86
Contreras-McGavin, M., 51, 172
Cooper, J. E., 11–12
courses. *see also* leadership development
    programs
  case-in-point training, 110
  religion, 134–136
Crosby, B. C., 28–29
cultural competency, 200–202
Cultural Leadership in Higher Education, 17
cultural sensitivity, 16–17, 18
culture, campus, 16–18, 19
curricula
building multiculturalism into, 81–83
exploring religion and spirituality in, 137–138
HERS, 43–53, 59
leadership development, 12–13, 24–33, 152–
    154, 226–228

Dalton, John, 131
Davis, J. R., 206
Deal, T. E., 3, 17, 201
Deegan, W. L., 188
Dinnerstein, D., 120–121
discrimination, 125–127, 156, 161–162

diversity
  developing through leadership programs,
    74–77
  in leadership, developing, 65–66, 78
  in team building, 159–161

Early, Vivian Nix, 52–53
education
  character, 131
  globalization of, 178
  religion and spirituality in, 131–149
emotions, role of, 20–21
employment trends, academic leadership,
    66–70
empowerment
  and career development for women, 54–58
  integrating into leadership development
    programs, 22–25, 29
  revolutionary leadership and, 5–8
environments
  changing organizational, 12
  complex, 6
  shared power, 7
ethics, 19–20
Executive Leadership in Academic Medicine
    (ELAM), 220–229
Executive Leadership Institute, 195, 196
Expanding Leadership Diversity in the Com-
    munity College, 196, 203, 204
Experiential Learning in Organizations, 111

faculty
  of color, 70–71
  funding, gender differences in, 124–125
  gender differences across disciplines,
    119–122
  in STEM disciplines, 118–122
  women, 70–71, 121–122
Faculty Women's Caucus (FWC), 170–171,
    174–175
funding, gender differences in, 124–125
Future Leaders Academy, 190

gender
  differences across disciplines, 119–122
  differences in funding, 124–125
Gillette, J., 111

global
    collaboration, 29–30
    leadership, 25–28
Global Leadership and Organizational Be-
        havior Effectiveness (GLOBE), 26
"Global Leadership: Women Leaders",
        27–28
globalization of education, 178
Goleman, Daniel, 21, 111
Gould, L. J., 111
grassroots
    activism, 169–183
    leadership, 172–174
"Green River Community College: A Differ-
        ent Kind of Leadership", 9–10
Greenleaf, R. K., 19
group dynamics, 111–113
Groups in Context, 111

Hamrick, F. A., 141
Hartog, Den, 26
Hayden, C., 111
Heifetz, R. A., 11, 111, 112–113
Higher Education Resource Sources
        (HERS), 236
    attributes of, 59–61, 214
    career mapping and, 54–58
    curricular format, 43–51, 59–60, 75–76
    global perspectives within, 53–54
    history of, xvi, 39–51
    Localized Leadership Project, 46
Hispanic Association of Colleges and Uni-
        versities (HACU) Leadership Fellows
        Program, 76
Hispanic Leadership Fellows Program, 203
Hogan, Katie, 177
Hornig, Lilli, 41
Hull, J. R., 190

Ideta, L. M., 11–12
*Individuals, Groups, and Organizations Be-
        neath the Surface*, 111
Institute for Community College Develop-
        ment, 203
Institute for Educational Management
        (IEM), 214

institutional
    fit, 56
    transformation, 122, 127–128
interpersonal skills, developing, 101–102

Jackson, J. F. L., 79

Katz, Judith, 52–53
Keim, M. C., 190
Keller, E. F., 121
Kellogg MSI Leadership Fellows Program,
        76, 77
Kellogg, W. K. Foundation, 76, 186–187, 197
Kezar, Adrianna, 17, 18, 51, 172, 188, 237
Kidder, Rushworth, 19
Knowles, M. S., 205
Komives, S. R., 15

Laking Institute for Mentored Leadership,
        203
leaders
    assessing worldview of, 142–143
    attributes of, 132–133
    role of, 9–10
leadership. *see also* leadership development
        programs
    adaptive, 11
    vs. authority, 97–98
    characteristics, 26–28
    collaborative, 13–16, 22
    contextual, 202–203
    as a cultural process, 18–19
    defined, 6
    development, recommendations for, 110
    global, 25–28
    grassroots, 172–174
    vs. management, 97
    nonpositional, 153–154
    professional associations and, 72–73
    qualities that encourage spiritual discus-
        sions, 143–149
    research, 2
    revolutionary assumptions, 5–8
    for social justice, 179–182
    training, 110–111
*Leadership and the New Science: Discovering
        Order in a Chaotic World*, 11

Leadership Can Be Taught, 111
leadership development programs
  ACE Fellows Program, 74–75
  ADVANCE initiative, 119, 122–129, 220
  assumptions of, 3–8
  audiences for, 215–222
  cost of, 222–226
  current offerings, 215–218
  curriculum, 226–228
  designing, 159–166
  Donna M. Bourassa Mid-Level Management Institute, 75
  Executive Leadership in Academic Medicine (ELAM), 220–229
  HACU Leadership Fellows Program, 76
  HERS, *xvi*, 39–62, 75–76, 214
  Kellogg MSI Leadership Fellows Program, 76, 77
  Millennium Leadership Project, 76
  Minority Undergraduate Fellows Program (MUFP), 74–75
  NASPA Undergraduate Fellows Program (NUFP), 74–75
  pedagogical strategies for, 13, 20, 28–33
  recommendations for, 110
  resources for, 74–77, 111
  team building, 220
Leadership Fellows Program, 76
Leadership on the Line, 111
Leadership Reconsidered: Engaging Higher Education in Social Change, 23–24
Leadership Without Easy Answers, 11, 111
Leading Forward initiative, 187, 189, 191
Leading Forward Initiative, 204
Leading From Within: Reflections on Spirituality and Leadership, 3
Leading With Soul, 3
League for Innovation in the Community College, 190, 195–197
learning
  adaptive, 6, 103–105
  organizational, 3, 8–10
  ways of, 206
Leland, C., 172–173
Lessons in Leadership: Executive Leadership Programs for Advancing Diversity in Higher Education, 69

Lewin, R., 134
Linsky, M., 111, 112
Lipman-Blumen, J., 28
Love, P., 133, 140
Lucas, N., 15

Management Institute for Women in Higher Education, 10
McCollom, M., 111
McDade, Sharon, *xi*
McMahon, T. R., 15
mentoring, 74–76, 83–85, 123–124
Meyerson, Debra, 23, 174
Millennium Leadership Project, 76
Minority Undergraduate Fellows Program (MUFP), 74–75
Molenkamp, R. J., 111
Montoya, A., 77
morality and leadership, teaching, 134–137
movements, social, impact of, 5–8
multiculturalism, building into curricula, 81–83

Nash, Robert J., 138
NASPA Undergraduate Fellows Program (NUFP), 73–75, 133
National Association for Equal Opportunity (NAFEO) Kellogg Leadership Fellows Program, 76
National Association of Student Personnel Administrators, 10
National Association of Student Personnel Administrators (NASPA), 133
National Institute for Leadership Development, 197
National Science Foundation (NSF) programs, 122–129
Nelson, S. J., 20, 173
Neumann, A., 14, 21, 188

O'Conner, P. M. G., 14
Olivet Case study, 9–10
organizational
  change toward career flexibility, 151–154, 156–159
  culture, 19

dynamics, 94–95, 103–110
learning, 3, 8–10

Palmer, Parker, 3, 20
Parks, Sharon Daloz, 111, 142
Pawlak, K., 201
pedagogical strategies, 13, 20
    program design, 28–33
    role playing, 14, 18, 25
    teaching morality and leadership, 134–137
pedagogy, case-in-point, *xvii*, 95, 98–106
personal skills, developing, 101–102
power
    addressing abuses of, 154–156
    issues in team building, 160
Presidents Academy, 190
problems, adaptive, 95–96
professional associations, role in leadership
    development, 72–73
program design. *see* curricula
programs, leadership development. *see* lead-
    ership development programs
public good, serving, 234–238

"Quaker College: Collegiality, Culture and
    Tradition", 17
Quinn, L., 14

radicals, tempered, 23, 174
Re-engineering Female Friendly Science, 121
*Redesigning Collegiate Leadership: Teams and
    Teamwork in Higher Education*, 14
reflection, 206–207
Regine, B., 134
religion and spirituality, exploring, 137–138,
    143–149
religious
    instruction, 134–137
    pluralism, 136–137, 140–141
resources, for leadership development, 111
*Rethinking the "L" Word in Higher Education:
    The Revolution on Research on Leader-
    ship*, *xii*, 172
revolutionary assumptions, leadership, 5–8
Rhoads, R. A., 17–18
Roddick, Anita, 28
role playing, 14, 25

roles, organizational, 106–110
Rural Community College Initiative
    (RCCI), 202

science
    disciplines, need for women leaders in,
        117–120
    as masculine domain, 120–121
science, technology, engineering, mathemat-
    ics (STEM), women faculty in, 117–120
Scott, David, 133
Scully, M. A., 23
Secor, Cynthia, 42, 43, 56
self-awareness, 107, 111–112, 206
Senge, P. M., 9
service, valuing campus, 176–178
skills, developing intra- and interpersonal,
    101–102
social change
    and HERS, 52–53
    leadership for, 22
    strategies for, 23–25
*A Social Change Model of Leadership Develop-
    ment*, 23
social intelligence, 111
social justice, 19, 179–182
social movements, impact of, 5–8
spirituality
    exploring, 137–138, 143–149
    and leadership, 19–20
Stamm, Liesa, 132
Stapley, Lionel, 111
Starratt, R. J., 19
Stein, M., 111
succession strategies
    for community colleges, 203–205
    and leaders of color, 71
Summer Institute for Women in Higher Ed-
    ucation Administration, 42

Talbot, D., 133, 140
Taliaferro, B., 77
Tavistock Primer, 111
teaching
    morality and leadership, 134–137
    strategies. *see* pedagogical strategies
team building, 159–161

technology disciplines, need for women leaders in, 117–120
Tempered Radicals: How Everyday Leaders Inspire Change at Work, 23
Tierney, W. G., 17–18
Tillery, D., 188
Tinsley, A., 54–55
Tobias, Shelia, 41
training, leadership, 110–111
Twombly, S. B., 188

values conflicts, managing, 94–95
van Ameringen, Hedwig Executive Leadership in Academic Medicine (ELAM), 220–229
VanDerLinden, K., 204
Vaughan, G. B., 189

Ward, Kelly, 161, 177
Watt, S., 173
Wellesley College Center for Research on Women, 42
Wheatley, Margaret, 8–11, 13
Wolf-Wendel, L., 161
women
    Association for Women Faculty (AWF), 170–171, 174–175, 181
    and career flexibility, 151–154
    empowerment and career development for, 54–58
    faculty, 40, 70–71, 121–122
    Faculty Women's Caucus (FWC), 170–171
    in science, technology, engineering, mathematics (STEM), 118–122

Understanding College and University Organization
Theories for Effective Policy and Practice / Two Volumes
James L. Bess, Jay R. Dee
Foreword by D. Bruce Johnstone

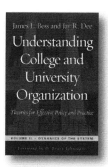

Volume I: The State of the System, hardcover
Volume II: Dynamics of the System
Available as a set

"I highly recommend this textbook to master's level instructors who seek to foster critical thinking about theory and practice."—***Cheryl J. Daly***, *Director, College Student Personnel master's program, Western Carolina University*

"Quite simply a tour de force. Not only have the authors written by far the broadest and deepest theoretical analysis of college and university organization I've seen, but they have clearly organized a complex topic, and written it engagingly. This will be seen as a landmark work in the field. It should be required reading for all who claim to understand higher education institutions and the behavior that goes on inside and around them."—***David W. Leslie,*** *Chancellor Professor of Education, The College of William and Mary*

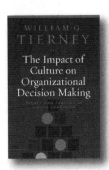

The Impact of Culture on Organizational Decision-Making
Theory and Practice in Higher Education
William G. Tierney

An organization's culture is reflected in what is done, how it is done, and who is involved in doing it. It concerns decisions, actions, and communication on an instrumental and symbolic level. This book considers various facets of academic culture, discusses how to study it, how to analyze it, and how to improve it in order to move colleges and universities aggressively into the future while maintaining core academic values.

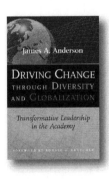

Driving Change Through Diversity and Globalization
Transformative Leadership in the Academy
James A. Anderson
Foreword by Ronald A. Crutcher

"On rare occasions one finds a book that reframes prior visions. Such books one does not merely read, but one returns to study. [This] is such a book. The first three chapters provide a framework for understanding diversity and globalization, which moves beyond the limits of affirmative action, ethnic studies, and overseas study tours. The theoretical discussion is rooted in the premise that universities' (read also society's) ability to work with diversity and globalization will determine the nature of their futures. Following a discussion of principles, Anderson moves from theory to practice, giving illustrations of campuses that have embraced some facet of this new vision applying it either in terms of teaching strategies and methods, curricular organization, and/or student development. The fact that Anderson is able to draw on working applications gives credence to his theoretical propositions."—*Irene Hecht, Director, Department Leadership Programs, ACE*

22883 Quicksilver Drive
Sterling, VA 20166-2102